Reflective Planning, Teaching, and Evaluation for the Elementary School

A Relational Approach

Third Edition

Judy W. Eby
Reflective Action Research Center, San Diego

Debra Bayles Martin
San Diego State University

Merrill
Prentice Hall

Upper Saddle River, New Jersey
Columbus, Ohio

Library of Congress Cataloging-in-Publication Data

Eby, Judy W.
 Reflective planning, teaching, and evaluation for the elementary school : a relational approach / July W.
 Eby, Debra Bayles Martin.—3rd ed.
  p. cm.
 Includes bibliographical references and index.
 ISBN 0-13-022695-5
 1. Elementary school teaching. 2. Thought and thinking. 3. Educational tests and measurements. 4.
 Educational planning.   I. Martin, Debra Bayles.
 LB1555.E29   2001
 372.1102—dc21   00-025308

Vice President and Publisher: Jeffery W. Johnston
Editor: Debra A. Stollenwerk
Editorial Assistant: Penny S. Burleson
Production Editor: Mary Harlan
Copy Editor: Lorretta Palagi
Design Coordinator: Robin G. Chukes
Photo Coordinator: Sherry Mitchell
Cover Design: Elvia van de Sande
Text Design: ReNae Grant, PageCrafters
Illustrations: Elvia van de Sande; Tom Kennedy
Production Manager: Pamela D. Bennett
Electronic Text Management: Marilyn Wilson Phelps, Karen L. Bretz, Melanie N. Ortega
Director of Marketing: Kevin Flanagan
Marketing Manager: Amy June
Marketing Services Manager: Krista Groshong

This book was set in Transitional 511 by Prentice Hall. It was printed and bound by R. R. Donnelley & Sons
Company. The cover was printed by Phoenix Color Corp.

Photo Credits: Scott Cunningham/Merrill: pp. 90, 176, 200, 220; Kenneth P. Davis/PH College: p. 252;
Anthony Magnacca/Merrill: p. 156; Barbara Schwartz/Merrill: pp. 1, 49; and Anne Vega/Merrill: pp. 20, 69,
109, 137.

Merrill
Prentice Hall

10 9 8 7 6 5 4 3 2
ISBN: 0-13-022695-5

Preface

We all have a powerful desire for meaningful, mutually satisfying relationships in our lives. Nowhere is this more true than in the elementary classrooms of schools around the world. Every time a new school term begins, children wake up, brush their teeth, put on their clothes, eat their breakfast, and walk out the door with the same hopeful longing: "I hope I get a good teacher."

What does the child mean by a *good* teacher? When we were in elementary school, it meant a teacher who was happy to see us, smiled at us, made us feel welcome on the first day of school. In later weeks, having a good teacher meant that you looked forward to going to school each day because you knew that the teacher looked forward to being there also, and expressed that joy by designing attractive bulletin boards and thinking up new and interesting ways to practice those terrible "basic skills," the spinach of elementary education. We especially looked forward to the nice things the teacher had to say about us, that our work was good, that we said interesting things in discussions, that we were obviously capable of learning to read and write and do mathematics. We basked in the good teacher's positive outlook and encouragement.

This has not changed. As every new school year approaches, students still have the same hope as they walk into a school building: "I hope my teacher likes me." Now that we have both been teaching for many years ourselves, we can share a lesser known secret with you, our readers. Every new school year, beginning teachers walk into the same school buildings, and they are thinking similar thoughts, having similar feelings: "I hope my students like me, and I hope the other teachers like me, too." The new teacher knows that to do well, it will all be easier and more enjoyable if there is a sense of being accepted and appreciated for one's self and the efforts, not always entirely successful, that one puts into the work of being a teacher.

We do not want to overstate the importance of being liked. There are other, equally important aspects of being a good teacher, such as knowledge of the subject matter and an understanding of how to plan lessons and present the material to students so that they are able to "get it." But, we want to make the point that good teaching is very much about good relationships, and we have revised this textbook with that in mind.

No, you won't find cookbook recipes here for getting students to like you. That is not how it works. When you cross the line from being the student to being the teacher, the responsibility for the relationship becomes yours. It is up to you to create an environment that is perceived as welcoming and encouraging. It is up to you to do the "liking" (read: appreciation, encouragement, offering suitable and stimulating learning experiences, satisfying students' curiosity, enabling them to solve problems and be successful.)

What we offer you in this textbook is our combined experience as both learners and teachers and our analysis of the best practices in research that can enable you to approach your new role as teacher with the confidence that you can succeed. We offer you our original model of how caring, relational teachers think and feel on the job. We call it *reflective action*. It is based on Kounin's (1977) powerful concept of *withitness*. You will find it highlighted in Chapter 1, and then referred to again and again throughout the book. Essentially, it is a teaching/learning process that prepares you to combine and alternate perceptiveness of your students' needs with periods of reflection, getting support and feedback from trusted colleagues, action, reflection on your action, and acting again, each time with more care and precision than the time before.

Conceptual Framework

We are excited about this concept. We hope that you are too. We have written this book believing that teaching is, and always will be, a marvelous marriage of science and art. Through careful study and experimentation, we will continue to learn more about how people learn and thus how we can better teach them. We have shared some of that knowledge with you in the pages of this text in the form of educational theory and teaching strategies. However, we also acknowledge the existence of an almost "magical" side to teaching—the "art"—and it is here that we have also tried to offer you some ideas as you enter this wonderful profession. Part of the art, we believe, is founded on coming to know oneself as an individual, and on coming to understand the uniquely human characteristics we all share.

When a teacher understands himself or herself as someone who wants to care for others and to be cared for in return, he or she is more likely to approach students as the miracle they are—unique and feeling individuals who want the very same things. Great teachers know themselves, know their students, know their disciplines, and weave them together in beautiful relational mosaics. A good part of the art of teaching, we believe, lies in its relational nature. Great teachers care about the world, ideas, and people, and caring is the passion that fuels their personal growth as well as that of their students.

If you gain nothing else from this book, we hope that you will come away from its pages more aware of your own need to care and be cared for—and convinced that within the enterprise of teaching are myriad opportunities to do just that. Teaching is a relational venture, and as you read we hope you will gain important insights that bring joy and vigor to your teaching and to your own learning—for a lifetime.

Features of This Edition

Relational Aspects of Teaching and Learning

In this edition, we have drawn on the literature and our own experiences to describe the positive effects of creating good relationships between teachers and students, teachers and parents, teachers and their colleagues. We describe practical methods and strategies teachers can use to relate well to others, especially by increasing their withitness to understand the needs of others. The model of Reflective Action presented in Chapter 1 also encourages teachers to confer with colleagues and ask for feedback when reflecting on dilemmas in teaching. Relationships are the key to good teaching, and so they are a major emphasis of this book.

CLAD

Many teacher education programs have Crosscultural, Language, and Academic Development (CLAD) requirements so that beginning teachers will be able to address the needs of students from very diverse households. We have provided CLAD-type strategies and chronicled the experiences of practicing teachers who use these strategies in their classrooms to stimulate cooperation, interaction, and appreciation of differences among children from very diverse backgrounds.

Professional Portfolio

At the end of each chapter in the book, we have provided active experiences for your own professional portfolio to clarify and communicate your unique educational philosophy to prospective employers or colleagues. The suggestions for reflective actions that we provide can be used to document the many accomplishments you have made and the strengths and talents you have to offer. Your professional portfolio will be quite impressive if you take the time to clarify your goals, create unit and lesson plans, and reflect on the issues and materials that you choose to include in it. You can take your portfolio with you on employment interviews.

Acknowledgments

We wish to express our gratitude to those who reviewed the text and made many helpful suggestions for this edition: Margaret Ferrara, Central Connecticut State University; Sylvia Holub, University of Houston; Honor Keirans, Chestnut Hill College; and Clifford Russell, National University.

References

Kounin, J. (1977). *Discipline and group management in classrooms.* New York: Holt, Rinehart and Winston.

About the Authors

Elliot Eisner described the role of an *educational connoisseur* in his book *The Educational Imagination* (3rd edition, 1994, Merrill/Prentice Hall). "The major distinction between connoisseurship and criticism is this: connoisseurship is the art of appreciation, criticism is the art of disclosure" (p. 215). He goes on to say that experience counts in the development of connoisseurship. "To develop connoisseurship one must have a desire to perceive subtleties, to become a student of human behavior, to focus one's perception" (p. 216). We'd like to believe that this book was written by two very enthusiastic educational connoisseurs.

Judy Eby began teaching in 1969 and has been a classroom teacher, coordinator of a gifted program, a teacher educator (De Paul University, University of San Diego, and San Diego State University), and a mentor teacher in the Beginning Teacher Support Academy with the San Diego Unified School district. Now retired, she still enthusiastically pursues her role as a connoisseur of the best educational practices. She actively searches out and researches best practices and shares her experiences and perceptions with other educators. She offers her experience to school districts as an educational consultant, specializing in the development of reflective action and professional portfolios for teachers.

She also volunteers in children's literacy programs on both sides of the San Diego–Tijuana border. Her most treasured project is the Tecolote Centro de Comunidad, a children's center in Tijuana, where she has created and runs a children's library for the community. She also participates in before- and after-school programs on both sides of the border.

Because Judy knows that teacher educators deserve to have the ideas of someone currently immersed in teacher education, she invited Debra Bayles Martin to co-author this new edition. Debra entered the education profession in 1980 as an intern teacher and completed a dual bachelor's degree in Educational Psychology and Elementary Education. Her Educational Psychology background included work with students who were deaf or hard of hearing, students with speech and articulation difficulties, and educationally challenged individuals.

As an elementary school teacher, Debra wrote and directed school musicals and dramatic productions and organized several after-school programs for students in photography, music, physical fitness, and other interest areas. Debra has been involved in teacher education at the university level for 11 years, teaching

Reading/Language Arts methods courses and supervising student teachers. She received her M.A. in Reading from Brigham Young University and her Ph.D. in Language and Literacy Studies/Curriculum and Instruction from the University of Texas at Austin.

In 1996, Debra helped develop and direct a new teacher education program at San Diego State University (the Accelerated Block), and she still works closely with local school districts to determine ways the university can help schools address educational needs at local and state levels. In 1997 Debra was named Director of the SDSU Community Reading Center, which is part of the Master's program in Reading/Language Arts. Debra teaches graduate assessment and instructional intervention courses at the Center. Community members of all ages and backgrounds are assessed and tutored at the Center by credentialed teachers enrolled in the Master's program. Center clients make excellent literacy growth during tutoring and experience the warm ethos of care that infuses the program.

Debra is involved in a number of professional teaching and research organizations, regularly consults on a local and national level, and maintains an active research agenda. She studies how teachers learn to teach and regularly presents her research at national conferences and through professional publications. Debra is the author of a literacy program for illiterate adults and a handbook on creating professional teacher portfolios; she is currently co-authoring a series of instructional materials for young, at-risk readers.

Debra enjoys working with teachers, students, and parents at the Center, and welcomes opportunities to counsel students, advise them in independent projects, and introduce them to research processes in their own classrooms or at the Center. She was named Outstanding Faculty Member for the School of Teacher Education in 1999.

Discover the Companion Website Accompanying This Book

The Prentice Hall Companion Website: A Virtual Learning Environment

Technology is a constantly growing and changing aspect of our field that is creating a need for content and resources. To address this emerging need, Prentice Hall has developed an online learning environment for students and professors alike—Companion Websites—to support our textbooks.

In creating a Companion Website, our goal is to build on and enhance what the textbook already offers. For this reason, the content for each user-friendly website is organized by topic and provides the professor and student with a variety of meaningful resources. Common features of a Companion Website include:

For the Professor—
Every Companion Website integrates Syllabus Manager™, an online syllabus creation and management utility.

◆ **Syllabus Manager™** provides you, the instructor, with an easy, step-by-step process to create and revise syllabi, with direct links into Companion Website and other online content without having to learn HTML.

◆ Students may logon to your syllabus during any study session. All they need to know is the web address for the Companion Website and the password you've assigned to your syllabus.

◆ After you have created a syllabus using **Syllabus Manager™**, students may enter the syllabus for their course section from any point in the Companion Website.

◆ Clicking on a date, the student is shown the list of activities for the assignment. The activities for each assignment are linked directly to actual content, saving time for students.

◆ Adding assignments consists of clicking on the desired due date, then filling in the details of the assignment—name of the assignment, instructions, and whether or not it is a one-time or repeating assignment.

◆ In addition, links to other activities can be created easily. If the activity is online, a URL can be entered in the space provided, and it will be linked automatically in the final syllabus.

◆ Your completed syllabus is hosted on our servers, allowing convenient updates from any computer on the Internet. Changes you make to your syllabus are immediately available to your students at their next logon.

For the Student—

◆ **Topic Overviews**—outline key concepts in topic areas

◆ **Electronic Bluebook**—send homework or essays directly to your instructor's email with this paperless form

◆ **Message Board**—serves as a virtual bulletin board to post—or respond to—questions or comments to/from a national audience

◆ **Chat**—real-time chat with anyone who is using the text anywhere in the country—ideal for discussion and study groups, class projects, etc.

◆ **Web Destinations**—links to www sites that relate to each topic area

◆ **Professional Organizations**—links to organizations that relate to topic areas

◆ **Additional Resources**—access to topic-specific content that enhances material found in the text

To take advantage of these and other resources, please visit the *Reflective Planning, Teaching and Evaluation for the Elementary School* Companion Website at

www.prenhall.com/eby

Brief Contents

Contents

Chapter 3
Diversity Equals Opportunity   49

Chapter 4
How Teachers Plan School Programs   69

Chapter 5
Planning Thematic Units for Authentic Learning   *90*

Chapter 6
Lesson Planning and Sequencing   *109*

Chapter 7
Authentic Teaching and Learning   137

Chapter 8
Discussion and Questioning Strategies   156

Chapter 11
Assessing Student Accomplishments   **220**

Chapter 12
Relational Teachers and the School Community   **252**

1

Reflective Action in Teaching

*I*t is the end of the first day of school in her first teaching assignment, and Shanisha is exhausted. She sinks to the chair near her desk and tries gallantly to hold back the tears burning behind her eyelids. "What went wrong?" she asks herself again and again. "My lesson plans were ready, I had the children help me create our class rules, and almost all the children seemed comfortable by the end of the day. But no matter what I did, Jaime would not look at me or respond to my questions. Instead, he sat there mute, too shy or afraid to look at me. I don't understand it!"

Just as Shanisha experienced, puzzling and disturbing events occur almost every day in every classroom. Students misbehave for no apparent reason. A lesson that seemed so right on paper does not go well. Students may appear to be bored, confused, or restless. The teacher hears whispered comments complaining about life in this classroom, or feels, like Shanisha, that it is impossible to get through to a particular student.

These dilemmas may seem overwhelming. Teachers may hear their own voices rising in an attempt to control the students' behavior. They may feel strong emotions of fear, anger, or embarrassment at being seen as ineffective. Some teachers seem to respond by resenting their students and blaming the system. If they talk about it at all, it is to complain to other teachers about the lack of family values in the community or the overcrowded conditions at the school. In other words, faced with a dilemma they cannot immediately resolve, they choose to blame others for the situation and try to convince themselves and others that there is nothing they can do to remedy the situation. They conclude that classroom problems are clearly the responsibility of others who are not doing their jobs.

However, other teachers react quite differently. Like Nel Noddings (1992), they recognize that occasional conflict in classrooms may be unavoidable and that it is difficult to create good relationships instantly. These teachers believe that education is a relational venture and that students and teachers can learn to care about themselves, about ideas, and about one another. They recognize that "the desire to be cared for is almost certainly a universal human characteristic. Not everyone wants to be cuddled or fussed over. But everyone wants to be received, to elicit a response that is congruent with an underlying need or desire" (p. 17). Caring is a way of being in relation, not a set of specific behaviors.

When confronted with a student who does not seem to respond, reflective and caring teachers do not take it as a personal insult. They understand that learning how to care is not something every child has had an opportunity to learn, and that people have various capacities for caring (Noddings, 1992). Such teachers realize that good teaching takes time and understanding. They recognize that much of the personal frustration in teaching arises when a teacher cares about a student and the student fails to respond in a way the teacher understands.

Good teaching also resembles good parenting in that both require long periods of time and continuity to develop. Good parents and teachers start by creating an environment that encourages trusting relationships and work continually to strengthen that foundation of trust (Noddings, 1992).

Most teachers have felt frustrations and anxieties like Shanisha's at one time or another. If these situations continue, they can grow worse with each passing day. In such cases, the frustrated teacher is likely to suffer from "teacher burnout"—a form of emotional stress that is so strong that it causes teachers to choose another profession. But other teachers survive and even thrive under very similar classroom conditions. Why do some teachers burn out while others succeed?

This book describes classroom strategies and methods that you can use to become a caring and reflective teacher so you will thrive in your chosen career. We believe that two major traits help teachers achieve the kind of caring relationships that encourage students to relate to ideas, to their peers, and to others in their worlds. The first trait is known as *withitness*, which refers to a combination of caring and perceptiveness that allows teachers to focus on the needs of their students. The second trait is rooted in withitness. It is the ability to monitor your own behaviors, feelings, and needs and to learn from your mistakes. We call it *reflective action*. One of the most important things you can do to develop withitness and reflective action is to get to know yourself and understand your own needs and desires to be cared for. We will return to this theme repeatedly because your need to receive respect and affection from your students is something you must come to recognize and deal with effectively before you can care for others.

We begin by examining the concept known as withitness and then describe reflective action.

Withitness

Kounin (1977) videotaped classrooms in action in order to discover the differences between well-managed, smoothly functioning and poorly managed, disorderly functioning classrooms. Although he expected to find that smoothly functioning classrooms were governed by certain rules and discipline strategies, he found no such relationship. Instead, he found that the most smoothly functioning classrooms were those led by a teacher whose management style was characterized by a high degree of alertness and the ability to pay attention to two things at the same time.

Kounin labeled the teacher characteristic that distinguished good classroom managers from poor ones *withitness*. The good managers he observed knew what was going on in their classrooms at all times. They were aware of who was working and who was not. They were also able to overlap their instruction with monitoring of student behavior. As a result, they were able to alter a presentation at the first sign of student restlessness or boredom. If a minor disruption occurred between students, the teacher perceived it immediately and was likely to move a student or otherwise prevent the disruption from growing.

Withitness is expressed more through teacher perceptiveness and behavior than through words. Eye contact, facial expressions, proximity, gestures, and actions such as stopping an activity demonstrate teacher withitness to students. These teachers are able to continue teaching a lesson while gesturing to a group or standing next to an overactive student who needs to refocus on the lesson. These are examples of the concept of *overlapping*, in which the teacher is able to deal both with student behavior and the lesson at the same time.

Kounin also studied what he called the *ripple effect*, a preventive discipline strategy that he found to be particularly useful in elementary classrooms. Kounin observed a student in his own college class reading a newspaper during the lecture. When Kounin reprimanded the student, he observed that his remarks caused changes in behavior among the other members of the class as well. "Side glances to others ceased, whispers stopped, eyes went from windows or the instructor to notebooks on the desk" (1977, p.

1). In subsequent observations in kindergarten classrooms, Kounin found that when teachers spoke firmly but kindly to a student, asking that student to desist from misbehavior, the other students in the class were also likely to desist from that behavior as well. When teachers spoke with roughness, however, the ripple effect was not as strong. "Children who witnessed a teacher desist another child with anger or punitiveness did not conform more nor misbehave less than those witnessing a teacher desist another without anger or punitiveness" (p. 10).

Reflective Action Builds on Withitness

Withitness is an essential foundation for becoming a reflective teacher. Perceptive teachers constantly observe conditions and gather information to make good judgments about what is happening in a classroom and what can or should be done to address it. Withitness continually raises the quality and level of reflective thinking because it helps teachers observe more accurately and collect more complete information about classroom conditions. Reflective teachers plan for variations in student response, constantly monitor students' reactions to classroom events, and are ready to respond when students show confusion or boredom. Reflective teachers actively monitor students during group activities and independent seatwork, looking for signs that students need clarification of the task or the teacher's expectations. They also consider the quality of developing student relationships, and note how students interact with ideas, with their peers, and with others in various settings.

Can withitness and reflective action be learned? We believe so. If you are willing to examine the cause-and-effect relationships in your classroom honestly and search for reasons for students' behaviors, you are likely to develop your withitness in the process. If you are willing to ask other adults to observe your interactions with students and give you feedback on how you respond to various situations, you will be able to make changes and improve the quality of your withitness radar and responses. If you are willing to discuss classroom problems openly and honestly with your students, in a problem-solving manner, you are likely to learn from them what their signals mean.

For example, Judy once visited a second-grade classroom where a teacher planned the morning activities to go from reading to math to science without a break. By the time the teacher asked the students to put away their math books and take out their science books, the grumbling and murmuring and shuffling of feet had grown to intolerable proportions. With no trace of withitness, this teacher's voice went higher and higher as she scolded the children and told them to be quiet and listen, keep their hands and feet still, sit up, and pay attention. This happened over and over again until lunchtime. A reflective, caring teacher using withitness as a tool would have perceived that student grumbling signaled a planning problem—one that could be easily solved by allowing the children to move and stretch for a few minutes before starting another lesson.

Principals and supervising teachers often note that withitness and reflective thinking grow with experience. They grow in a symbiotic way. The more withitness teachers develop, the more reflective they are likely to become. Similarly, the more that teachers reflect on the needs of their students, the more withitness they are likely to display. Few first-year teachers exhibit consistent and accurate withitness. It is gradually developed by teachers as they actively reflect on the effects of their actions and decisions on their students' behavior.

For example, a beginning teacher may gradually become aware that her lessons are too long for the students' attention spans. From that time on, she will be sensitive to whether a particular lesson is moving too slowly or lasting too long. On another day, the teacher may notice that whenever a certain student is made to establish eye contact, the student ceases to misbehave; the teacher reflects on this and actively begins to use eye contact as a way to connect not only with this student but with others. Then, after further observation and discussion with a colleague, the teacher may also become aware that in some cultures children avoid making eye contact with adults as a sign of respect. In response to a serious disruption, the teacher may notice that using a strong, confident voice causes the students to pay attention, whereas using a tentative, meek voice causes their attention to wander. Through reflecting on these experiences, the teacher develops two effective strategies for redirecting student behavior, and begins to learn which is more effective in a given situation. Her active self-reflection is the first step toward developing greater withitness, and her increasing withitness contributes to greater self-reflection.

Reflecting on Your Ethics and Principles

Reflective action is a time-consuming practice that may involve a personal risk for the individual willing to engage in it. Personal examination of why you do something, how you can do something better, and an honest look at the effects of your actions from others' points of view can result in feelings of discomfort. When you engage in reflective thinking about actions you have just taken or are about to take, you may become critical of your own behavior or your motives. Peters (1991) observed that reflective practice involves a personal risk because it requires that practitioners be open to an examination of beliefs, values, and feelings about which there may be a great sensitivity.

When teachers are engaged in reflection about their decisions, actions, and behaviors, they are likely to begin asking themselves questions such as "Why do I have this rule?," "Why do I care so much about what happens in my classroom?," and "How did I come to believe so strongly about this element of my teaching?"

When teachers ask themselves these types of searching questions, they may find a need to reexamine their beliefs and values. For example, a teacher who has been raised and schooled in traditional settings where children were "seen but not heard," unless they were responding to a direct question by an adult, may expect the same type of behavior from his or her students. But imagine that same teacher observing a classroom where students are allowed to interact, discuss their ideas with other students, and take part in very spirited discussions with the teacher. Based on past assumptions, the beginning teacher may feel very uncomfortable in a classroom with this noise level and consider the behavior of the students to be rude. If, however, the teacher is willing and able to ask, "Why am I uncomfortable with this noise level? Is it because I was never allowed to speak up when I was a child? How did I feel about the rules when I was a child? How do I feel about them now? What are the differences in the way these children are learning and the way I learned? What do I want my future students to learn, how to be quiet and orderly or how to be curious and assertive?"

When teachers confront confusing and ambiguous questions like these with honesty, they are becoming "real." Honest self-reflection can lead to new understandings of how your beliefs influence your present choices and actions. Continued reflective thinking can lead you to begin to clarify your philosophy of life and teaching and your ethical standards and moral code.

Do you think that it is necessary for you as a teacher to know what you stand for, what you believe and value? Is it important that you be able to state clearly the ethical and moral basis for your decisions? Strike (1990) notes two important reasons why teachers should have a well-articulated philosophy of teaching and code of ethics: (1) They work with a particularly vulnerable clientele and (2) the teaching profession has no clear set of ethical principles or standards. Strike believes that, in the matter of discipline and grading, the most important ethical concepts are *honesty, respect for diversity, fairness,* and *due process.* He also believes that teachers must be willing to consider the ethical implications of equity in the way teachers distribute their time and attention to students, avoiding playing favorites. Are these part of your personal code of ethics?

It is likely that you believe your students ought to have the attributes of honesty, respect for diversity, and fairness. If so, it is very important that you demonstrate these behaviors for them, because it is well known that teachers are important models of moral and ethical behavior for the students they teach. As Ryan (1986) noted,

> . . . research has now confirmed what humankind long ago recognized intuitively: People with power and prestige are imitated by those around them. And, although some teachers may not think of themselves as people with power and prestige, the children they teach certainly see them as such. Children watch their teachers to find out how grown-ups act. Therefore, teachers need to be constantly aware of the powerful influence that their actions in the classroom have on students. (p. 231)

Your students are your clients. They are quite vulnerable to the influence of their teachers' beliefs and ethics. Teachers are very important role models for behavior and character. In classrooms that we observe, the teacher's character and moral code set the standards and the tone or climate for the classroom. If the teacher is fair, students are influenced to treat others fairly. If the teacher is impulsive and selfish, students are likely to behave in the same way. When teachers demonstrate a willingness to listen openly and honestly to others' points of view, students begin to respect the opinions of others as well. When teachers are closed and rigid in their approach to teaching and learning, students mold their behavior into a search for right answers and rote learning.

Gilligan (1982) asserts that the concepts of caring and responsibility are essential elements of moral development. Teachers may express these qualities by showing respect for students' feelings and taking responsibility for meeting students' needs without shifting the blame for their low performance to other factors. Noddings (1992) expresses the need for ethical caring in schools because schools are places where human beings learn how to interact. She proposes that caring is the basis of the Golden Rule. Caring as a moral attribute is probably high on the list of most aspiring teachers. Many people choose the career of teaching because they care deeply about the needs of children in our society. They are also likely to feel responsible for meeting the needs of their students. Occasionally, you may observe teachers who seem to have lost the ability to care for others because they are overwhelmed with meeting their own needs. They tend to blame others when their students do not behave or achieve. But reflective, caring teachers willingly accept that it is their responsibility to design a program that allows their students to succeed. They work every day to balance their own needs with the needs of their students. To achieve this goal, they are willing to learn systematic ways of reflecting on their own practice so that they can enhance their students' likelihood of succeeding.

Definitions of Reflective Thinking and Action

In *How We Think: A Restatement of the Relation of Reflective Thinking to the Educative Process*, John Dewey (1933) defined reflective thinking as the "active, persistent and careful consideration of any belief or supposed form of knowledge in light of the grounds that support it" (p. 9). An analysis of this carefully worded statement creates a powerful verbal image of the reflective thinker and correlates with the concept presented here of a person consciously choosing to use reflective action in teaching.

The first descriptive adjective, *active*, indicates one who voluntarily and willingly takes responsibility for considering personal actions. Reflective action includes an energetic search for information and solutions to problems that arise in the classroom. Dewey's use of the word *persistent* implies a commitment to thinking through difficult issues in depth, continuing to consider matters even though it may be uncomfortable or tiring to do so. Although some teachers may begin to seek knowledge and information, they may be satisfied with easy answers and simple solutions. In contrast, the reflective teacher is rarely satisfied with quick answers. Instead, he continually and persistently seeks to fine-tune and improve ways to teach students and manage classroom events.

The careful thinker is one who has concern for both self and others. Teachers who use reflective action care deeply about ways to improve their own classroom performance and how to bring the greatest possible benefit to the lives of their students. They believe that teaching is relational—meaning that the quality of interactions in the classroom sets the tone for learning. Using reflective action, such teachers set out to create positive, nurturing classroom environments that promote high self-esteem and concern not only between the teacher and her students, but also among students and their peers. Less caring teachers are likely to consider their own needs and feelings to be of greater importance than those of their students. Because they do not reason with care, they may make unreasonable demands on their students or fail to sense and address important student needs.

Dewey's phrase "belief or supposed form of knowledge" implies that little is known for sure in the teaching profession. The teacher who uses reflective action recognizes the value of informed practice, but maintains a healthy skepticism about various educational procedures and theories. While a less reflective teacher might be persuaded that there is only one right way to teach, the reflective teacher observes that individual students may need different conditions for learning and a variety of incentives in order to be successful. A less reflective teacher might adopt each new educational fad without questioning its value; the reflective teacher greets each of these new ideas with an open but questioning mind, considering whether it is valuable and how it can be adapted to fit the needs of the class.

The final phrase in Dewey's definition, "in light of the grounds that support it," directly relates to the reflective thinker's practice of using evidence and criteria in making judgments. Whereas less reflective teachers may jump to conclusions very quickly based on initial observations or prior cases, the reflective teacher gathers as much information as possible about any given problem, weighs the value of the evidence against suitable criteria, and then draws a tentative conclusion. After a conclusion is made, the less reflective teacher may stick to it rigidly, but the reflective teacher will reconsider his judgments whenever new evidence or information becomes available.

Although persistent and careful thinking is important to the reflective teacher, such thinking does not automatically lead to change and improvement. Dewey also acknowledged the importance of translating thought into action, and specified that attitudes of open-mindedness, responsibility, and wholeheartedness are needed for teachers to translate their thoughts into reflective actions.

Schon (1987) concurs with Dewey's emphasis on action as an essential aspect of the reflective process. He defines the reflective practitioner as one who engages in "reflection-in-action." This kind of thinking includes observing and critiquing our own actions and then changing our behaviors based on what we see. Reflection-in-action gives rise to on-the-spot experiment. We define a problem, consider how we have addressed it in the past, and think up and try out new actions to test our tentative understandings of them. This process helps us determine whether our moves change things for the better. An on-the-spot experiment may work, or it may produce surprises that call for further reflection and experiment.

Schon also notes that reflectivity in teaching leads to "professional artistry," a special type of competence displayed by some teachers when they find themselves in situations full of surprise, ambiguity, or conflict. Just as physicians respond to each patient's unique array of symptoms by questioning, inventing, testing, and creating a new diagnosis, Schon believes that reflective teachers also respond to the unexpected by asking questions such as "What are my students experiencing?," "What can I do to improve this situation?," and "How does my students' performance relate to the way I am teaching this material?"

Often, during the process of reflection, individuals find that a new, surprising event contradicts something they thought they already "knew." When this happens, the reflective individual is able to cope with paradoxes and dilemmas by reexamining what they already know, restructuring their strategies, or reframing the problem. They often invent on-the-spot experiments to put their new understandings to the test or to answer the puzzling questions that have arisen from the event.

Reflective action is made up of many elements and is related to an individual's willingness to be curious and assertive in order to increase self-awareness, self-knowledge, and new understandings of the world in which we live and work. It is not something that occurs easily for most of us and it takes time to develop. Writing of this idea, Brubacher, Case, and Reagan (1994) cite the children's story of the Velveteen Rabbit to suggest that becoming a reflective practitioner has much in common with the process of becoming "real." As the Skin Horse explained to the Rabbit, becoming "real" takes time, and happens after a toy has been loved so much that it loses its hair and becomes shabby. In the same way, becoming a truly reflective teacher involves time, experience and, inevitably, a bit of wear around the edges!

Graphic Model of Reflective Action in Teaching

Consider that as writers, it is our responsibility to connect with you in the same way teachers must connect with their students. We reflect on our memories of ourselves as beginning teachers and think about what we wanted to learn and needed to know in order to be successful. In this, the third edition of the book, we use feedback from readers of previous editions as well as our own continuing research, to fine-tune the material we want to present.

We know that sometimes students learn better by seeing a picture or a graphic model of a complicated idea. The model of reflective action we present in this edition has changed from the first and second editions because we are continually reflecting on how to make it more understandable and usable. Still, we recognize that any model is oversimplified and relies on the readers to fill in details and examples with their own imagination. With feedback from you, we will continue to refine our thinking in future editions. This is exactly how your own teaching can improve over the years if you are willing to seek critical feedback and to reflect and grow as a result of your experiences.

When you think of your school years, no doubt several of your own past teachers come to mind. Maybe you had a favorite teacher who reached out to you in a way that made you feel valued and important. Perhaps one of the reasons you are reading this book is because your interactions with a caring teacher helped instill in you the desire to influence others in the same way you were influenced. On the other hand, you may also have had a negative experience with a teacher and determined that you would enter the teaching profession to help ensure that more caring individuals become the teachers of the future. You have probably heard the term *the art of teaching*. One aspect of the art of teaching is that each of us enters the teaching profession with a set of unique experiences with people and with institutions. From these individual experiences, each teacher develops a unique perspective, or set of expectations, through which we view the world and from which we determine what we think life in a classroom should be like.

In the field of education, our perspectives or expectations work a little bit like the visual artist's perspective. For example, imagine that three different artists have been asked to paint the same landscape. Figure 1.1 shows the artist on the left painting the scene as she views it. Notice how she has chosen to depict the boat in relation to the sunset and the lake. In contrast, note how the middle artist's view differs. He focuses on a close-up of the pine tree, with the boat further in the distance. If you compared the two paintings, you might not realize from the first that there were pine trees in the original scene. Finally, look at the third artist's canvas. How does her view compare to the first two? There is no lake at all in her painting.

Over time, artists develop particular perspectives that become associated with their style of art. In the same way, your unique teaching and learning perspective will lead you to notice some things and overlook others—during your teacher preparation courses and throughout your teaching career. There is nothing wrong with having a perspective or set of expectations about teaching; in fact, you cannot help but have one. However, it is important to remember that one's personal perspective is not the only view or interpretation of events. In fact, there are at least as many different perspectives for an event as there are participants in it!

Why does the existence of different perspectives matter in becoming an effective, reflective teacher? Let's explore what happens to a teacher who fails to recognize how to take advantage of different perspectives, as compared with one who does.

Teacher Enters with Expectations

A teacher preparing a lesson works from a personal perspective or set of expectations about what makes a good lesson, how students should act, and what effective teachers do. When it is time to actually teach the lesson, this set of expectations functions almost like a mental picture of what is about to occur (Figure 1.2).

Figure 1.1 Different perspectives create a point of view.

Figure 1.2 Teacher has a view of how a lesson will proceed.

Figure 1.3 Students' responses do not match what the teacher expected.

Unforseen Problem Occurs

Unfortunately, students do not always share the teacher's perspective for a lesson (Figure 1.3). This can occur for a number of reasons. Perhaps the students' experiences with school differ greatly from those of the teacher, or perhaps a physical need (e.g., hunger, fatigue) prevents a student from paying full attention to the teacher's input. For any number of reasons, an unforeseen problem or challenge can (and often does!) arise during even the best-prepared lessons.

Unaware Teacher Continues

Like an artist who chooses to paint a close-up of a figure, some teachers focus only on those students or events that are doing what they expect or want to see (Figure 1.4). These teachers lack withitness. They fail to notice disruptive students' behaviors or

Figure 1.4 Some teachers focus only on students who fulfill expectations.

needs. For example, the teacher pictured here focuses only on the student who is attending to the lecture. Perhaps you have been in a classroom like this where the teacher does not interrupt the planned lesson flow to address unexpected, and often undesirable behaviors. Sometimes the teacher seems completely unaware that there is even a need to change the pace or interact with a particular student. How long will students continue to learn in such a setting?

Caring Teacher Uses Withitness

In contrast, the most effective, caring teachers monitor the ever-changing climate of the classroom by paying close attention to students' nonverbal and verbal responses (Figure 1.5). We use the term *withitness* to describe the combination of caring and perceptiveness that such teachers possess. When events deviate from expectations, a withit teacher responds by changing pace in a lesson, moving about the room, and making eye contact with students in an effort to refocus their attention on learning.

Figure 1.5 Teacher notices behavior of all students and responds quickly to unexpected events.

Figure 1.6 Teacher reviews the event and creates a tentative explanation for it.

Teacher Puts the Problem into Perspective

Successful teachers do not stop thinking about a problem when the bell rings. Effective teachers have learned the value of reflecting on negative classroom events and considering how those events might have been prevented. You will often find reflective teachers reviewing an event, seeking to explain for themselves what caused the problem to occur (Figure 1.6). For example, as the teacher in this drawing reviews the math lesson, the teacher may blame it all on a particular student who is known as a *troublemaker*. This easy solution can be supported by recalling several instances in the past when the student exhibited disruptive behaviors. As with most easy solutions, this one may only cover up the real issues. Reflective teachers will not be satisfied with such a hasty conclusion.

Teacher Widens the Perspective

A caring and reflective teacher understands that a particular point of view can limit perceptiveness and withitness (Figure 1.7). This teacher examines the first conclusion about the *troublemaker* in class, and recalls that this student seems to exhibit this behavior about 5 minutes before the lunch bell. Thinking back to the students' schedules, the teacher suddenly realizes that the misbehaving student (and several others) helps in the cafeteria on Tuesdays and Thursdays. Perhaps the math lesson deteriorates as students grow anxious about arriving on time for their special lunchroom jobs. Recognizing that a different perspective exists for the classroom event, this teacher then rules out the troublemaker idea and looks further into the event, wondering if there was anything about the way the lesson was presented that also contributed to student restlessness.

From this example, you can see how vitally important it is to spend some time on self-reflection. By rushing out the door to another appointment, or turning your attention away from the problems you face to do paperwork, you may miss valuable opportunities to develop your capacities for withitness and reflective action. We cannot empha-

Figure 1.7 Teacher reexamines tentative explanation and considers alternatives.

size enough the importance of this first step. Without reflection, there is unlikely to be any growth of withitness. Without reflection, there is little motivation to take action.

Teacher Invites Feedback

In our example, the teacher's honest self-reflection leads to the first important action step, inviting the feedback of respected colleagues or looking for other resources to help explain the unexpected classroom event (Figure 1.8). In this case, the concerned teacher shares the math experience with a colleague, who has a different perspective to offer. "Did you have something besides the chalkboard for students to look at?" the colleague asks. "Perhaps they needed something more concrete to focus on. I would use some blocks to demonstrate the mathematical operations more concretely."

Figure 1.8 Teacher turns to colleagues and other sources for feedback on the problem.

Figure 1.9 Teacher gathers new information to create a new perspective for the problem.

Teacher Redefines the Problem

Rather than simply adopt someone else's interpretations, the reflective teacher gathers information and uses it to help reexamine earlier thinking (Figure 1.9). In this case, the reflective teacher's willingness to redefine the problem results in a completely new perspective, and suddenly she realizes that the students may have needed *their own* blocks to understand the concept. "Empty hands!" thinks the teacher. "They lost focus and misbehaved because they had *nothing to do with their hands!*"

Teacher Creates New Action Plan

Once the reflective teacher widens the perspective and redefines the problem in terms of students' needs, the next step is to create an action plan to meet their needs (Figure 1.10). The teacher imagines the students working with manipulatives at their own desks. This leads to more action steps of locating the needed materials and getting them set up in the classroom in time for the next math lesson.

Figure 1.10 Teacher makes a new plan that sets up new expectations.

Figure 1.11 Teacher plans for possible surprises that could occur.

Teacher Predicts Possible Outcomes

However, reflective teachers do not just devise an action plan and rush back to the classroom to carry it out. Rather, they continue with their self-reflection long enough to consider the potential outcomes of their new plan, considering possible pitfalls or problems that may arise as they put their new plan into action (Figure 1.11). As this teacher reflects on the desirable effects of using manipulatives in her math lesson, there is also a need to address the possibility that students could easily misuse the materials, causing noise and disruption to occur. By imagining the plan in action and visualizing potential problems, the teacher is able to take steps to prevent any new problems. The reflective teacher tries to imagine passing out the blocks and rehearses the procedures and rules to be used. "When Juanita hands you your blocks, you are to leave them alone until I tell you what to do next." Thinking ahead like this is one of the most important aspects of reflective action that helps teachers gain confidence in their own effectiveness. Each successful cycle of reflective action results in enhanced withitness, heightened enthusiasm, greater expectations for success, and greater maturity as a teacher.

Professional Standards for Teachers

The reflective action model we have presented here is our way of articulating a set of thought processes and action steps that encourage self-understanding and professional growth. As a beginning teacher, you may want to be able to demonstrate your professional growth and your unique teaching style, talents, and abilities to others. You may need to do this in order to earn your teaching credential or, after that, to compete successfully for a teaching position. The National Board for Professional Teaching Stan-

dards (NBPTS) (1999) proposes *five propositions of accomplished teaching* as fundamental requirements for professional teachers to be able to demonstrate. The NBPTS
believes that "excellence in teaching is the sum of human qualities like judgment and
improvisation, expert knowledge and skill, and unflagging professional commitment."
These are the five NBPTS propositions:

1. Teachers are committed to students and their learning.
2. Teachers know the subjects they teach and how to teach those subjects
   to students.
3. Teachers are responsible for managing and monitoring student learning.
4. Teachers think systematically about their practice and learn from experience.
5. Teachers are members of learning communities.

We hope you can see the links between these five core propositions of excellence in
teaching and the processes we have described as reflective action steps. To clarify these
links, we believe that teachers who are committed to their students are those who use
withitness to perceive their students' needs and are further willing to reflect alone and
collegially to meet those needs. Teachers who are determined to be sure that they know
the subjects they teach and how best to teach them are willing to use reflective action
steps to do research and examine and reexamine the problems that arise in their classrooms. Teachers who want to grow in their management capabilities are willing to ask
colleagues for feedback on management problems and issues and consider contingencies before they arise to prevent management problems from occurring.

The fourth core proposition is that teachers think systematically about their practice
and learn from experience. What does it mean to "think systematically"? We have tried
to offer one version of systematic thinking in this chapter. Our reflective action model
is just that—a system of thinking and acting in order to improve your practice and learn
from your experience. Our model is purposefully collegial as we concur with the fifth
core proposition that teachers are members of learning communities.

Creating a Professional Portfolio

If you want to be able to demonstrate your professional accomplishments as well as
your ability to think systematically and learn from experience, there is no better vehicle
than the creation of a professional portfolio. At the end of each chapter, we have provided suggestions for pages that you may wish to include in your professional portfolio.
For example, in this chapter, we make suggestions that will allow you to clarify and
articulate your unique philosophy of teaching and learning. We suggest that you use
our model of reflective action in teaching as the basis for demonstrating your systematic thinking as well. Because the underlying idea of reflective action is that actions
change as a result of our reflection, we do not expect that you will write one philosophy
of teaching today and keep it for many years. Rather, we believe that you will write one
draft of your philosophy today and revise it many, many times over the course of your
career. When you feel that your philosophy has changed, it is important to come back
to that page in your portfolio and revise it accordingly.

Reflective Actions for Your Professional Portfolio

My Philosophy of Teaching

Use Your Withitness to Observe and Respond

Visit a classroom and use all your senses to observe and describe how the teacher uses space and other resources. How are the students' desks arranged? Where is the teacher's desk? Does the room feel crowded or spacious? Are there activity spaces? If so, for what purpose are they used? Observe and describe the use of light, color, and decorations. What do you hear when you walk into this classroom? How does the room smell? Are there any tastes associated with your visit?

Put Your Philosophy into Perspective

Take photos or draw a sketch of this classroom and include them in your portfolio, along with your written reflections. As soon as possible after your classroom observation, draw a sketch of how you would arrange this classroom to make it fit your preferences.

Widen Your Perspective

Would you like to be a student in the classroom you visited? Why or why not? Would you like to be a student in the classroom you sketched for yourself? Why or why not?

Invite Feedback

Ask yourself, "How does the classroom environment demonstrate one's philosophy of teaching?" Discuss your question with colleagues. Brainstorm with colleagues to create a list of moral and ethical attributes that are highly valued by humankind (for example, honesty, courage, fairness).

Redefine Your Philosophy

Select four to six of the qualities you brainstormed that represent the attributes that you value most. Describe how your classroom environment will represent these values.

Create an Action Plan That Reflects Your Philosophy

Write a paragraph or two about why each value you identified is important to you and how you will attempt to model and teach those concepts to your students. Consider this paper a first draft of your teaching philosophy. For additional pages, remember that teaching is a very creative career. Some of the creative talents that teachers use include art, music, interior design, drama, photography, and cartooning. What are some creative talents that you will use to create a unique and welcoming classroom environment for your students? Include sketches of the bulletin boards, centers, or class projects that you will design to enhance your classroom environment.

Predict Possible Outcomes

After you write the first draft of your philosophy, consider again what the likely effects of your philosophy will be on your students' experience. What elements of your philosophy will your students welcome and respond to in a positive way? What elements of your philosophy might be a "hard sell" for your students? How will you convince them of the importance of these elements? Add a paragraph that describes your understanding that philosophies change with experience and that you intend for your philosophy to be a dynamic one, based on your future experiences and the needs of your students. Also, write a statement about how you will plan for contingencies and learn from your mistakes. Revise and refine your philosophy as the year goes by. The final draft goes in your portfolio.

References

Brubacher, J., Case, C., & Reagan, T. (1994). *Becoming a reflective educator: How to build a culture of inquiry in the schools.* Thousand Oaks, CA: Corwin Press.

Dewey, J. (1933). *How we think: A restatement of the relation of reflective thinking to the educative process* (rev. ed.). Lexington, MA: D. C. Heath.

Gilligan, C. (1982). *In a different voice.* Cambridge, MA: Harvard University Press.

Kounin, J. (1977). *Discipline and group management in classrooms.* New York: Holt, Rinehart and Winston.

National Board for Professional Teaching Standards. (1999). *What teachers should know and be able to do.* Washington, D.C.: Author. Access on-line at http://www.nbpts/standards/intro.html.

Noddings, N. (1984). *Caring: A feminine approach to ethics and moral education.* Berkeley: University of California Press.

Noddings, N. (1992). *The challenge to care in schools.* NY: Teachers College Press.

Peters, J. (1991). Strategies for reflective practice. *Professional and Continuing Education, 51,* 83–102, San Francisco: Jossey-Bass.

Ryan, K. (1986). The new moral education. *Phi Delta Kappan, 67,* 228–233.

Schon, D. (1987). *Educating the reflective practitioner.* San Francisco: Jossey-Bass.

Strike, K. (1990). The legal and moral responsibility of teachers. In J. Goodlad, R. Soder, & K. Sirotnik (Eds.), *The moral dimensions of teaching* (pp. 188–223). San Francisco: Jossey-Bass.

Chapter

2

Planning a Healthy, Safe Environment for Learning

When you walk into a classroom, you can sense a particular climate or environment within a few moments. The way the room is arranged, its messiness or neatness, wall decorations, movements and noises made by the students, and the smell of chalk dust or an animal cage all combine to create a unique flavor or climate in the classroom. The behavior, body language, and facial expressions of the teacher and students give you the most important clues about what life is like in this classroom. You may sense healthy elements such as excitement, energy, joy, cooperation, and pride, or you may sense debilitating elements such as fear, aimlessness, frustration, and tension. These are all components of the classroom environment, which is largely established by the teacher during the first days and weeks of the school year.

Teachers who have committed themselves to use withitness and reflective action make hundreds of decisions a day to promote a healthy classroom climate that promotes student achievement and satisfaction. By carefully considering the psychosocial needs of their students, they are able to structure classroom expectations and incentives that promote students' achievement and interest in school.

A Good Beginning for the School Year

Studies show that it is the teacher who establishes the particular climate of each classroom. Given identical classrooms in the same school, identical materials and resources, and the same clientele, each teacher creates a unique learning environment by drawing from personal expectations, beliefs, attitudes, knowledge, and effort. As a student, you have experienced the power of the teacher for many years. It is likely that you still enter every classroom on the first day of a new course hoping that the teacher will be interesting, fair, knowledgeable, and caring.

Many people think that inner-city schools serving less affluent students are oppressive and sterile, whereas suburban schools serving middle-class students are vital and stimulating. In reality, though, a great variety of classroom environments exist within every school. No matter where they teach, reflective, caring, and creative teachers know they can make a significant difference in students' lives, and they work especially hard to create a positive, healthy classroom environment to counteract the effects of poverty, discrimination, and neglect.

Organizing the Physical Environment

The classroom appearance makes a statement about the extent to which the teacher cares for the environment in which the class lives and works. It may be untidy, neat, colorful, drab, filled with objects, plants, animals, and children's art or left undecorated and unkempt. No two classrooms are alike; each has its unique environment. However, some classrooms (and their occupants) bloom with health, vitality, and strength, while others appear sickly, listless, and debilitated.

Studies of teacher planning show that during the days immediately preceding the school year, teachers are primarily concerned with setting up the physical environment of the classroom. Reflective teachers want to come to school several days before their contracts call for them to be there. They hang posters, decorate bulletin boards, and carefully consider ways to arrange the students' desks, tables, bookcases, and other furniture to fit their curriculum plans and the needs of their students. You know from your many years in classrooms that a bright, colorful, cheerful, and stimulating classroom suggests that school will be interesting and that the teacher celebrates life and learning. You also know that drab, undecorated spaces lead to expectations of dullness and boredom.

How to arrange the desks is a complex issue. Often the room contains many more desks than it was designed to hold comfortably. The number of students in a classroom may vary from 15 to 35, and the precise number of students is not known until the last minute, making preplanning difficult. Generally, though, teachers know approximately how many students they will have in their classrooms, and they arrange the desks in a way that uses space economically and strategically. Their plans are governed by an image of themselves and their students in teaching and learning experiences. While arranging the classroom, reflective teachers envision in their minds the "activity flow" of the classroom—how things will work when the students arrive.

This imaging process helps reflective teachers decide how to arrange the furniture in the room. As with other important decisions, every organization decision has both advantages and disadvantages. Desks can be arranged in rows, circles, semicircles, and small groups. Each arrangement influences how students work and how they perceive their environment. Rows of desks provide an advantage in keeping order but leave little space for activities (Figure 2.1). A large circle of desks can be used if the teacher envisions teaching and learning experiences taking place in the center of the circle, but it will be difficult for all students to see the chalkboard (Figure 2.2).

Doyle (1986) reports that open arrangements (i.e., those not in rows) result in students spending more time working together, initiating their own tasks, and working without teacher attention than students in traditional rooms. Teachers who value cooperative learning experiences over teacher-centered learning experiences often use clusters of four to six desks (Figure 2.3).

Jones (1987) recommends organizing the classroom into shallow concentric circles, no more than three rows deep (Figure 2.4). In this setting, the teacher can maintain eye contact with all students and is able to move quickly to the side of any student who needs assistance or a reminder to pay attention. The increased physical proximity allows the teacher to circulate more easily to provide individual help.

Activity and work spaces can be arranged by using bookcases and room dividers or simply by arranging tables and chairs in the corners of the room. Some teachers bring in comfortable furniture and rugs to design a space just for quiet reading. Computer or listening stations are also designated. Room arrangement and the use of space are highly individualized decisions. Teachers make these decisions to fit their personal image of what a classroom should be, by considering what they value most highly and how the room arrangement fits their values, and by considering the curriculum and grade level of the class.

Reflective teachers also consider the effects the physical arrangement of the room will have in developing a healthy classroom environment. Rows of desks connote order and efficiency but do little to build a sense of community. Clusters of desks promote cooperation and communication among groups of students. Large circle or concentric circle arrangements encourage communication and sharing among the entire class. Many reflective teachers change their room arrangements from time to time, depend-

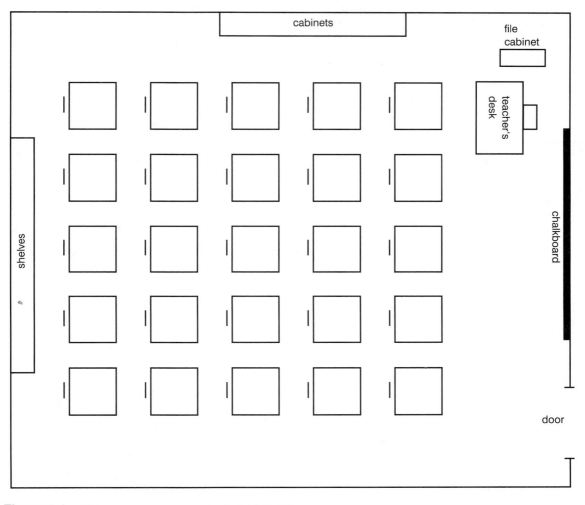

Figure 2.1   Classroom arrangement: rows of desks.

ing on the goals of a particular learning experience, and thus create a variety of class-room environments to fit a variety of purposes.

The First Day of School

The physical environment and schedule of the classroom may lead students to expect certain things about the way teaching and learning will occur during the school year. Thus, as you will recall from your own experiences, students look forward to meeting their new teacher for the first time so that they can discern what life will be like in this classroom. Students create lasting expectations during the first few minutes of the first

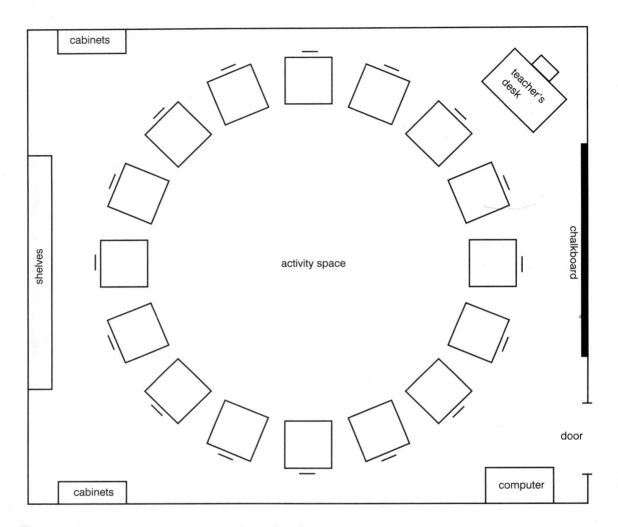

Figure 2.2   Classroom arrangement: circle of desks.

day of school. For example, consider Figure 2.5, which describes students' experiences on their first day of school in four hypothetical elementary classroom scenarios.

You probably recognize the teachers in these opening day scenarios and may even be able to give them different names and faces from your own experiences in school. You have been exposed to a variety of teaching styles, methods, attitudes, and philosophies as consumers of education. Now you will soon become teachers yourselves. What style will you have? How will your students perceive you? What values and principles will you model? How will your students feel when they walk into your classroom on the first day of school?

Each scenario depicts a variation of what we call a *teaching style*. A teaching style is a highly individualized and complex concept made up of personality, philosophy, val-

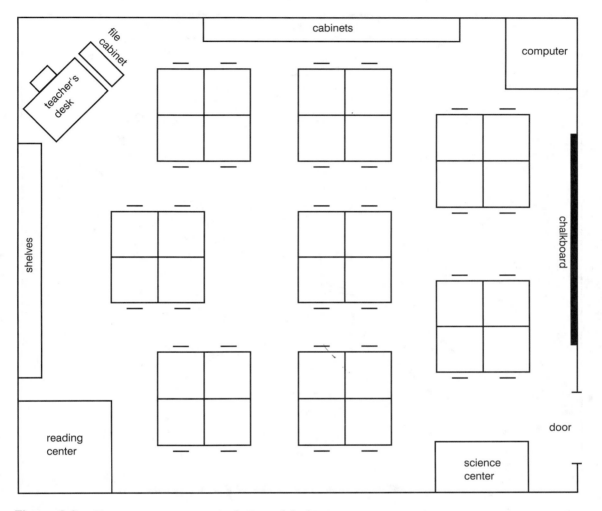

Figure 2.3   Classroom arrangement: clusters of desks.

ues, physical and emotional health, past experiences, and current knowledge about the effects of a teacher's behavior on the classroom environment.

Perhaps you are considering this important question: "Is it possible to control and decide on my teaching style, or is it simply a function of my personality?" The more information you can gather about how teachers create healthy climates for learning, the more power you have to gain self-understanding and control over this and other important matters pertaining to teaching and learning. Evertson (1989) has demonstrated that when teachers learn to examine their own practices and behaviors, they can learn to use more productive and positive classroom practices and discontinue the use of less effective methods.

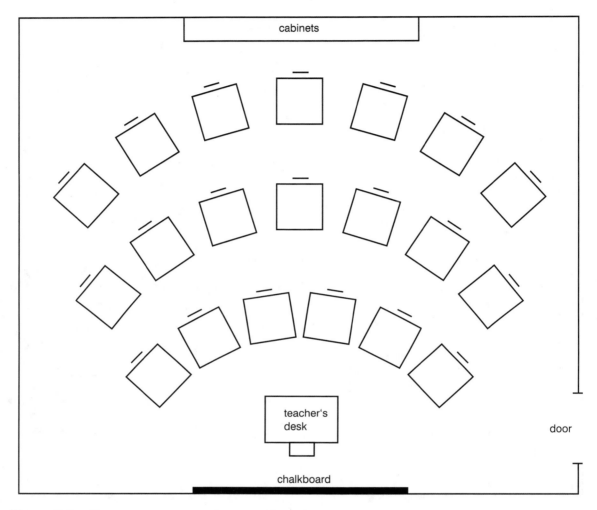

Figure 2.4   Classroom arrangement: concentric circles.

To identify the most effective classroom management strategies, Evertson and Harris (1992) reviewed and evaluated the findings of many major studies on classroom management strategies. They found that even under the best circumstances, half or less of the school day is used for instruction. They also noted that the more effective classroom managers were able to conserve instruction time and minimize noninstruction time by appropriately sequencing, pacing, monitoring, and providing feedback for student work. The most effective managers were those who had rules and procedures planned for their classes. During the first week of school, the more effective managers spent a major part of the first day and much time during the next 3 weeks helping their students adjust to their classroom expectations and learn to understand the rules and procedures established for the class. Like Miss Adams and Mr. Catlin, as soon as most students had arrived, the teachers began describing the rules and procedures they had carefully chosen. In some cases, students were asked to suggest rules for the class. The rules and procedures were explained clearly, with examples and reasons.

More effective managers did not rely simply on a discussion of the rules. They spent a considerable amount of time during the first week of school explaining and reminding students of the rules. One of the most effective ways to communicate your expectations to your class is to lead them through a rehearsal on how to follow the procedures. More effective teachers take time to rehearse procedures such as how to line up for lunch or what students should take out of their desks for math class. Many teachers teach students to respond to specific signals, such as a bell or a hand signal to call for attention. Evertson and Harris (1992) observed that the more effective managers begin the school year by clearly establishing themselves as the classroom leaders. They prepare and plan classroom procedures in advance, communicate their expectations clearly, and demonstrate their withitness by communicating their awareness of student behavior when it occurs. After the first three weeks, teachers who used these methods had few major discipline problems for the rest of the year.

The reflective teacher, guided by moral principles, also recognizes that it is not simply a matter of establishing leadership that is important; the style of leadership counts as well. Miss Adams and Mr. Catlin quickly established that they were the classroom leaders, but Mr. Catlin's style of leadership best exhibited the underlying moral principles of caring, consideration, and honesty as he interacted with his students. The result is that students in such an environment return the caring, consideration, and honesty to the teacher and exhibit it in their interactions with one another.

In contrast, less effective managers (exemplified by Mr. Baron) did not have well-thought-out classroom procedures. Although teachers like Mr. Baron always have rules, the rules are often vague and the teachers tend to tell the class the rules and procedures quickly without spending time discussing and rehearsing what they really mean. Others, like Mrs. Destry, try to move quickly to academic matters. They seem to expect the students to be able to comprehend and retain the rules from a single, brief statement. They do not teach the class routines and procedures. As a result, they often waste many, many hours of class time during the year as they remind the students again and again to behave.

The way the two groups of teachers monitor the behavior of their students is also a critical factor in establishing a clear set of expectations for students. The Evertson and Harris (1992) study disclosed that less effective teacher-managers did not actively monitor students' behavior. Instead, they busied themselves with clerical tasks or worked with a single student on a task while ignoring the rest of the class. The consequence of vague and untaught rules and poor monitoring was that the children were frequently left without enough information or a good enough example to guide their behavior.

From this study, you can conclude that if you expect your students to obey the rules of your classroom, you must give them clear directions, allow them to rehearse the procedures until they get them right, and actively monitor your students at work, showing them that you expect them to pay attention to the task and do their work. Remember the sad finding that less than half of the school day is actually used for teaching and learning itself. Resolve to use your time as effectively as possible by using your withitness and other strategies to prevent time from being wasted unnecessarily.

The scene is an elementary school. It is the first day of the new school year. In one corridor, several classroom doors are open. We see and hear four teachers greet the students in their classes.

Room 101

Miss Adams is standing at the doorway. As children walk in, she says, in a calm, even-toned voice, to each of them, "You'll find your name on a desk," as she gestures toward six clusters of desks. "Sit in that desk and wait quietly." The children obey and the room is quiet within. When all the children have entered, Miss Adams goes into her classroom and quietly shuts the door behind her. The beginning bell rings at precisely that moment.

Room 102

Mr. Baron is nowhere to be seen. Children enter the classroom looking for him, but when they don't see him, they begin to talk and walk around the room. The desks are arranged haphazardly in ragged rows. Two boys try to sit in the same desk, and a scuffle breaks out. The beginning bell rings. Suddenly Mr. Baron comes running down the hall, enters the room, and yells, "All right, you guys, sit down and be quiet. What do you think this place is? A zoo?"

Room 103

Mr. Catlin is standing at the door wearing a big smile. As each child enters, he gives the child a sticker with his or her name on it. "Put this sticker on a desk that you like and sit in it," he says. The children enter and quickly claim desks, which are arranged in four concentric arcs facing the front of the room. They talk with each other in the classroom. When the bell rings, Mr. Catlin enters, leaving the door ajar for latecomers.

Room 104

Mrs. Destry is sitting at her desk when the children enter. Without standing up, she tells the children to line up along the side of the room. They comply. When the bell rings, she tells a student to shut the door.

If we were able to enter the classrooms with the students, this is what we might see, hear, and experience.

Room 101

Miss Adams stands in front of the class. She has excellent posture and a level gaze. As she waits quietly for the children to find their seats, she looks each child in the eye. They settle down quickly. When the classroom is perfectly quiet, she begins to talk.

"I see that you have all found your desks. Good. Now we can begin. I like the way you have quieted down. That tells me that you know how to behave in school. Let's review some of the important rules of our classroom."

Pointing to a chart entitled "Class Rules," she reads each aloud and tells the children its significance. "Rule 1: Students will pay attention when the teacher is speaking. This is important because we are here to learn and there can be no learning if you do not hear what the teacher is saying. Rule 2: Students will use quiet voices when talking in the classroom. This rule is important because a quiet, orderly classroom is conducive to learning. Rule 3: No fighting, arguing or name calling is allowed."

The children listen attentively to all items. They do not ask questions or comment on the rules. After the rules are read, Miss Adams assigns helpers for class jobs. The newly appointed monitors pass out the reading books, and the children begin to read the first story in their books. Miss Adams walks quietly from desk to desk to see that each child is reading.

Figure 2.5 Scenarios of the first day of school.

Room 102

Mr. Baron rushes in and slams some books and papers on the desk. Some of them land on the floor nearby. Stooping to pick them up, he says, "Sit down, sit down or I'll find cages for you instead of desks." The children sit down, but the noise level remains high.

"Enough! Do you want to begin the school year by going to the principal's office? Don't you care about school? Don't you want to learn something?" Gradually, the noise diminishes, but children's voices continue to interrupt from time to time with remarks to their teacher or to fellow classmates.

Mr. Baron calls roll from an attendance book. He does not even look up when a child says "Here" but stares intently at the book. He has several children pass out books at one time, resulting in more confusion about whether each child received all the necessary books. Finally, he tells them to begin reading the first story in their reading books. Some do so, others do not. Mr. Baron begins looking through his file cabinet, ignoring the noise.

Room 103

Mr. Catlin walks throughout the room as he talks to the class. From time to time, he stops near a child and puts his hand on the child's shoulder, especially a child who appears restless or insecure. This action seems to help the child settle down and pay attention.

"Welcome back to school! This year should be a good one for all of us. I've got some great new ideas for our math and social studies programs, and we'll be using paperback novels to supplement our reading series. But first, let's establish the rules for our classroom. Why are we here?"

A student raises her hand. Mr. Catlin reads the name tag sticker on her desk and calls on her by name. "To learn," she says timidly.

"Exactly!" Mr. Catlin agrees. "And, what rules can help us to learn the most we've ever learned in a single year?"

Several children begin to call out responses at the same time.

"Wait a moment, class. Can we learn anything like this?"

A chorus of "No's" is heard.

"Then what rule do we need to solve this problem?"

A child raises his hand, is called on, and says, "We need to raise our hands before we talk."

"What a fine rule," Mr. Catlin says with a broad smile. "How many agree?" The hands of most children go up. Mr. Catlin spots one child whose hand is not raised. He walks over to that child, kneels next to the child's desk and says, "Do you agree that this rule will help you learn this year?" "Yes," says the child and his hand goes up.

After the class has established and agreed on several other class rules, Mr. Catlin talks about the reading program. He offers the children their choice of five paperback novels, distributes them, and tells the children to begin reading. As they read, he circulates around the room, stopping from time to time to ask questions or make comments about the stories to individual children.

Room 104

Mrs. Destry regards the children in their line with an unfriendly gaze. When a child moves or talks, she gives that child a withering stare. From a class list, she begins to read the students' names in alphabetical order, indicating which seat they are to take. The students sit down meekly. No one says a word or makes a sound.

"Now, class, you will find your books in your desks. Take out your reading books and turn to the first page." Going down the rows, each child reads a paragraph aloud while the other children sit silently and listlessly, following along in their books.

Figure 2.5 *Continued*

Preventive Discipline Strategies

Teachers' Body Language

Jones (1987) found that effective classroom management and control of student behavior depends a great deal on the teacher's body language. Strong, effective teachers are able to communicate many important things with eye contact, physical proximity, bodily carriage, gestures, and facial expressions. These teachers do not have to be 6 feet 5 inches tall and weigh 230 pounds. Indeed, it is fascinating to observe teachers who are small in stature manage classrooms with a glance by standing next to a student who is disturbing the classroom.

Consider the eye contact of the teachers in the first-day scenario. Miss Adams had a level gaze and met the students' eyes as she looked at each of them at their first meeting. In a positive and nonthreatening manner, she communicated that she was aware and in control. In contrast, Mrs. Destry gave the students "withering stares" that probably caused them to feel anxious and fearful about the year ahead. Mr. Baron never met the eyes of his students at all, communicating his lack of preparedness and confidence to manage the classroom.

Mr. Catlin used physical proximity as well as eye contact to put his students at ease and to communicate that he was in charge. Jones (1987) recommends the concentric circle desk arrangement that Mr. Catlin used because it causes students to focus their attention on the teacher and enables the teacher to provide help efficiently by moving quickly to the side of any student who is having difficulty. A teacher can help students allay their fears and turn the focus to the classroom activity by moving close to the restless student and placing a hand on the student's shoulder. However, to use physical proximity effectively, the teacher must be able to step quickly to the side of the restless student, as Mr. Catlin did. Thus, room arrangement can help or hinder a teacher's ability to manage children's behavior.

A teacher's personal bearing also sends messages to students. The strong, straight posture of Miss Adams reinforced the students' perception that she was an authority worthy of their respect. Good posture and confident bodily carriage convey strong leadership, while a drooping posture and lethargic movements convey weakness, resignation, or fearfulness (Jones, 1987).

Gestures are also a form of body language that can communicate positive expectations and prevent problems. Teachers can use gestures to mean "stop," "continue," or "quiet, please" without interrupting their verbal instruction. When used with positive eye contact, physical proximity, bodily carriage, or facial expression, gestures can prevent small disruptions from growing into major behavior problems.

Facial expressions also vary greatly among teachers. They can show enthusiasm, seriousness, enjoyment, and appreciation, all of which encourage good behavior; or they can reveal boredom, annoyance, and resignation, which may tend to encourage misbehavior (Jones, 1987). Facial expressions that display warmth, joy, and a sense of humor are those that students themselves report to be the most meaningful. You may even want to look in the mirror to see how students will see you when you are happy, angry, feeling good about yourself, or upset.

Establishing Rules and Consequences

In a healthy democratic community, the citizens understand and accept the laws that govern their behavior. They also understand and accept that if they break the laws, certain consequences will follow. Healthy democratic classrooms also have laws that govern behavior, although they are usually called rules. In the most smoothly managed classrooms, students also learn to understand and accept the consequences for breaking a rule from the very first day.

In the first-day scenarios, each teacher established rules and consequences for the classroom differently. Miss Adams established a set of rules before school began. She read them to the class and explained why each was important. Neither Mr. Baron nor Mrs. Destry presented a clear set of rules. Their actions indicated that they expected the students to discover the rules of the classroom. These are likely to be quite consistent in Mrs. Destry's classroom, but in the case of Mr. Baron, we suspect that the rules may change from day to day. Mr. Catlin had planned an entire process for establishing rules. His process involved the students in helping to establish the class rules based on shared expectations and consequences.

Two different types of consequences are used to guide or shape student behavior. Natural consequences are those that follow directly from a student's behavior or action. For example, if a student gets so frustrated while working on an assignment that he rips the paper in half, the natural consequence is that he will have to redo the work from the beginning. If another student wakes up late, the natural consequence is that she misses the bus and has to walk to school, arrives late, and suffers the embarrassment of coming to class tardy. In these cases, there was no adult intervention; the consequence grew directly from the student's behavior.

Logical consequences are those the teacher selects to fit students' actions; they are intended to cause students to change their behavior. For example, a teacher may decide that the logical consequence of not turning in a paper on time is that the student must stay in for recess or miss another activity period to finish the paper. When the paper is turned in, the logical consequence is that the student may go out to recess or take part in the activity period.

The difference between a punishment and a consequence is that a consequence is not arbitrary and it is not dispensed with anger or any other strong emotion. To work effectively, logical consequences must be understood fully by the students. The teacher must describe them and explain the connections between the action and the consequence so that students understand the justification of the consequence. They must be applied consistently to all students who exhibit the behavior.

In many classrooms, teachers write a set of rules on a large piece of posterboard that is prominently displayed. Many teachers try to word the rules in positive ways, describing what they expect rather than what they forbid. Many teachers also write very specific consequences for each rule on the same poster for all students to see. For example, an elementary teacher may display these rules:

Our class rules	*Consequences if you choose not to follow this rule*
We wait in line courteously	You will go to the end of the line
We listen to the teacher	You will lose 5 minutes of free time
We turn in work on time	You will do your work at free time
We work and talk quietly	You will take a time-out
We treat others with respect	You will write a letter of apology

Using Positive Consequences and Rewards

Jones (1987) focuses on preventing discipline problems by helping students to develop self-control. One way to assist students in developing self-control is through the use of positive consequences or incentives for learning and behaving cooperatively. To this end, Jones has examined familiar and widely used teacher practices and has recommended ways to refine these practices to make them more effective and to eliminate negative side effects. For example, he examined the familiar incentive systems of grades, gold stars, and being dismissed first and discovered that these systems appear to benefit only the top achievers; they are not genuine incentives for students who cannot realistically meet the established criteria.

Jones also noted that if teachers offer incentives that are not particularly attractive to many students, the incentives will not positively affect student behavior or achievement. He uses the term *genuine incentives* to distinguish those that students perceive as both valuable and realistic for them to earn from those that students perceive to be of little benefit or impossible to achieve.

Jones uses the phrase "Grandma's Rule" to describe a familiar teaching practice: "First, eat your dinner; then you can have dessert." Applied to the classroom, this rule requires that students first do what the teacher expects; then they can do something that they genuinely want to do. Examples of genuine incentives that many students prize are computer activities, videos, or free time in which students can choose and play games in small groups; and learning experiences in art, drama, and music.

If students are to continue to perceive these favored activities as genuine incentives, they must be delivered as promised. Some teachers promise the incentive but run out of time and do not deliver on their promises. Another counterproductive practice is to continually threaten to reduce or eliminate the incentive if students do not cooperate. Still others deliver the reward even when the work is not done acceptably. When this occurs, the students learn that they can have dessert even if they do not eat their dinner—that is, they can get the reward without doing their work. This practice can destroy the balance of trust between student and teacher, so that when the teacher establishes incentives, the students are skeptical that they will be delivered as promised.

When delivered as promised and as earned, genuine incentives can promote increased achievement among individuals and groups and can cause peer pressure to encourage good behavior. Caring, reflective teachers attempt to understand the real needs and desires of their students and to provide incentives that meet these needs.

Many schools have designed school-wide systems of behavior management based on the Canters' (1976) theory known as *assertive discipline*. According to this theory, teachers have the right to expect good behavior from their students. In these schools, the rules and consequences are the same in every classroom. A set of procedures is established for the first, second, and third infraction of each school rule. For example, the first offense causes the student's name to go on the board and serves as a warning. If students are disciplined for the second time, a check goes by their name and they must write the rule 25 times. For a third offense, students lose recess or stay after school and parents are notified of the student's behavior.

In assertive discipline systems, individuals or classrooms often can earn positive rewards for demonstrating their cooperation with the rules. For example, a school may establish a Friday afternoon movie with popcorn for students who have not received any citations for misbehavior during the week.

Two-Way Communication with Parents

Discipline problems are less likely when teachers communicate their expectations to students and parents so that everyone is working with the same set of expectations. Communication with parents needs to occur early in the school year and continue on a regular basis. Teachers should clearly explain the policies, procedures, and rules that govern the classroom and should establish procedures for parents to ask questions and voice their concerns.

Vernice Mallory teaches fifth grade in a neighborhood of small homes and apartments that houses a very diverse population of African Americans, Caucasians, and recent immigrants from Asia, Mexico, and Central America. In the Reflective Action Case 2.1, Vernice describes the ways she builds effective two-way communication with the parents.

Case 2.1 ⊃ Reflective Action

Establishing Two-Way Communication with Parents

Vernice Mallory, Fifth-Grade Teacher, Edison Elementary School, San Diego, California

Use Withitness

At the beginning of this year, I noticed that many of my students were not turning in their homework on a regular basis. I knew I had to attack this problem right away before a pattern was established.

Define the Problem

I have been teaching for many, many years and I have found that one thing hasn't changed. To prevent discipline problems, it is absolutely necessary to establish good-quality two-way communication with parents early in the school year.

Put the Problem into Perspective

This policy holds true for every ethnic group. What has changed is that there seems to be less and less supervision at home because so many parents are working so hard to support their families these days.

Parents are the child's first teachers and I feel that children respond better when they know their parents are behind them. When I hear other teachers criticize parents and say that they won't come to conferences, I believe that it often occurs because teachers erect barriers between themselves and the parents. They don't try to understand how the parents feel. For example, many African-American parents come from an old school: God first, preachers second, and teachers come right next to God and the preacher. So it isn't that they don't respect the school or the teacher. Something else comes between them and feeling comfortable visiting their children's classes. Some African-American parents may believe that when they send their children to school, the teacher is the boss and has the right to do whatever it takes to make the child learn. But I'd rather work as partners with parents so I build a partnership.

Invite Feedback

For me, teaching has been a learning process from day one until the day I retire. I've read many books about teaching and discipline systems in my career and I've attended many workshops to learn new methods, but I know I still have a lot to learn. In this case I think I learned the most from the parents themselves. They were the ones who could best tell me how to meet their needs.

Redefine the Problem

Each year, I have to learn what the parents of my students are thinking about. I don't wait for the fall open house.

Create an Action Plan

In the second week of school, I send home a notice inviting all the parents to come to my classroom for coffee or a get-together. I don't make the note formal or threatening. It might look something like this:

> Hi
>
> I'm your child's teacher this year and I want to get to know you. Let's all get together and discuss the plans for this year. In Africa, there is a saying that it takes a whole village to educate a child, and this goes for our neighborhood too. So come next Wednesday at 1:00 to meet your child's classmates and their parents. We'll discuss homework policies, attendance, parent involvement and whatever else piques your interest.
>
> Vernice
>
> _____ Yes, I can attend
>
> _____ No, I cannot attend. A more convenient time for me is _____ .

When the parents come for my get-togethers, they may be skeptical at first, but when I greet them in a friendly way, they respond with enthusiasm. I always do a survey of my parents at the meeting. I ask the question "What are your strengths and interests?" Then I try to make a place for them in my classroom, putting their strengths to work. By the way, this get-together includes the students, too. I want my students to see their parents at school and to have positive role models in their homes and neighborhood.

In the middle of the year, I call another meeting. We sit down and discuss anything the parents are concerned about or are not pleased with. We discuss class parties and schedules. I remind them of my expectations. If a new parent has moved to the neighborhood, the meeting gives them a chance to meet the other parents. A feeling of community bonding develops.

At the end of the year, I invite parents to help us make class ribbons and autograph books. The culminating activity of the year is something I developed to celebrate the diversity of our classroom and to bring all of us together again. I have a pot luck and the parents make food representing their cultures.

Getting back to my problem with homework supervision: At the first parent get-together, with the students sitting there listening, I tell their parents to expect homework every day. I show them how I write the homework assignments on the board and then I tell them that they are expected to sign their names on the students' finished homework every day. In this way, we all understand each other, and I am confident that the parents know what I expect.

After the first meeting, I invite the parents to come be part of the program, based on their strengths and interests. For example, one parent loved math, so she led a math tutorial. Another parent wrote that her main interest was African-American culture. She taught all the students to wrap material around their heads into authentic African crowns. Another parent volunteers to do physical education because his strength is physical fitness. One even teaches ballroom dancing. If the parent has to bring in a small child, I let her. I'd rather have her bring her child and do her good work for our classroom than stay at home. My classroom has a variety of dolls and games the young child can use to keep busy while the parent works with the students.

Predict Possible Outcomes

The majority of parents come to the meeting, but for the ones who don't I follow up and ask them to come in at their convenience. I don't limit them to any time of day. I make time for them. I make myself available because I feel that getting my students' parents to work with me is one of the most important parts of my job.

When parents have had bad experiences with other teachers, and they have made up their minds that they don't trust schools or teachers, I have to build trust. I had a parent who was absolutely irate because the child's homework was too hard for him to understand and he couldn't help his child. I tried to convince him that the homework was not for him, it was for his child, but that if he really wanted to learn, he was welcome to come in while we were doing math. A few weeks later, he walked in my classroom and I nodded him to an available seat. He sat very quietly. When the class was over, I went to him and he said, "Math isn't the way it was when I was in school." He started coming in every day for about 2 months. I asked him if he wanted to sit by his son and he did. He sat by his son and they learned fractions together.

At the end of the year, during the pot luck, every child in my classroom gets a special award, even if he just sharpened a pencil for me. And at the same time, I present awards for positive parenting to the parents. We all feel proud of our village of children that we have worked together to raise.

Discipline Systems That Build Character and Self-Esteem

Lickona (1992) confronts a very complex issue that teachers face today in his design of a system called *moral discipline*. Like Glasser, he acknowledges that fewer students come to school with attitudes of respect for adults or schools: " . . . many are astonishingly bold in their disrespect for teachers and other authority figures" (p. 109). He has observed student teachers and first-year teachers confront the harsh realities of working with students who bring their anger and resentment to school each day.

Lickona (1992) believes that the teacher is the central moral authority in the classroom, and for many children the teacher functions as the primary moral mentor in their lives. "Exercising authority, however, doesn't mean being authoritarian. Authority works best when it's infused with respect and love" (p. 111).

To create a moral discipline system for your classroom, Lickona (1992) suggests involving your students in establishing the rules in a cooperative, mutually respectful manner. He describes how Kim McConnell, a sixth-grade teacher at Walt Disney Elementary School in San Ramon, California, develops rules with her students on the second day of school.

She arranges her classroom into groups of four students each because she believes it is important for students to have a support group. She asks each group to brainstorm rules that will help them:

1. Get our work done.
2. Feel safe.
3. Be glad we're in school.

When they have written their rules on large pieces of paper, she shows them the list she has created. As a group, the class synthesizes the best elements into one list that serves as the class rules for that year.

Lickona (1992) compares the system of moral discipline with the system of assertive discipline, and observes that assertive discipline is a fixed system that uses the same consequences for all types of behavior. Moral discipline, in contrast, focuses on the specific needs of each class and uses logical consequences that help students understand what they have done and what they must do to improve their moral conduct.

For example, with a rule such as "Use respectful language in this classroom," the consequences (designed by the students in cooperation with their teacher) might be:

First occasion: Take a time-out of 5 minutes and state or write the language you used that was disrespectful. Tell why it was disrespectful and to whom.

Second occasion: Write a letter of apology to the person or class to whom you were disrespectful.

Third occasion: Bring up your own behavior at a class meeting; ask for feedback about how you can stop using this type of language. Write a plan for improving your language and present it to the class.

Humor in the Classroom

Csikszentmihalyi and McCormack (1986) recognized the importance of enjoyment in the learning process in a study they conducted on the influence of teachers on their students. When they asked students to tell them who or what influenced them to become the kinds of people they are, 58% mentioned one or more teachers, with descriptions such as this:

Mrs. A. was influential because her (English) class was a lot of fun. After all these years, I found out for the first time that I really liked English—it was really fun—and I've kept up my interest even though I'm not doing as well as other kids. (p. 419)

Diane Loomans and Karen Kolberg (1993) have written a book called *The Laughing Classroom*, which is filled with motivating strategies for teachers to use in all areas of the curriculum. They identify four different styles of humor-oriented teaching. The Joy

Master is a teacher who inspires students to become warmhearted and humane toward one another. She might use a strategy such as creative debate in which students are assigned a role and debate an issue. Abe Lincoln may be debating on one side and Charlie Chaplin on the other.

The Fun-Meister uses slapstick and clowning as a motivational technique. When teaching a mathematical operation, the teacher may pretend to make mistakes so that students catch them, thereby giving the students a reason to monitor the teacher's demonstration more carefully. Peals of laughter may fill the room as the students point out the teacher's error. This style of teaching, however, can have its dark side, because Fun-Meisters sometimes mock others, including their students, causing students to laugh at one another's mistakes.

A third type of humorous teacher is the Life Mocker, and this type is almost entirely negative from the students' viewpoints. Teachers who are cynical and sarcastic may cause a few laughs, but the students may experience this style as coldhearted and dehumanizing.

A fourth style is the Joke Maker. Teachers who have a way with telling stories and jokes are always entertaining for their students. These stories can be very instructive and provide insight as examples of an abstract concept. Teachers must take care, however, not to use jokes or stories that could be interpreted as insults or stereotypes by their students.

The Laughing Classroom is an excellent resource for teachers at all grade levels and can assist you in planning humorous activities that are supportive, positive and healing.

Building Self-Esteem and Intrinsic Motivation

The Enhancing Effects of Success

All individuals want to win or succeed. Virtually all students who walk into a classroom on the first day of school hope that this year will be the year, that this grade will be the grade, and this teacher will be the teacher who will make it possible for them to succeed. Some enter secure in the knowledge that they have succeeded before, but they are still anxious to determine whether they can duplicate that success in this new situation. Others enter with a history of failure and harbor only a dim, hidden hope that maybe they could succeed, if only they could overcome their bad habits and learn how to succeed.

Winning and success are the most powerful motivations for future effort and achievement that we know of. As Glasser (1969) noted:

> As a psychiatrist, I have worked many years with people who are failing. I have struggled with them as they try to find a way to a more successful life. From these struggles I have discovered an important fact: regardless of his background, his culture, his color, or his economic level, he will not succeed in general until he can in some way first experience success in one important part of his life. Given the first success to build upon, the negative factors . . . mean little. (p. 5)

It is possible to restate Glasser's message as a significant principle of teaching and learning: When an individual experiences success in one important part of life, that person can succeed in life regardless of background, culture, color, or economic level. Glasser's book, *Schools Without Failure*, has caused researchers and practitioners to reflect on the fundamental goals of education and to reexamine what students need from the school environment to succeed.

Raths (1972) also identified eight emotional needs that people strive to satisfy: the need for love, achievement, belonging, self-respect, freedom from guilt, freedom from fear, economic security, and self-understanding. Raths believes that children whose needs are not satisfied exhibit negative, self-defeating behaviors such as aggressiveness, withdrawal, submissiveness, regressiveness, or psychosomatic illness.

Raths (1972) recognizes that teachers cannot expect to satisfy the many unmet needs experienced by all the students in their classrooms. However, he does believe that "children cannot check their emotions at the door and we should not expect them to. If unmet needs are getting in the way of a child's growth and development, his learning and his maturing, I insist that it is your obligation to try to meet his needs" (p. 141). His book, *Meeting the Needs of Children*, contains many pages of specific suggestions about what teachers can do to help meet children's emotional needs so that they are free to learn.

Meeting Students' Affective Needs

In *Motivation and Personality*, Abraham Maslow (1954) first described a hierarchy of human needs. Maslow recognized that people have basic physical and emotional needs that must be satisfied before the individual can attend to the higher need for achievement and recognition. If the lower needs are not satisfied, the individual is preoccupied by trying to meet them, and other, higher level, needs are pushed into the background. This explains why hungry or tired students cannot learn efficiently. All their capacities are focused on satisfying the need for food or sleep. To satisfy the real hunger needs experienced by many students, some schools provide breakfast or snacks so that students can pay attention to school tasks.

But what happens when the student has plenty of food and adequate shelter and is well rested? Then "at once other (and 'higher') needs emerge" (Maslow, 1954, p. 375) and these become dominant. Once basic physiological needs are met, humans need safety and security. Next come the needs for love and belonging. Imagine two classrooms, one led by an autocratic or permissive teacher, in which students feel threatened, insecure, and isolated, and the other led by a democratic teacher, in which students feel safe, secure, cared for, and connected with other members of the class-community. In the latter setting students are more likely to have their needs met and therefore be ready and able to achieve greater success in academic work.

Glasser (1969) believes that students need to feel safe, happy, and proud of themselves in a classroom if they are going to become convinced that schoolwork is worth the time and effort. To enlist their support, he recommends that you allow your students to know you as a human being, not just as an authority figure. Isn't it true that the better you know someone and the more you like them, the harder you will work for that person? Glasser asks you to use that same principle when establishing the expectations and procedures for your classroom. He suggests that during the first few months you are with your students, you look for natural occasions to tell them:

1. Who you are.
2. What you stand for.
3. What you will ask them to do.
4. What you will not ask them to do.
5. What you will do for them.
6. What you will not do for them. (1993, p. 32)

Teaching Students How to Resolve Conflicts

In many schools, conflicts have escalated to violent confrontations. Students bicker, threaten, and harass one another. Conflicts among racial and ethnic groups are on the rise. Truancy is epidemic in some areas. Traditional discipline programs, involving scolding and suspensions, do not appear to improve such situations. What can we do? What will you do when you are confronted with these situations? In some learning communities, teachers are teaching students how to be peacemakers and to resolve conflicts for themselves and their peers. Johnson and Johnson (1991) provide a curriculum for such programs in their book titled *Teaching Students to be Peacemakers*. Through the use of role plays and other learning opportunities to practice conflict resolution skills, students learn how to negotiate and mediate when conflicts arise.

Laurie Mednick, a fifth-grade teacher at Kellogg Elementary School in Chula Vista, California, teaches fourth-, fifth-, and sixth-grade students the communication skills they need to resolve conflicts peacefully. Based on the belief that conflict is inevitable and can even be healthy if dealt with in an honest and caring manner, Laurie sponsors the Peace Patrol program at her school. She describes this program in Case 2.2.

Case 2.2 ⊃ Reflective Action

Teaching Students to Resolve Conflicts

Laurie Mednick, Fifth-Grade Teacher, Kellogg Elementary School, Chula Vista, California

Use Withitness

I was very troubled by the apparent lack of concern my students felt for other people. Instead of treating one another with respect, many of my students were involved in behaviors such as fighting, tattling, putting each other down, and interrupting when others were talking.

Put the Problem into Perspective

My original belief was that the students were mirroring the prejudices of the society in which we live.

Widen the Perspective

Not willing to accept or perpetuate these behaviors, I asked myself: "How can I help these children to understand that people are different and have different ideas and perceptions, but that they are still very important? How can I help them learn to resolve their own conflicts? How can I teach them to make better choices for themselves?"

Invite Feedback

I went to see mentor teachers in my district who were investigating a new Peace Education curriculum and asked them what programs or methods were helpful in building self-esteem. I gained an enormous amount of insight and information from these people as well as an enthusiasm to continue my search.

I did a literature search at a university library on the topic of Peace Education and found from the articles that I read that this topic is of major concern to teachers across the country and that a number of programs are designed to address this issue. This search took about 2 months. I became so interested in the topic that I wrote my master's thesis on the subject as well.

Redefine the Problem

I decided that this problem was larger than my own classroom. My students would benefit most if the whole school got involved. This decision was a direct reflection of my values because I believe that each individual is important and must be shown respect and value, even if you don't agree with them. I also believe that there are alternatives to violence and that we need to teach these alternatives to our students.

Create an Action Plan

I began my new effort by teaching my students to be more attentive listeners and how to solve problems among themselves without telling the teacher. We also began to practice sharing our feelings using "I" messages (e.g., "It hurts my feelings when you call me that name. I don't like it.")

Then I began to use role playing three to four times a week to involve my students in sharing feelings and practicing conflict resolution by listening to each other with respect. The students were very receptive to the curriculum. They loved being treated with respect by their peers. The class as a whole became very cohesive and helpful toward one another.

After implementing these strategies in my classroom, I selected 30 other fourth, fifth, and sixth graders from other classes to become part of a Peace Patrol program for the entire school. I taught them the same communication and conflict management skills that I had used in my classroom. I meet with the Peace Patrol twice a month for continued training. Each day they wear their blue jackets out on the playground and assist other students to resolve their conflicts peacefully.

Now, in our school, when a conflict occurs between students, the peace patroller acts as a "conflict manager" by taking the students involved in the conflict to a quiet corner or passageway to discuss the event. The patroller listens to each student and then asks them to suggest solutions. If a solution can be found by the children themselves, the patroller writes a brief report about the conflict and the solution. Copies of the report are given to the students, their teachers, and the principal.

Predict Possible Outcomes

I was concerned that not all teachers would take seriously the reports written by student peace patrollers, so I brought up this problem at a staff meeting. As a faculty, we have agreed that whenever we receive a Peace Patrol report, we show our respect for these successful conflict management encounters by congratulating the students for resolving their conflicts peacefully. I feel very proud of the role I took in developing this program for my school community.

Effective communication between teacher and student is based on mutual trust that grows from the basic moral principles of caring, consideration, and honesty. Reflective teachers who are guided by these moral principles express them in the classroom by listening empathetically, or as in the case of the Peace Patrol in Laurie's class, by teaching students to listen empathetically. Listening is one of the most important ways of gathering information about students' needs in order to make informed judgments about why students behave the way they do.

Discussions between teacher and student must be guided by consideration for the child's feelings and fragile, developing self-concept. There is also a great need for honest, open exchanges of feelings and information among all members of a classroom. A sense of community and shared purpose grows from a realistic understanding of each other's perceptions and needs.

Classroom Meetings

One method democratic teachers often use to build mutual caring, consideration, and honest expression of opinions and perceptions is to hold classroom meetings to discuss problems confronting the class. The classroom meeting was first described by Glasser (1969) in *Schools Without Failure.* Some teachers hold regularly scheduled classroom meetings each week; others schedule them only when necessary. When Judy taught fifth grade, she scheduled her meetings just before lunch on Wednesdays so that they were in the middle of the week. Debra scheduled hers on an as-needed basis. We both found that one of the most important effects of a classroom meeting is the sense of community created when the students and teacher sit down to solve problems together.

We give an abbreviated description of a class meeting in this chapter, and encourage you to refer to Glasser's book for a more detailed account of how to initiate and lead a class meeting. The seating arrangement for a class meeting is a single circle of chairs, so that each member of the class can see the teacher and all other members of the class. The teacher has the responsibility of establishing rules and consequences for the meeting. These usually consist of a rule about one person speaking at a time and accepting the ideas and opinions of others without criticism or laughter. It is very important that as the leader of the meeting the teacher be nonjudgmental. When expressing anger or other feelings, class members are encouraged to use "I" statements.

The meeting may be divided into several parts. For example, the teacher may choose to open with an unfinished statement such as "I sometimes wonder why" or "I am proud of" or "I am concerned about." Going once around the circle, every member of the class is encouraged to respond to this opening statement, while the teacher encourages communication from every member of the group. While all class members are encouraged to respond, the teacher makes it clear that any individual can simply say "Pass." Opening the class meeting in this way has the advantage of allowing everyone to speak at least once during the meeting and may bring out important issues that need discussion.

The second part of the meeting can be devoted to students' concerns. The teacher opens this discussion by asking who has a concern. When a problem is expressed, the teacher moderates discussion on that issue alone until it is resolved. Issues are seldom resolved easily in one meeting, but class members can raise a problem, express different ideas and opinions, then offer possible solutions. When a reasonable solution is worked out, the teacher's role is to restate the solution and suggest that the class try it for a time and discuss how it worked at the next classroom meeting. Other student concerns can then be expressed.

The third part of the class meeting can address the teacher's concerns. The teacher can bring up a problem by expressing personal feelings or stating expectations for future work. Students' responses can be brought out and discussed and solutions proposed. The sense of community that develops from expressing needs and opinions, hearing other perspectives, and solving problems together is translated into all aspects of life in the classroom. When an argument occurs during recess or when students perceive something as unfair, they know they can discuss it openly and freely in a class meeting. When the teacher needs mo. e cooperation or wants higher quality work, this issue can be brought up in a class meeting. Mutual understanding, tolerance for opposing views, and developing a way to resolve conflicts results in a strong sense of ownership and commitment to the academic, social, and emotional goals of the class as a whole.

The Self-Fulfilling Prophecy

Children are extremely perceptive. They understand and react to subtle differences in adult expectations. This effect has come to be known as the *self-fulfilling prophecy*. The process appears to work like this: (1) The teacher makes a decision about the behavior and achievement to be expected from a certain student; (2) the teacher treats students differently depending on the expectations for each one; (3) this treatment communicates to the student what the teacher expects and affects the student's self-concept, achievement motivation, and aspirations either positively or negatively; (4) if the treatment is consistent over time, it may permanently shape the child's achievement and behavior. High-expectation students tend to achieve at higher and higher levels, whereas the achievement of low-expectation students tends to decline.

What is it that teachers do to communicate their high or low expectations for various students? This is the question that interested Good and Brophy (1987), who found that some teachers treat low achievers this way:

1. Seat them far away from the teacher.
2. Call on them less often.
3. Wait less time for them to answer questions.
4. Criticize them more frequently.
5. Praise them less frequently.
6. Provide them with less detailed feedback.
7. Demand less work and effort from them. (p. 55)

Scheduling Time for Active Learning

Daily and Weekly Schedules

Teachers at all levels believe they cannot fit everything they want to teach into the school day. Charles (1983) cites "dealing with the trivial" as one of teachers' greatest time robbers (p. 243). When teachers simply try to fit everything into the day, they are as likely to include trivial matters as important ones. A reflective teacher weighs the relative importance of each element of the school program and allocates time accordingly. This may mean eliminating certain items entirely and carefully scheduling the minutes of the day to meet students' most important needs.

Schedules differ from grade to grade, depending on the relative importance of the subject at that grade level and the way the school is structured and organized. The most frequently used structure in elementary schools is to place students into grade-level self-contained classrooms in which one teacher has the responsibility for teaching all academic subjects. In other cases, students may have a homeroom, but their academic subjects are departmentalized, meaning that teachers specialize in one academic area and students move from class to class during the day.

For example, the primary grades are usually structured as self-contained classrooms, and primary teachers often schedule reading and language arts activities for up to one-half of the school day. The intermediate grades may be self-contained or departmentalized, but in either case, math, science, and social studies activities are usually given more time than they are at the primary grades. In junior high school, the schedules are likely to be departmentalized, meaning that each teacher specializes in one subject and teaches it to several classes of students during the day.

No two schedules are alike. Teachers in self-contained classrooms are usually allowed great discretion in how they allocate time. Typically, state requirements mandate how many minutes per week are to be allocated to each of several subjects, but teachers make varied plans within those prescriptions. For example, the state may require a minimum of 150 minutes of math per week. Teacher A may schedule 30 minutes per day; teacher B may schedule 40 minutes for 4 days; teacher C may schedule 45 minutes on Mondays, Wednesdays, and Fridays with brief review periods on other days.

Elementary class schedules may be rigid or flexible. They may be the same every day or vary greatly. They may be governed by bells or by the teacher's own inner clock. Charles (1983) recommends that regardless of how it is determined, "the daily classroom schedule should be explained in such a manner that students know what activities are to occur at each part of the day and how they are to work and behave during those activities" (p. 10). When students know the schedule, they can learn to manage their own time more efficiently. A teacher who uses a consistent schedule may create a permanent display of the schedule on a bulletin board; a teacher who varies the schedule from day to day can write the current schedule on the chalkboard each morning.

The conventional wisdom of teachers is that the most difficult subjects should be scheduled early in the day when students are most likely to be attentive. Reading/language arts is often the first subject of the day in a self-contained classroom, followed by math. Science, social studies, art, computers, and music fill the afternoons. This may be the preferred schedule, but often school constraints make it difficult to achieve. Physical education, art, computers, and music may be taught by other teachers in separate classrooms. The schedule for these special classes may affect the classroom teacher's schedule. Some groups must be scheduled for special classes in the morning, causing classroom teachers to adjust their plans.

Planning Time

Teachers may be annoyed when special classes interrupt their scheduled lessons, but they appreciate one important side effect: When the class leaves for art, computers, music, or physical education, the classroom teacher often has a planning period. Planning time is generally part of the teacher's contract and is designed to provide opportunities for individual or collegial planning. Teachers of self-contained classrooms usually have complete discretion over their planning time, but departmentalized teachers frequently hold meetings during their planning time to discuss how they will plan and deliver their shared curricula.

Teachers use planning time in various ways, some productive and others less so. Charles (1983) recommends that teachers use this time as efficiently as possible by "prioritizing tasks, giving attention to those that are absolutely necessary, such as planning, scoring papers, preparing for conferences, and preparing instructional materials and activities. Also high on the list should come those tasks that are difficult or boring, leaving for later those that are most enjoyable" (p. 244). Less efficient teachers may use the time for socializing, complaining, smoking, eating, reading magazines, or making personal telephone calls. Later they complain that the school day is too short and that they have too much work to do at home.

Charles (1983) recommends that routine tasks such as watering plants, cleaning the room, feeding animals, and distributing materials should not be done during planning time or by the teacher at all. The teacher who is an efficient time manager delegates as many of these routine tasks as possible to student helpers. This has two effects that contribute to a healthy classroom environment: (1) It reduces the stress teachers feel about time and (2) it provides a sense of responsibility and meaningful accomplishment for the student helpers.

Most reflective teachers want to create a classroom in which students can meet their basic human needs for belonging and achievement. To accomplish this, they consider every aspect of the environment as it relates to children's needs. They arrange the furniture to meet students' needs for a sense of belonging, they create rules and schedule time to meet students' needs for security, and they provide opportunities for students to write about and discuss their other feelings and needs. They do this because they want to create a nurturing sense of community in their classroom as a means of enhancing successful achievement.

Reflective Actions for Your Professional Portfolio

A Sample of Your Classroom Management System

Use Withitness

Visit a classroom and observe and record how time is used. Is a schedule posted? If so, is it followed rigidly or flexibly? If not, how is the schedule determined? Keep a record of how much time is spent on academic, nonacademic, and classroom management concerns. Also, observe what the rules are in this classroom and how the rules are communicated to students. Do the students seem to understand and accept the rules?

Put the Problem into Perspective

Create a schedule that you would use if this were your classroom and you had control over the resource of time.

Widen the Perspective

How do you want time to be used in your classroom? What are the rules you consider most important to establish for your students?

Invite Feedback

Read articles about the classroom management strategies in which you are interested. Visit and talk with a teacher using them. Ask the teacher to give you feedback on the strategy.

Redefine the Issue

Write your ideas of how you will incorporate these strategies into your classroom.

Create an Action Plan

Create a schedule that incorporates the best of your ideal use of time with the realities of your school environment. Write about the balance you try to achieve with this revised schedule. Write down the rules you believe are most effective. Write the consequences or incentives that fit each rule. Describe how you can explain these rules to your class and how you can incorporate students' suggestions into the class rules. Include these pages in your portfolio.

Predict Possible Outcomes

Ask some students to look at your schedule and rules. Ask them to tell you how effective they think your plan is. Be prepared to make alterations if you receive some useful feedback.

References

Canter, L., & Canter, M. (1976). *Assertive discipline: A take charge approach for today's educator.* Santa Monica, CA: Canter & Associates.

Charles, C. (1983). *Elementary classroom management.* New York: Longman.

Csikszentmihalyi, M., & McCormack, J. (1986). The influence of teachers. *Phi Delta Kappan, 67*(6), 415–419.

Doyle, W. (1986). Classroom organization and management. In M. Wittrock (Ed.), *Handbook of research on teaching* (3rd ed., pp 392-431). New York: Macmillan.

Evertson, C. (1989). Improving elementary classroom management: A school-based training program for beginning the year. *Journal of Educational Research, 83*(2), 82–90.

Evertson, C., & Harris, A. (1992). What we know about managing classrooms. *Educational Leadership, 49*(7), 74–78.

Glasser, W. (1969). *Schools without failure.* New York: Harper & Row.

Glasser, W. (1993). *The quality school teacher.* New York: Harpers Perennial.

Good, T., & Brophy, J. (1987). *Looking in classrooms* (4th ed.). New York: Harper & Row.

Johnson, D., & Johnson, R. (1991). *Teaching students to be peacemakers.* Edina, MN: Interaction Book Co.

Jones, F. (1987). *Positive classroom discipline.* New York: McGraw-Hill.

Lickona, T. (1992). *Educating for character.* New York: Bantam Books.

Loomans, D., & Kolberg, K. (1993). *The Laughing Classroom.* Tiburon, CA: H. J. Kramer.

Maslow, A. (1954). *Motivation and personality.* New York: Harper & Row.

Raths, L. (1972). *Meeting the needs of children.* Upper Saddle River, NJ: Prentice Hall.

Diversity Equals Opportunity

Diversity. You've probably heard this word a number of times. What comes to mind when you hear it? What does it mean for teachers in today's schools? For some, the word *diversity* is synonymous with race or ethnicity. For others, the concept is broader. It includes everything from personality and socioeconomic background to learning preferences and personal mannerisms. It is the second, more inclusive kind of diversity that we wish to celebrate in this chapter. For the simple truth is that each human being is a perfectly unique individual, living a never-to-be-repeated life (Bakhtin, 1993).

Caring, reflective teachers will tell you that one of the greatest joys of teaching is the opportunity to interact with so many unique individuals, from students and their families to colleagues. They are also likely to counsel you that the quality of your interpersonal relationships is determined, in large part, by the attitudes and beliefs you bring to your teaching. Consider this story.

A teacher had moved from one city to another and was being interviewed by a principal in the new community. "Do you have any questions for me?" asked the principal at the end of the interview.

"Yes," answered the teacher. "What are the people like in this neighborhood?"

Rather than give the teacher a direct answer, the principal turned the question back by asking, "What were they like where you taught before?"

"Oh they were wonderful!" responded the teacher. "They were so friendly and always offered to help in the classroom. You know I learned a lot from some of the parents of my students. They had many great suggestions that improved my teaching."

"Well," replied the principal, "I believe that's how you'll find them here."

Later that afternoon, the same principal interviewed another prospective teacher who had also just moved into town. At the end of that interview, this teacher also asked the principal, "What are the people like in this community?"

"What were they like where you taught before?" responded the principal.

"Whew," said the teacher with a sigh. "I'm glad to get away from them. They were very unfriendly and critical of everything I did. They never supported me one bit."

"I'm sorry to hear that," answered the principal, putting the teacher's file at the bottom of the pile. "That's exactly the way you'll find them here."

In this chapter we encourage you to celebrate the diversity in your classroom and learn ways to help your students gain valuable experiences by interacting with one another. We also encourage you to become what Noddings (1992) calls relational in your teaching. *Relational* means the process of establishing relationships with your students in such a way that the students know that you care for and value them as unique and special human beings. As you recall your days as a student, you will undoubtedly think about how much you liked certain teachers. Usually, students like their teachers because they feel that their teachers like them. Students who feel that they have a positive, mutually enjoyable relationship with their teachers are highly motivated to do well in school. In this chapter, we discuss several ways you can build relationships with your students. We also describe ways in which students resemble one another, some ways they may differ, and some considerations for how you, as a relational teacher, will want to direct your interactions with all of your students.

Observing Individuals and Groups

If you sit on a bench at a local school and simply observe groups of students on their way to class, you are likely to experience a number of impressions. Your gaze may fall on various modes of dress, the way individuals move (fast or slow, in small groups or alone), and whether some students are more mobile and energetic than others. If you listen closely to the bits of conversation that drift by, you may notice a number of language patterns and accents. Perhaps some children are speaking in Hmong, others in Spanish. Some speak rapidly in confident tones, while others murmur softly. Some propel themselves in motorized wheelchairs, while others meander with apparent aimlessness. What if all of these students were headed to your classroom? Could you create an environment in which each child would feel comfortable, safe, and willing to learn? How would you communicate with students who speak a primary language other than the one you habitually use?

Celebrating Diversity in the Classroom

Some people are very critical of the growing diversity among children in our schools. They seem to believe that the ethnic groups commonly known as minority groups may hold back or prevent other children from learning. There are many fallacies in this argument, not the least of which is that in many school districts today, no ethnic group holds a numerical majority. Instead, several ethnic groups may each have about 20% to 30% of the total population.

Rather than view diversity as a potential hazard or drawback to teaching, we believe that the greater the diversity in our classrooms, the greater the opportunities for each person to learn from others, and this includes teachers as well as students! The potential for positive interactions is limitless if you approach teaching as a *relational* venture. The reflective teacher considers traits his or her students may share, and also explores ways in which students may differ. This teacher realizes that sometimes a common ground must be attained across and among students, and so constantly seeks productive ways to address differences to create a warm, inclusive environment. Reflective teachers also seek to celebrate diversity in positive ways that help each individual feel valued, safe, and able to learn.

Traits All Students Share:
Physical and Affective Needs

Although it was proposed more than 40 years ago, Maslow's theory of motivation (1954) is still very helpful for teachers as they consider ways in which their students may be alike. According to Maslow, all humans have unconscious physical and emotional needs that must be met or satisfied before a person is able to pay attention to anything else.

First among these are the physical needs of food, shelter, and warmth. In other words, your students will all share the need to be fed, sheltered, and clothed comfortably. A student who is hungry or cold is unlikely to participate fully in class or benefit from course activities, no matter how well planned and creative the lessons may be.

The same is true for students with other physical needs. For example, a student who has difficulty hearing will function more capably in an environment where he or she is able to see the face and gestures of any speaker, to read charts and blackboards easily, etc. Reflective teachers know that the need for physical well-being and comfort is something that all students share. Such teachers realize that it is important to learn about each of their students, their potential needs, and how those needs can be addressed.

Along the same lines, Maslow suggested that once their physical needs are met, humans must feel safe, be part of a group, and know that they are accomplishing and growing. Meeting these affective needs helps people to become what Maslow termed *self-actualized*. A self-actualized person has learned how to learn, to interact in society, and to meet his or her own needs. This individual feels worthwhile and looks forward to life with expectancy and hope.

Related to this idea is a similar motivational concept known as *efficacy* (Bandura, 1977). Persons who develop a high degree of self-efficacy realize that their achievements are affected by the effort they put forth. They realize that they are capable of changing their circumstances, and they believe they have the ability to set and achieve goals.

Our students will bring with them not only their physical needs (which are relatively easy to discover and address) but also their affective needs. As Nel Noddings (1992) notes: "To care and be cared for are fundamental human needs. We all need to be cared for by other human beings. At every stage we need to be cared for in the sense that we need to be understood, received, respected, recognized" (p. xi). Addressing students' affective needs is not something teachers can do just once. Helping students feel safe, function as part of positive groups, and see that their efforts result in personal and group achievement are ongoing goals reflective teachers set as guiding principles. Although they do not expect to create classrooms full of self-actualized students, they rely on their belief in the value of these goals to guide their choices in all areas of teaching. Throughout this text, we will refer back to these principles, suggesting ways teachers can support the development of affective well-being among all their students.

Ways Students Differ: Differences in Linguistic and Cultural Backgrounds

During the past decade, the number of students in our schools who speak a primary language other than English has grown remarkably. This growth is significant not just because you may not speak some of these languages, but because of the fact that differences in language background often suggest other differences in the way people view their world, define their values, and interact with others. When a student comes from a home where the values and accepted ways of interacting are similar to those found in the classroom, it is likely that the student will feel comfortable at school. This comfort level allows students to take the risks associated with learning without undue fear of misunderstanding or error. It allows them to function in predictable ways in a familiar environment. However, the reverse is also true: Students whose home backgrounds differ greatly from the school environment are likely to feel tense, overwhelmed, perhaps even defensive in the school setting. It is essential to establish a classroom environment that supports all learners, regardless of their background and culture.

How should English language learners be taught subjects such as math and science? This question has become a very controversial one at the beginning of the 21st century. Many experts in bilingual education believe that students from homes where a language other than English is regularly spoken should, when possible, receive much of their early educational experiences in their familiar, primary language. Many bilingual policy makers also believe that reading instruction for young children should first be taught in the primary language. They reason that it is difficult enough to discover the principles of reading in one's native tongue, without having to learn new vocabulary with every word read! Over time, these bilingual proponents believe, a student should receive instruction partly in English, partly in his or her native language. After a student achieves a relatively strong foundation in English, which may take as many as 5 to 7 years, he or she can be transitioned to the English-only classroom.

This is not, however, the only point of view guiding policy decisions related to teaching and learning English. Many laypeople express doubts about the bilingual policies in America's schools. This group believes that in order to become a fluent English speaker, a child must be immersed in the new language at once. They want students learning English to have sheltered English classes for a very brief time and then transition to a regular, English-only classroom. Some of the proponents of this idea are people who immigrated to the United States themselves and learned English in schools that did not have highly structured bilingual classes. They reason that to assimilate into the culture of America as quickly as possible, it is important to learn English as early as possible.

You will no doubt find yourself facing this issue as you begin to teach, especially if you choose to teach in a large, urban school district. One of the other challenges you will face in teaching English language learners involves the question of just how much English they have really learned. Often, a student learns to communicate about day-to-day issues in relatively fluent English. This can give listeners a false impression of the student's overall grasp of the language for academic learning. Teachers who work regularly with English language learners distinguish between a student's ability to speak day-to-day English and that same student's understanding of complex academic terms that are less common in daily speech. To succeed in an English-only classroom, students must understand and be able to use academic language as well as more casual conversation.

One way teachers help students learn and use more complex academic terms is to incorporate an approach to teaching known as *sheltered* instruction. In sheltered classrooms, teachers use simplified English vocabulary to introduce more complex academic concepts and their associated terms. They also support their English instruction with gestures, activities, and other means of communication that help students better understand what is being taught. During your teaching career, it is likely that you will encounter students who speak a number of primary languages other than English. By becoming aware of sheltered English techniques, you can better support the academic and linguistic development of your students.

Even if all of your students speak fluent English, you will want to remember that each individual comes from a unique home with individual and family values that may differ from your own values and beliefs, as well as from those of other class members. Divergent values and beliefs can be a source of conflict among students, or they can be a source of growth. Your approach to cultural differences is likely to have a great impact on the comfort and growth of your students as well as your own.

Often, a first response to someone who seems *different* is to withdraw or find fault with that person in some way. This can be true of someone who simply differs with regard to a physical characteristic (e.g., red hair versus brown or black hair) or to differences in belief systems (e.g., religions, holidays, etc.). Noddings (1992) addresses this typical human response to differences:

> Why do we tend to draw circles around groups to which we belong and attribute uncomplimentary qualities to people outside our circles? One reason is our deep and natural desire to be in caring relations. We want to be cared for—loved in the inner circle, recognized and respected in a somewhat larger circle, and at least safe to move about in huge impersonal circles. The problem is that most of the people outside our circles feel the same way we do. They, too, cherish caring relations and feel the need to protect themselves against external attack. When we understand why we draw circles and erect barriers, we can begin to explore the differences between belonging and encountering, between established relations and potential relations. (p. 117)

As you consider the circles and barriers that may exist in your own classroom, you will want to ask yourself, "How will I break down the barriers and help students feel safe in my classroom? How will I encourage the development of caring relationships among students, ideas, and adults?"

Many teachers seek to address the goal of helping students from different backgrounds better understand and interact with one another by adopting multicultural education techniques. As you are probably aware, these techniques vary in depth and commitment. Some teachers have students read an occasional book featuring a character from an ethnically diverse background or celebrate a particular holiday with students in honor of a certain cultural group. Although this is certainly a beginning step toward understanding one another, you will probably agree it is only that, a first step.

Other teachers teach a *curriculum unit* on multiculturalism, perhaps focusing on African-American history, or on the role of Chinese-Americans during the settlement of the American western frontier. More in-depth study of the challenges and feelings of a particular group of individuals is likely to provide greater insights for students regarding shared and differing world views. Indeed, Banks (1994) urges teachers to seek to transform the mainstream curriculum into an integrated approach that celebrates all individual cultures and views and avoids attempts to coerce students into accepting as *normal* or *better* a white, Anglo-Saxon view of the world.

Although Banks's ideas are both compelling and exciting, helping students understand and accept individuals they first perceive as different than themselves can be a challenge. Maintaining a relational view can help us in our efforts, as Noddings (1992) notes:

> One purpose of global education and multicultural education is to supply students with knowledge of other people and their customs. We suppose that knowledge will reduce misunderstanding, stereotyping, and the almost instinctive fear of strangers. But knowledge alone is unlikely to establish caring relations. Knowing something about other cultures is important and useful, but it is not sufficient to produce positive relationships. Knowledge is important, but it is best acquired in relation. It is useful to know something about a group's literature and art, its historical and contemporary sufferings, its myths and images. But students need motivation to undertake such studies energetically. A powerful source of motivation is an invitation from living others. One good reason for studying a particular selection of literature is that people we care about ask us to read it. (pp. 113–114)

As a reflective teacher, you will want to celebrate the wonderful diversity you find among your students, realizing that as they build positive relationships with one another, they become more adept at building relationships among groups of individuals as well. In like manner, every child who brings to the classroom a different view or set of experiences brings to you, the teacher, an invitation to grow and develop within yourself as well.

Differences in Approaches to Academic Learning

Just as your students may differ in the language they speak and in the values and traditions they honor, so too they will differ in their preferred ways for understanding and remembering academic material. The ability to understand, remember, and utilize new information is often referred to as *intelligence*. For many years, people believed that intelligence was a single entity—an unchangeable ability or degree of brightness that was genetically endowed. They referred to measures of intelligence as one's "intelligence quotient" or "IQ." In recent years, however, that concept has been supplanted by the notion that there are several distinctly different *ways of knowing*, preferred learning patterns by which an individual perceives information, links it to already known information, and stores it for retrieval and later use.

Howard Gardner (1983) successfully challenged the concept of a single IQ when he documented the presence of at least seven distinctly different forms of intelligence or ways of knowing. He identified these intelligences as linguistic (ability to work with words), logical-mathematical (logical reasoning and math ability), musical (musical talent and ability), visual-spatial (ability to visualize the use of space and aesthetic principals), interpersonal (ability to communicate with others effectively), intrapersonal (self-knowledge and awareness), and bodily-kinesthetic (graceful movement and athletic ability). Others have suggested that there may be more than seven intelligences. In fact, Gardner himself has suggested the addition of an eighth that he calls a naturalist (understanding of the natural world). In her research, Eby (Eby & Smutny, 1990) describes another that she calls *mechanical/technical inventiveness,* which is the ability to visualize how mechanical objects work and invent new systems for solving technical problems.

Whether the number of approaches to learning is hypothesized as two or two hundred, the important concept to a reflective teacher is that students probably learn and remember in unique ways. By planning your lessons and interactions with students to allow for multiple avenues of information gathering, response, and use, you will encourage greater growth among all your students.

In addition to exhibiting various ways of knowing, your students will also differ in the *rate* at which they learn. Some students in your classroom will learn more easily and rapidly than others. Some of these students may excel in only one subject area. For example, one student may perform brilliantly in math computation and problem solving, but encounter great difficulty writing a short essay. Another may show a strong sense of leadership and understanding of social interactions in the classroom, and yet struggle with singing a song on pitch.

Students who exhibit an ability to learn and perform easily in a particular area are sometimes referred to as *gifted.* In recent years, many schools have established various programs to address the learning needs of individuals with special talents or abilities. Many of these programs have been founded on the idea that the regular classroom cannot serve the needs of such students. Some gifted programs stress accelerated curricula in an area such as math. Students with standardized test scores in the 95th to 99th percentile range are often placed in these programs to allow them to learn advanced mathematical concepts at a rapid pace. Other students may be placed in special enrichment classes focusing on literature and writing. Others may be placed in special programs that allow them to work with a mentor in a field such as science or government (Cox, Daniel, & Boston, 1985). In some schools, gifted programs are not subject specific. They are pull-out programs (meaning that the students are pulled out of the regular classroom) that allow students to work on independent activities or group projects that stress higher level thinking, research skills, and creativity.

As a classroom teacher, you may be asked to help identify students for the school's gifted program or for other intervention programs (extra help with reading, etc.). You may be asked to observe a particular child's behaviors in several settings and provide ratings or other feedback. Careful reflection is needed in recommending a child for any program. In addition to special programs, it is recommended that you create your own academic program to meet the needs of high-achieving and talented students in your classroom, as well as to address the needs of students who may struggle in particular areas.

In the book, *A Thoughtful Overview of Gifted Education,* Eby and Smutny (1990) suggest that regular classroom teachers can provide enriched materials and activities for students who easily complete regular class work. Within the regular classroom you can have students work at an accelerated (or slowed) pace, provide students with materials from a different grade level (higher or lower), and conference with students on an individual basis about what they are doing and learning. You can also team up with colleagues to allow students with particular needs to receive instruction from another teacher in another setting (e.g., going to a seventh-grade classroom for math and returning to your sixth-grade classroom for other subject instruction). Use of cooperative groups, workshop approaches (for reading and writing), and other project-based instruction can also help you address the wide range of academic needs found in any classroom.

Regardless of the ways in which your students best learn and best express themselves, it is important for you, as their teacher, to maintain high expectations for them. Ylianna Romo, who teaches fifth grade at Washington School in downtown San Diego, discovered the value of believing in her students through one-on-one experiences such as this:

> *My best advice is to have high expectations for all your students. When you demonstrate that you expect the best, you are more likely to get the best. As soon as a teacher starts to flounder and think, "Oh, they really can't do this work. It's too hard," is when the teacher loses her edge. I refuse to do that. I often struggle with this decision. Sometimes I feel pity for a child because his mother is not home very much or her dad is an alcoholic. But when I start to waiver and expect less, I always try to think, "If this was my child, what would I expect?"*
>
> *My first year of teaching was the hardest because at that time, my strongest value was not to hurt their self-esteem. Sometimes a student would turn in a paper I couldn't even read and I really struggled with the conflict of which was more important: to expect high-quality or not damage their self-esteem.*
>
> *The turning point came for me when a boy turned in a very short writing assignment that I couldn't read. I thought about what this boy really needed from me and I asked him to do it again. He took the paper away and when he turned it in again, it was much better—neater, longer, more interesting. That's what made me realize that I need to do this for all of my students—have high expectations for their work and require them do it over until it meets those expectations.*

Physical Differences

Although some physical differences among your students will be obvious (e.g., hair color, eye color, absence of a limb), other differences may be less apparent. For example, some students have a great deal of energy and find interaction with others to be energizing. Others move more slowly, finding quiet reflection the ideal mode for learning. As with any other difference among students, these differences are likely to reveal themselves over time, as you come to truly know and understand the youths with whom you work.

For example, some individuals have a need for physical activity. This need can be easily misdiagnosed as a behavior disorder. For example, Fadley and Hosler (1979) found that teachers frequently refer students to psychologists for hyperactivity or attention deficit disorder (ADD). The teachers complained that the students were unable to sit quietly and pay attention during lessons. The psychologists in the study reported that most of the referred students were not clinically hyperactive at all; they were normal students in need of movement.

Other studies have found that when previously restless youngsters were reassigned to classes that did not require passivity, their behaviors were rarely noticed. Teachers report that certain students thrive in activity-oriented classrooms, while others remain stationary, despite frequent attempts by teachers to coax them to move. Reflective teachers are willing and able to use their withitness to detect when children who have short attention spans display a need for physical movement. They respond to the cues of restlessness among their students not with anger or resentment, but with opportunities for active learning that involve physical movement.

Showing That You Care

As a reflective, caring teacher, you will want to become aware of as many of your students' needs as possible. Will you be able to address each of these needs during the school year in a way that supports maximum student growth? Probably not. It is unrealistic to cast yourself as a combination social worker/psychologist/medical doctor/educator. However, through careful observation, wise interaction with students and their families, and continued reflective action, you'll be able to make a positive difference in the lives of many students in a number of ways. You will rely on several skills to help you achieve this goal, including listening, observing, and interacting with genuine respect and care.

Meetings with parents provide an excellent opportunity to sharpen your listening skills, and to gain important information to help you create a safe and comfortable environment for all students. Take advantage of opportunities to speak both formally and informally with parents (as well as with students!). Pay special attention to their hopes and fears and to their dreams and challenges. If possible, you may want to complete some home visits. Try to understand how your students interact with family members, and how they learn in their home settings. For example, does the family work together in joyous and spirited interaction? Or do family members tend to scatter to various corners of the home and work quietly at individual tasks? Are hands-on activities valued more than verbal descriptions (e.g., doing something versus speaking about something) or is the reverse true? Each of these insights can help you plan curriculum activities that support different ways of knowing among your students.

On occasion, you may find that students and/or their families reveal more than you can comfortably assimilate. Difficult issues of poverty, divorce, abandonment, or other damaging social conditions may cause you to feel overwhelmed or helpless to serve the best interests of a particular student. In cases of severe social and emotional problems, it is a good idea to refer the student and/or the family to other school personnel who can assist them in addressing pressing needs. Regardless of where or when you encounter information about a family, remember to treat your insights with care. Information about families should remain confidential, shared only with other school personnel when appropriate.

Avoid Labeling Students

Another important consideration in discerning and addressing student needs involves the use of various labels. Whether you gain information about your students through formal assessments or informal interactions, it is important to avoid the temptation to categorize or stereotype particular students. You can probably recall a time in your own life when you were burdened with a label you resented. Perhaps you dealt with a nickname you detested or with an academic designation that failed to capture your real potential. Being able to learn about your students and act in their best interests without labeling requires a great deal of care and reflection. How often has a quick perusal of a student's cumulative file, a glance at a standardized test score, or a few days of observation in the classroom led a teacher to label a student as a *slow learner, behavior disordered,* or *underachiever*? These labels can stick for life! When communicated to a student and his or her family (whether indirectly or directly), such labels can have disabling effects all by themselves. Many labels imply that a student is deficient in some way and contribute to a self-fulfilling prophecy where further erosion of self-concept and self-confidence causes even more severe learning difficulties.

Students with excellent school performance can also suffer from labeling. Some teachers refer to their most capable and willing students as *overachievers*. This pseudoscientific term is attached to students whose test scores are only moderate, but whose grades and work habits are excellent. The implication is that these students are working beyond their capacity, and this is somehow seen as a negative characteristic by some teachers (and some peers).

Students with high test scores on standardized tests, especially IQ or achievement tests, are frequently labeled as *gifted students*. At first glance, this label may appear very positive; certainly many parents seek it for their children. But careful reflection reveals that this label can be as damaging as any other. Rimm (1986) notes that "any label that unrealistically narrows prospects for performance by a student may be damaging" (p. 84). Being labeled a gifted student tends to raise the expectations for performance for that student to a constant state of excellence. Any performance less than excellent can be interpreted by the student (and/or the parent) as unacceptable.

The *gifted* label also has other negative implications. If 2% to 5% of the students in a given school are labeled as *gifted*, then what are the other 95% to 98% of the students? Not gifted? What is the hidden consequence for a sibling or a very good friend of a *gifted student*? Or what about the student who scores a few percentage points below the cutoff score for a particular gifted program? What do we call him, *almost gifted*?

Broader labels also carry damaging consequences. The term *minority* carries a connotation of being somehow less than other groups with respect to power, status, and treatment. Terms such as *economically disadvantaged, culturally deprived,* and *under-*

privileged may also create stress and anxiety among those to whom they are applied. These may be especially insidious because they fail to acknowledge the value and unique contributions of various individuals or groups.

As you become aware of the various strengths and needs among your students, you can work to address them without relying on labels. Students who are learning English can be joyfully released to work with a special tutor and be warmly welcomed back to the classroom. Children who encounter difficulty working in large group settings can spend part of their day in small groups and build interaction skills in larger groups under carefully designed conditions. Children who learn more quickly can be challenged to extend their thinking through engaging inquiry projects. Regardless of their unique needs, our students can be welcomed to our classrooms as valued individuals— labeled only as important, cared for, and wanted.

Interpreting Data from Students' Cumulative Files

So, now you have agreed with us that labeling students is a dangerous and counterproductive practice to be avoided at all costs. It would be relatively easy to follow this principle except for one thing: standardized test scores that follow students from one grade to the next. A record of information, called the *cumulative file* (often referred to as a *cume file*), is kept on each student in a school. Each year, the classroom teacher records in the students' files such data as information about the student's family, standardized test scores, reading levels, samples of written work, grades, and notes on parent–teacher conferences. At the end of a school year, the cume files are stored in the school or district office until the next year when they are redistributed to the students' new teachers.

Obviously, these files contain much useful information for teachers to use in preliminary planning. By studying them, the teacher can make judgments about placement in reading, math, or other study groups before meeting the students. Alert teachers may discover information about a student's home environment, such as a recent divorce or remarriage, that can help them when communicating with the student. Some files may reveal little about the students; others may be overflowing with records of conferences and staffings that signal that the student has exhibited a special need or difficulty.

Yet, many teachers resist looking at their students' cume files before meeting the class. Tracy Kidder's (1989) *Among Schoolchildren* provides a realistic look at the entire school year of a fifth-grade class in upstate New York. In the opening chapter, which describes the beginning of the school year, the teacher, Chris Zajac, reflects on the value of cume files as she ponders what to do with a student named Clarence, whose negative attitudes toward school have become apparent on the first day of school:

> Chris had received the students' "cumulative" records which were stuffed inside salmon-colored folders known as "cumes." For now she checked only addresses and phone numbers, and resisted looking into histories. It was usually better at first to let her own opin-

ions form. But she couldn't help noticing the thickness of some cumes. "The thicker the cume, the more trouble," she told Miss Hunt. "If it looks like *War and Peace.* . . . " Clarence's cume was about as thick as the Boston phone book. And Chris couldn't help having heard what some colleagues had insisted on telling her about Clarence. One teacher whom Chris trusted had described him as probably the most difficult child in all of last year's fourth-grade class. Chris wished she hadn't heard that. (pp. 8–9)

While data and observations about students made by former teachers can be a valuable resource for planning, many reflective teachers, like Chris Zajac, are aware of the power of the self-fulfilling prophecy, in which their own expectations may influence the way their students behave or achieve in school. Good and Brophy (1987) define *teachers' expectations* as "inferences that teachers make about the future behavior or academic achievement of their students" (p. 116) and show that the self-fulfilling prophecy occurs when "an originally erroneous expectation leads to behavior that causes the expectation to become true" (p. 116).

When cume files contain data and descriptions of low academic achievement or misbehavior, nonreflective teachers may assume that the students are unteachable or unmanageable. On the first day of school, the teacher may place them at desks set apart from the rest of the class or hand them textbooks from a lower grade. These teacher behaviors tell the students how the teacher expects them to behave and perform in this class. If these expectations are consistent over time, they are likely to affect the students' self-concepts and motivations in such a way that they achieve poorly and behave badly. In contrast, consider the possible effects of warm and encouraging teacher behavior on these students. If the teacher builds rapport with the students, includes them in all classroom activities from the first day, and works with them to establish their achievement levels and needs, it is likely that their behavior and achievement will improve during the year.

Reflective teachers who understand the great influence of their expectations on their students prefer to assess the strengths and needs of each student independently in the first few weeks of class. They may read the cume folders at the end of September to see how their assessments fit with those of the students' previous teachers.

A good case can be made for either point of view: using cume folders for preliminary planning or waiting to read them until the students are well known to you. This is an issue that you will need to consider and decide for yourself. Perhaps if you understand the power of teacher expectations, you can find a way to use the information in the files to establish positive expectations and resist the tendency to establish negative ones.

Interpreting Standardized Test Results

In many ways the teacher's role in diagnosing students' needs is similar to the role of the medical doctor in evaluating patients' health. Doctors get information from observing and talking with patients about their medical histories. Similarly, teachers observe and talk with their students to assess their learning histories. But some important information needed for an accurate diagnosis cannot be observed or discussed. Just as doctors may find that laboratory tests provide them with valuable information about the patient, so teachers may find that achievement tests and other assessment procedures can provide them with valuable data about their students.

Some tests, known as *criterion-referenced tests,* are created by teachers themselves. They are designed to fit the subject being taught. Questions and problems on the tests are drawn directly from the teacher's lessons and criteria for success are established by the teacher. For example, after a week of geometry lessons, the teacher presents the students with a test consisting of 20 geometry problems that are similar to those studied during the week. As criteria for success, the teacher establishes a grading system of A = 90% correct, B = 80% correct, C = 70% correct, and so forth. From tests like these, teachers are able to discern which students have learned the previous lessons and which students need reteaching.

A second type of test that is frequently used as a diagnostic tool by teachers is the *norm-referenced achievement test batteries* given to students in a school district once a year. These test batteries consist of reading, spelling, English, mathematics, science, and social studies exams given over a period of several days. The teacher does not write the questions or establish the criteria to fit a particular classroom. Instead, the tests are created by nationally recognized testing companies, and the items are written to approximate what is taught across the nation in each subject area at each grade level.

Statistical calculations of test scores provide information about a student's performance. The score may be translated into a percentile or a grade-equivalent score. These interpretations are done by comparing the student's raw score with the raw scores of the sample population. A *percentile rank* tells you what percentage of the people tested scored below a given score. For example, if Joe receives a percentile rank of 78, this means that 78% of the students at Joe's grade level scored lower than he did.

Grade-equivalent scores were created by test publishers especially for use in schools. The results are reported as a function of grade level. For example, if Sally receives a grade-equivalent score of 4.2, this means that her performance is similar to that of students who are in the second month of fourth grade. If Sally is in the fourth grade, her score tells the teacher that Sally is doing about as well as she is supposed to be doing. If Sally is in the second grade, the score tells the teacher that Sally is capable of functioning like students who are 2 years above her present grade level. But if Sally is in sixth grade, her score alerts the teacher that Sally is functioning like students who are 2 years below her present grade level.

The use of standardized tests varies widely from district to district. In some schools, they are used to identify learning difficulties so that corrective measures can be taken. In some school systems, the test results are published in local newspapers to compare how well students from different schools are doing in the basic skills. This practice is a controversial issue among educators. The tests were not designed to be used as a measure of excellence to rate schools, but some members of the public and the press have come to believe that they can be used that way.

For example, in elementary schools, the average test scores on standardized reading achievement tests for each school in a district may be compared. Educators know that these conclusions are misleading because there are many other contributing factors, such as the socioeconomic conditions of the families whose children attend each school and the degree to which the items on the test match the school's curriculum.

Another thing that achievement tests were not designed to do is to show the aptitude for learning or to predict the achievement of any student. Reflective, caring teachers recognize that the teacher's interpretation of a student's low achievement test results could contribute to a negative self-fulfilling prophecy. To avoid that problem, the reflective, caring teacher interprets the information gained on standardized achievement tests with great caution and uses the scores as only one of a number of items helpful in ascertaining a student's needs.

Achievement tests were designed to help you to gain a general picture of the current achievement level of your class so that you can plan lessons to begin at that level. These tests can help you pinpoint the students in your class who have low achievement in a certain subject so that you can plan a special course of action for them. These tests help you to identify the students who have mastered the basic skills in one or more subjects so that you can provide them with more challenging learning experiences.

Another form of standardized test that may be given in your school district is the *aptitude* or *ability test.* Some test publishers have created short, timed, paper-and-pencil tests that purport to test the student's innate ability, which is quite a different construct from achievement in school. The scores are reported in the same format as IQ tests, with 100 as the mean and a standard deviation of approximately 15. These scores look like IQ scores, but because of their brevity and mass production scoring, many educators are reluctant to give them much credence.

Achievement tests have been defined as measuring what the student *has* learned up to the moment of testing. Aptitude tests, on the other had, are said to measure the student's *ability* to learn in the future. Achievement and aptitude tests are not all that different. Indeed, you will probably discover that in format and content they are quite similar (Wick, 1973, p. 152).

Pretests

Interactive goal setting by teachers and students is probably the wave of the future in elementary education. When students are involved in planning and goal setting for their own learning, they are likely to be more highly motivated to achieve their goals. Individual goal setting leads quite naturally to journal writing and collecting evidence of student accomplishments for their individual portfolios. These systems also honor individual differences and allow teachers to plan for a wide range of diverse needs in a way that tests rarely do.

Assessment devices, such as pretests, provide teachers and students with useful information to plan what students need to learn and what teachers need to teach. At the beginning of a term or a unit of study, teachers often use pretests to determine what skills and knowledge pertaining to a particular subject have already been mastered by students. Pretests, also known as *readiness tests*, are designed to determine whether students have the skills and knowledge that will allow them to be successful in the new unit of study.

Some pretests and readiness tests, especially in the area of reading, are provided by textbook publishers to accompany their texts. Others are available separately through test publishers. Kindergarten and first-grade teachers frequently use reading readiness tests at the beginning of the year to determine which students are capable of succeeding in the complex task of learning to read. Certain skills, especially visual and auditory discrimination, have been shown to be essential prerequisites for learning to discriminate between letter shapes and sounds. Students who score very low on a reading readiness test may be provided with a curriculum designed to improve their visual and auditory discrimination skills before they even attempt to learn to read. Readiness tests, then, are designed to prevent students from failing by identifying those who need preliminary experiences to help them become ready for the academic curriculum.

Many textbooks, in a variety of subject areas, provide pretests that are matched to the content of the books themselves. Math textbooks may provide an initial pretest to be used at the beginning of the school year. English textbooks often provide pretests for each unit of study in the book, such as grammar, punctuation, sentences, and organization of paragraphs.

When pretests are not provided by the textbook publishers, the teacher can create them to fit virtually any unit of study. For example, prior to introducing a teacher-made unit on molecules and atoms, the teacher may write a brief pretest to determine what the students already know about this subject. Pretests can be designed to show the specific skills that a student needs to practice, leading to an individual diagnosis and a specific plan of action. The teacher, an aide, a classroom volunteer, or a more capable peer can then provide the student with feedback and activities to support student achievement. After mastering these skills, the student is then ready to join the class in the regular curriculum.

Students and teachers both need to reflect on the information gained from a pretest. The best use of pretests occurs when the teacher and the student discuss the results together and share their insights into what the student needs to do next. For example, a pretest may reveal a pattern of correctable mistakes in a mathematics operation. The teacher may be able to reteach the process quickly and the student will then be able to proceed successfully. In another instance, a pretest may reveal that the student has mastered the material already and the conference may then focus on an enriched or accelerated learning opportunity for that child while the other students are learning the material.

Placement and Grouping Decisions

Standardized tests and pretests are occasionally used to place students in special programs, tracks, or ability groups. Did your own educational experiences include being placed in a high, low, or average reading group? Were you placed in a gifted and talented program or did you miss the cutoff score? If so, what effects did your placement have on what you learned and how you felt about it?

Ability groups have been used in the teaching of reading, and sometimes math, in many elementary schools. Reading groups are formed, and students in each group are then taught the skills they have not yet mastered at a pace that appears to fit the group of similar or homogeneous students. Although teachers who use this approach may believe that the groups are temporary, expedient devices to allow them to teach more efficiently, research shows that the groups are likely to have a permanent effect on students' achievement. Studies show that the achievement gap between the low and high groups grows farther and farther apart each year.

Teachers may use data from pretests or standardized tests when creating cooperative teams or pairs for peer tutoring. To strengthen student motivation and interaction, many teachers employ the cooperative team concept. Cooperative groups typically consist of three to five students who are assigned a set of tasks to complete by cooperating with and assisting one another. In some classrooms, teachers use pretest data to decide which students to assign to each team. Often, teachers use cooperative groups to promote peer coaching and interactive assistance among their students. In this case, a team of four students may consist of one student with very strong performance, two with moderate performance, and one with relatively weak performance in the subject area. Similarly, peer tutoring dyads may consist of one skilled and one less skilled student. These are simply two examples; other types of cooperative group placement decisions, for different purposes, are possible as well.

Determining the Causes of Underachievement

Teachers who carefully structure their classroom lessons to ensure success are frequently baffled by the tendency of some students to fail to succeed even under optimal conditions. As Sylvia Rimm (1986) observes, "Millions of children who are very capable of learning—children with average, above average, even gifted abilities, including those from middle class homes where education is supposed to be valued—are simply not performing up to their capabilities" (p. 1).

There is no single cause for underachievement, nor is there a single cure. Also, no consistent characteristics are associated with underachievement. Some underachievers are bossy and aggressive; others are lonely and withdrawn. Some are slow and perfectionistic; others are hurried and disorganized. A few have adopted a behavior pattern of *learned helplessness* because of previous experiences in school, unusually high expectations at home, or a combination of both. These students perceive that they are certain to fail at whatever they try, so they have learned not to try.

Students from culturally diverse backgrounds or those raised in poverty may underachieve because of low self-esteem. Marc Elrich, a sixth-grade teacher in Washington, D.C., was frustrated to find that even though he and his colleagues had created a curriculum celebrating diversity and talking about it as a source of strength, he was unable to change his students' own preconceptions about their self-worth. One year 27 of his class of 29 students were either African American or Hispanic, and had been raised in low socioeconomic neighborhoods. Marc observed that even at age 10 or 11, most showed very low self-esteem and had low expectations for their future. He enriched his curriculum with many examples of African-American and Hispanic literature and other contributions to art and music. Still, the stereotypical view the students had of themselves did not seem to change.

In a discussion with his students exploring the issues of race, Marc heard his African-American students attribute negative racial stereotypes to themselves. They commented that "Blacks are poor and stay poor because they're dumber than whites (and Asians). Black people don't like to work hard. White people are smart and have money. Hispanics are poor and don't try hard because, like blacks, they know it doesn't matter."

Teachers like Marc are not willing to accept the status quo. They keep trying to create a healthy classroom environment that will encourage their culturally diverse students to raise their own hopes and expectations to appropriate levels. He reflected on how to teach them to like themselves. He considered the frequently used strategy of setting aside a month for studying Black history, but decided that this is not an adequate remedy. "These students aren't naive," he thought. "What are the other eleven months? White history months?"

Marc hasn't solved this problem yet. Neither has our society. But, you, as teachers will have an opportunity to confront this difficult issue and create new educational opportunities to improve your students' view of themselves and encourage our nation to grow together rather than apart.

Reflective Actions for Your Professional Portfolio

An Example of Your Student Needs Assessment Plan

Use Withitness: Create a Cultural Bridge

Arrange to interview one student. Select a student whose culture is very different from yours. Talk with the student about what is important and valued in his or her family. Share your own memories of growing up with that student. Look for common experiences and discuss your differences.

Ask questions to learn about how this student prefers to learn. Sample questions are provided here, but you may want to make up your own as well.

- Do you learn easily by reading about something?
- Do you learn well by listening to a teacher explain something?

- Do you need for the teacher to write examples on the board?
- Do you learn best by having somebody show you something or by working alone?
- Do you need a quiet room or can you work when others are talking or when the TV is on?
- Does it bother you when there is movement around you?

Put Issue into Perspective

From your interview, write an initial assessment of what conditions this student needs in order to learn and feel safe and comfortable in your classroom.

Widen Your Perspective

Ask yourself what else you need to know in order to make a thorough assessment of this student's needs. Ask yourself whether your own preferred way of learning may serve as a blinder in assessing students who are different from you. How do you learn how to meet the special needs of students with physical disabilities, learning difficulties, and cultural or language differences? What strategies can you use to meet their needs and provide them with opportunities to experience pride and success?

Assess your own strengths and talents according to Gardner's seven intelligences: verbal, mathematical reasoning, music, visual arts, physical-kinesthetic, interpersonal, and intrapersonal. Which are your greatest strengths; your weakest areas? Do you wish to strengthen your talents or overcome weaknesses in your own life? Do you believe it is more important to strengthen your students' talents or develop the areas in which they are weak?

Invite Feedback and Gather Information from Parents

If possible, try to meet the student's family and learn what the parents' hopes and expectations are for their child. Write in your journal what you have to teach this child and what the child can teach you.

Redefine the Issue

Write another draft of your plan to create classroom conditions that you believe to be important for this student to learn effectively. Include in your plan ideas for encouraging students with differences to feel safe and comfortable in your classroom.

Create an Action Plan

Design a learning experience that will allow your students to choose from a variety of learning activities that take into account several different ways of knowing or types of intelligence. Write a description of your plan that shows how students can use each type of intelligence to accomplish something of value.

Predict Possible Outcomes

Imagine yourself teaching the multiple intelligence learning experience you designed. Try to imagine the positive and negative effects on your students. What are they likely to gain from it? What could be the troublesome areas? Will they expand their strengths or weaknesses? What else can you do to improve your plan?

References

Bakhtin, M. (1993). *Toward a philosophy of the act*. Vadim Liapunov, Translator. Austin, TX: University of Texas Press.

Bandura, A. (1977). *Social learning theory*. Upper Saddle River, NJ: Prentice Hall.

Banks, J. (1994). Transforming the mainstream curriculum. *Educational Leadership, 51*(8), 4–8.

Cox, J., Daniel, N., & Boston, B. (1985). *Educating able learners*. Austin, TX: University of Texas Press.

Eby, J. & Smutny, J. (1990). *A Thoughtful Overview of Gifted Education*. White Plains, NY: Longman.

Fadley, J., & Hosler, V. (1979). *Understanding the Alpha child at home and at school*. Springfield, IL: Charles Thomas.

Gardner, H. (1983). *Frames of mind*. New York: Basic Books.

Good, T., & Brophy, J. (1987). *Looking in classrooms*. New York: Harper & Row.

Kidder, T. (1989). *Among schoolchildren*. Boston: Houghton Mifflin.

Maslow, A. (1954). *Motivation and personality*. New York: Harper & Row.

Noddings, N. (1992). *The challenge to care in schools*. New York: Teachers College Press.

Rimm, S. (1986). *The underachievement syndrome: Causes and cures*. Watertown, WI: Apple Publishing Co.

Wick, J. (1973). *Educational measurement: Where are we going and how will we know when we get there?* Columbus, OH: Charles Merrill.

Chapter

4

How Teachers Plan School Programs

One of classroom teachers' most important responsibilities is to plan the curriculum, the course of events and learning experiences for their students. To illustrate the complexity of the planning process, here is a brief account of some of the issues Lori Shoults faced during her first 3 months at Seth Paine Elementary School in Lake Zurich, Illinois:

When I first walked into my empty classroom in August, I was greeted by a big box of textbooks. I had been hired by this school district because of my interest in and enthusiasm for the whole language approach to teaching reading and writing. So I had the freedom to create my own curriculum rather than rely on the texts. With that freedom came a lot of hard work.

It was very hard to plan before knowing my students, especially the first year, when I didn't even know what second graders were like. I wanted the curriculum in my classroom to be fully integrated. I wanted science and social studies to be a part of reading and writing. What I did was examine all the textbooks in great detail. I made lists of skills that were taught in the English, phonics, and spelling books. From the science, social studies, and reading basals, I looked for topics. I divided the year into 2- or 3-week integrated units on topics such as plants, weather, light, magnets, dinosaurs, animals, and safety.

Within these units, I taught my reading and English skills every morning in a new poem that was related to the unit's theme. I distributed a poem to the students and they glued it into their folders. We read the poem once just to enjoy its ideas and sounds. Then each day, I focused on two or three new skills such as looking for examples of phonics rules, word structures, types of sentences and punctuation.

I allowed students to choose their own reading materials from the books in our room or in the library. To encourage them to read, I decided to use a reading incentive program, which gave credit or rewards for the number of books each student read. But when I considered this idea, it had a lot of drawbacks. Children who read short, easy books would appear to get more credit than those who read long, challenging books. I talked to other teachers to find out what they had tried. One teacher told me about a system of having students keep track of the number of minutes they read rather than the number of books. When I considered this approach, I concluded that it was more productive than focusing on the number of books read because my goal was for the students to read longer stories and books rather than just counting books. It also seemed more fair because students at different achievement levels read books of different lengths. This system gave equivalent credit to each student for time spent reading at every reading level.

The social studies textbook focused on the concepts of community and geography. I decided to have an overall theme of community, which I implemented by establishing a simulated community in the classroom. We had a teacher, a sheriff, a mayor, a meteorologist, a banker, and a gardener. Students signed up for the jobs they wanted and rotated every week. The learning stations in the class were community sites such as a post office (letter-writing center), a greenhouse (science center), a newspaper stand (writing center), a telephone company (listening center), a library (reading center), a toy store (learning games), and a computer lab.

My organizational problems were growing more difficult each day. At the beginning of the year, I tried to do it all at once. In addition to my regular reading, writing, and math programs, I set up five rotating math enrichment stations, the community stations, a geography program, and literature circles in which students discussed books they were reading on their own. I wasn't able to get to all of these things as I had planned. I kept running out of time during the day. The students were confused. They were always asking me when we were going to do different things.

So I sat down and planned for one special activity each day. On Tuesdays we would do community stations, on Wednesdays we had our literature circles, and on Fridays we had math enrichment stations. I thought it would be better to have a consistent schedule. The students wanted to know what to expect and I felt better knowing when to plan for each activity.

For mathematics, I examined the basal text and believed that I could cover the skills in more interesting ways. I wanted to teach with more hands-on activities and use fewer math pages. I decided to use the Everyday Mathematics program (Bell, 1990) for teaching concepts and use the textbook for practice and review. I also gave the tests from the math book. After using this approach for several months, I found that the students were able to do the textbook tests successfully. More important to me, they were enthusiastic about math. Even my lowest achieving students felt confident participating in math activities.

After 3 months of teaching, I believed that I was beginning to think like a teacher. At the beginning of the year, my schema for teaching and learning was rudimentary, leading me to make most decisions by trial and error. But later I felt I had expanded my knowledge and experience base to the point that when I reflected on a decision, I had a much better understanding of the consequences of my actions.

As Lori's account shows, teachers face a multitude of complex issues and judgments in their own classrooms. As a teacher, she has a great deal of freedom to decide what to teach and when to teach it, but behind the scenes, her decisions are influenced by many forces, both past and present. For one thing, history and tradition exert powerful influences over what is taught in schools. The three Rs have served as the basis for planning in U.S. schools for more than a century, and there are active and vocal groups of citizens who believe that the primary goal of K–12 schools should be to instill these basic skills in their students.

Some groups believe that schools are the custodians of the culture and that the primary goal of education should be to develop good citizenship and understanding of the great ideas and literature produced by Western civilization. Others believe strongly that the primary goal of a modern education is to teach students how to use reasoning, problem-solving, and communication skills as a means of learning how to learn, so that they are able to gather the information they will need in their lives.

Still others believe that the new wave of computer technology available to future generations makes older forms of learning obsolete. They call for an emphasis on the use of technology in K–12 schools to prepare students for a future that will be vastly different from the present. There is also a growing trend toward creating school programs that are multidisciplinary and multicultural by design, with a new emphasis on investigation, inquiry, research, experimentation, and conflict resolution.

Lori discovered how difficult it is to plan so many different types of school programs all at once. Like many beginning teachers, she wanted to incorporate the best ideas from all of the influential groups she had read about in her teacher education program.

At times the responsibility seemed so overwhelming that she might have wished that there was just one standard curriculum for all teachers to follow.

How School Curricula Are Planned

National Standards in the Planning Stage

Many nations have uniform standards for school curricula. When these standards exist, individual teachers plan their daily programs to coincide very precisely with the national expectations. In some countries, if you were able to visit several schools in various cities at the same time of the school year, you would find the students using the same textbooks and working on the same chapter as students in other cities and rural areas of that country. Periodically, all children attending the schools take national examinations as a means of testing whether they have learned the requisite material and, at the same time, whether schools are accomplishing their mission of teaching the national curriculum.

Other countries, including the United States, have no such tradition of a uniform mandated curriculum. Historically, the regulation and supervision of K–12 curriculum has resided with the states, and although many states have established curriculum guidelines and examinations, there has also been a strong public sense that the best curriculum is the one planned at the local level based on local interests, values, resources, and the needs of a particular group of students in each school district.

Recently, however, some school districts have been criticized by the media or by citizen watchdog groups because their students have performed poorly on a variety of tests and measurements of academic progress. As a result of the public's perception that some school districts prepare students for the world much better than do other school districts, a debate is growing over the value of establishing national standards for student performance. There is also a movement to establish national standards for the preparation of teachers and for teaching effectiveness.

In 1994, Congress formalized efforts to address school reform in its Goals 2000: Educate America Act (H.R. 1804; available on-line at http://www.ed.gov/legislation/GOALS2000/TheAct/intro.html). It was intended to improve learning and teaching by providing a national framework for education reform. Goals 2000 includes eight goals that have had a great impact on local, state, and national directions. The act was revised in 1996 and is likely to be amended in the future. Despite its changing nature, you will want to be familiar with the eight goals, which include provisions for these areas:

1. School readiness
2. School completion
3. Student achievement and citizenship
4. Teacher education and professional development
5. Mathematics and science

6. Adult literacy and lifelong learning
7. Safe, disciplined, and alcohol- and drug-free schools
8. Parental participation.

As you can see, each goal in the list is vital to the creation of a society of lifelong learners. You may even want to organize your own professional goals according to these eight areas, adding others you feel are also important.

In response to the public's desire to be able to measure and compare the progress of students across the nation, the U.S. Congress mandated the Department of Education to provide a set of assessment tools to measure K–12 students' subject-matter knowledge in five areas. They produced a document known as the National Assessment of Educational Progress (NAEP), which is commonly referred to as the nation's report card. NAEP provides benchmarks for each subject area. A *benchmark* is a statement describing what students should be able to do or demonstrate at various grade levels. NAEP updates its benchmarks on a cyclical basis. To view the latest benchmarks for the academic areas that interest you, log onto the National Center for Education Statistics web site (http://nces.ed.gov/nationsreportcard/site/home.asp) and click on the NAEP report that you want to read.

As is often the case in a vigorous, multicultural democracy such as the United States, there is little agreement about the form educational standards should take or how they should be used. Subject-area specialists, for example, argue that their disciplines are so different from each other that standardizing performance expectations across the disciplines would be impossible (Viadero, 1993).

Many other philosophical debates concern the purpose of national standards in education. Before they can establish one set of universally accepted standards, educators need to agree on such issues as whether the national standards and benchmarks ought to describe basic or minimal competency in each subject area or whether they ought to describe how experts perform. A national debate remains over the value of emphasizing content or process knowledge in most subject areas, and this causes the authors of standards and benchmarks to disagree about whether to assess content knowledge or performance standards.

State Curriculum Guidelines

In the United States, each state has a department of education that has traditionally taken responsibility for establishing guidelines for curriculum development. Many states are revising their curriculum guidelines by inviting representative teachers and administrators from all areas of the state to form a committee responsible for reviewing the standards and benchmarks created by national subject-matter councils and considering ways to incorporate these standards into the state's curricular goals for each major subject area. State departments of education publish and distribute the resulting documents to all of the school districts they serve.

Another source of updated information about national and state standards in education is a web site managed by the Putnam Valley Central Schools in Putnam Valley,

New York (http://putwest.boces.org/Standards.html). When you log on, you will have the choice of reviewing the latest national standards or viewing the most recent curriculum frameworks for each state.

Curriculum frameworks at the state level change frequently based on the latest research in education. They are also heavily influenced by political pressures and interest groups within the state. As a beginning teacher, you will be expected to become familiar with the latest curriculum frameworks for your state and implement them in your classroom.

Evaluation and Use of Textbooks

School textbooks have an enormous impact on the curriculum. Many elementary school textbooks are undergoing major revisions to meet the demand for updated, student-centered, active learning rather than the older emphasis on receptive, rote learning. These changes are controversial, reflecting the often divisive issues that are hot topics among adults in our society.

One of the greatest controversies regarding textbooks today is the rewriting of social studies textbooks to include multiple perspectives on history. Critics responsible for these changes view traditional textbooks as written from one perspective—that of a white European male. They believe students should learn history from multiple perspectives. Traditionalists believe that eliminating or ignoring content in the traditional textbooks will misrepresent history and that the subject will become diluted in an effort to please every ethnic group. Reflective teachers attempt to clarify their own values and their own curriculum orientations and beliefs as they make decisions about the curriculum they teach.

When most first-year teachers move into their classrooms, the textbooks are already there. Novice teachers have been told about the importance of individualizing education and meeting the needs of all students in their professional preparation programs. When reality sets in, they realize that many of the materials they need to plan a highly creative program that meets the students' individual needs are not in the classroom. A less reflective teacher will, without thinking, distribute the textbooks and begin teaching on page one, perhaps emulating former teachers, with the intent of plowing through the entire book by the end of the year.

Reflective teachers, however, are more inquisitive and more independent in their use of textbooks. They ask questions of other teachers: "How long have you been using these textbooks? How were they chosen? Which parts match the school or district curriculum guides? Which parts are most interesting to the students? What other resources are available? Where do you go to get your ideas to supplement the textbook? In your first year of teaching, how did you meet the individual needs of your students when you had only textbooks available to you?"

Less reflective teachers tend to accept without question that the "approved" or "correct" curriculum is the one found in textbooks because it is written by "experts." They attempt to deliver the curriculum as written, without adapting it to meet the needs of their own particular students.

More reflective teachers consider decisions about curriculum planning to be within their jurisdiction, their domain of decision making. They consult with others, but they take responsibility for deciding which parts of a textbook to use to meet the needs of their own particular class and to match the goals and learning outcomes their state and local curriculum committees establish.

Tyler's Basic Principles of Curriculum Planning

Tyler (1949) observed that in planning educational goals, teachers should first consider the needs of the learners, second the needs of society or what he termed "contemporary life," and then the suggestions or recommendations of subject-matter specialists. Since 1949, there has been consistent support for Tyler's elegant (simple but not simplistic) curriculum planning method. He proposed four fundamental questions that should be considered in planning any curriculum:

1. What educational purposes should the school seek to attain?
2. What educational experiences can be provided that are likely to attain these purposes?
3. How can these educational experiences be effectively organized?
4. How can we determine whether these purposes are being attained? (p. 1)

Reflective educators are very likely to use Tyler's basic principles in planning, organizing, and evaluating their programs because they are remarkably similar to the process of reflective thinking. Essentially, Tyler suggests that teachers begin curriculum planning by perceiving the needs of students, gathering information, making a judgment about an educational purpose, selecting and organizing the strategies to be used, and then evaluating the effectiveness of their curriculum plan by perceiving its effects on their students. These are very similar processes to those outlined in the model of reflective action presented in Chapter 1.

Although reflective teachers are not likely to memorize Tyler's four questions word for word, they are likely to carry with them the fundamental notion of each:

1. What shall we teach?
2. How shall we teach it?
3. How can we organize it?
4. How can we evaluate it?

Reflective teachers ask themselves these questions each year because they have probably noticed subtle or dramatic changes in their communities, subject-matter materials, students, or themselves from year to year that cause them to reexamine their curricula. On reexamination, they may confirm that they want to continue to teach the same curriculum in the same way or that they want to modify some aspects of the curriculum. As teachers grow in experience and skills, most greet each new year as an opportunity to improve on what they accomplished the previous year. Rather than continue to teach the same subjects in the same ways year after year, reflective teachers often experiment with new ways of teaching and organizing the curriculum.

An obvious contrast between more reflective and less reflective teachers is that after teaching for 20 years, a reflective teacher has accumulated 20 years of experience, whereas a less reflective teacher is likely to have repeated 1 year of experience 20 times. Reflective teachers want to have an active role in the decision-making processes in their schools, and curricular decisions are very important. They also display a very strong sense of responsibility for making good curriculum choices and decisions, ones that will ultimately result in valuable growth and learning for their students.

Bloom's Taxonomy of Educational Objectives

Benjamin Bloom, a student of Ralph Tyler's, extended Tyler's basic principles in a most useful way. Bloom and his colleagues Max Engelhart, Edward Furst, Walker Hill, and David Krathwohl (1956) attempted to respond to the first of Tyler's questions as completely as possible. In meetings with other teachers, they brainstormed and listed all the possible purposes of education, all the possible educational objectives that they could think of or had observed during many years of classroom experience. Then they attempted to organize and classify all of these possible objectives into what is now known as the *Taxonomy of Educational Objectives*. Their intent was to provide teachers with a ready source of possible objectives so that they could select ones that fit the needs of their own students and circumstances. It was also intended to help teachers clarify for themselves how to achieve their educational goals. A third purpose for the taxonomy was to help teachers communicate more precisely with one another.

The taxonomy first subdivides educational purposes into three domains of learning: cognitive, affective, and psychomotor. The *cognitive domain* deals with "the recall or recognition of knowledge and the development of intellectual abilities and skills"; the *affective domain* deals with "interests, attitudes, and values"; while the *psychomotor domain* concerns the development of manipulative and motor skills (Bloom et al., 1956, p. 7).

Clarifying Educational Goals and Outcomes

All three domains are considered to be important in the curriculum because together they support the growth and development of the whole student. Educators used to begin writing curriculum documents by carefully wording their educational goals. An educational *goal* is a general long-term statement of an important aim or purpose of an educational program. For example, most schools have a goal of teaching students how to read and write, another to ensure that they understand the cultural heritage of the United States, and another to help them develop attitudes and habits of good citizenship.

To translate goals into operational plans, however, most educators today prefer to specify what *outcomes* are expected as a consequence of being in school and taking part in the planned curriculum. Eisner (1994) alerts educators to be aware that goals express intentions but that other factors may occur that alter the intentions in the educational process. According to Eisner, "Outcomes are essentially what one ends up with, intended or not, after some form of engagement" (p. 120).

Outcomes are statements that describe what students will demonstrate as a culmination of their learning. Spady (1994) proposes that outcomes must specify "high quality, culminating demonstrations of significant learning in context" (p. 18). A high-quality demonstration means one that is thorough and complete, showing the important new learning the student has gained or demonstrating the mastery of a new skill or process. Outcomes are designed to be assessed at or near the end of a learning period.

Written outcome statements are used to translate goals into actions. They describe what students will be able do as a result of their educational program. If educators can envision what they want students to be able to do or know after a series of learning experiences, they can plan with that outcome in mind. Learning outcomes generally describe actions, processes, and products that the student will accomplish in a given period.

Cognitive outcomes are expressed in terms of students' mastery of content or subject-matter knowledge. For example, kindergartners are expected to master the alphabet, third graders are expected to master multiplication facts, and sixth graders are expected to show mastery of the history of ancient civilizations.

Educators also write many psychomotor outcomes, including strategies, processes, and skills that involve both the mind and the body in the psychomotor domain. For example, elementary students are expected to learn how to decode symbols to read, write, calculate, solve problems, observe, experiment, research, interpret, make maps, and create works of art, music, and other crafts.

Most teachers view affective outcome statements as being related to the development of character. Typically, schools emphasize the affective outcomes that deal with good citizenship, self-esteem, respect for individual and racial differences, and an appreciation of art, music, and other aspects of our cultural heritage.

Individual teachers may write outcome statements for their own classes, but when they work collectively to clarify a set of school-wide outcome statements, the effect on students is likely to be much more powerful and result in greater growth and change. This enhanced growth is a result of the consistency of experiences that students have in every classroom and with every adult in the school. Many school districts have statements of philosophy (often called mission statements) and outcome statements written in policy documents, but they may or may not be articulated and applied in the schools themselves. For effective change to take place, the school faculty must consider its educational purposes each year, articulate them together, and communicate them to the students through words and deeds.

In a classroom, each teacher has the right and the responsibility to articulate a set of educational outcomes for his or her own students. Working alone or with teammates at the same grade level or subject area, the classroom teacher may want to articulate approximately two to four yearly outcome statements in each of the three domains. Tyler (1949) encourages teachers to select a small number of highly important goals, "since time is required to change the behavior patterns of human beings. An educational program is not effective if so much is attempted that little is accomplished" (p. 33).

Writing Useful and Appropriate Outcome Statements

The wording of outcome statements must be general, but not vague. This is a subtle but important distinction. Some school documents contain goals such as "Develop the full potential of each individual." What does this mean to you? Can you interpret it in a meaningful way in your classroom? Can you translate it into programs? Probably not. This goal statement is so general and vague that it cannot be put into operation, and it would be very difficult to determine whether it is being attained.

An outcome statement should be general, in keeping with its long-term effects. It should also describe, clearly and precisely, how you want your students to change and what you want them to be able to do at the end of the term of study. Some examples of useful *cognitive* outcome statements are:

> Kindergarten students will be able to recognize and name all the counting numbers from 1 to 20.
>
> Fifth-grade students will demonstrate that they understand how technology has changed the world by creating a time line, graph, chart, or set of models to show the effects of technology on human experience.

Examples of *psychomotor* (sometimes referred to as skill or process) outcome statements are:

> Third-grade students will be able to measure and compare a variety of common objects using metric units of measurement of length, weight, and volume.
>
> Sixth-grade students will be able to compose and edit written works using a word processing program on a computer.

Examples of *affective* outcome statements are:

> Second-grade students will demonstrate that they enjoy reading by selecting books and other reading materials and spending time reading in class and at home.
>
> Students at all grade levels will demonstrate that they tolerate, accept, and prize cultural, ethnic, and other individual differences in human beings by working cooperatively and productively with students of various ethnic groups.

In many school programs, outcome statements are intended to be accomplished over the course of a school year. Yearly outcome statements can be written for one subject or across several disciplines. Outcome statements can also be written for a shorter period such as a term or a month. They are used as guides for planning curriculum and learning experiences for that length of time. At the end of a given time, the teacher assesses whether students have successfully demonstrated the outcome. If not, the teacher may need to repeat or restate the outcome statement to ensure that it can be met.

Some outcome statements may need to be modified because they are too vague. Compare the first vague statement with the improved second statement:

> *Original outcome statement:*   Students will be able to demonstrate that they understand the U.S. Constitution.

> *Improved outcome statement:*   Students will be able to describe the key concepts in the articles of the U.S. Constitution and give examples of how they are applied in American life today.

Other outcome statements may need to be modified because they are too difficult for the students. Compare these:

> *Original outcome statement:*   Fourth-grade students will demonstrate that they know the key concepts of the Bill of Rights by creating a time line showing how each has evolved during the past 200 years.

> *Improved outcome statement:*   Fourth-grade students will be able to create an illustrated mural showing pictorial representations of each of the articles in the Bill of Rights.

Some outcome statements may need to be improved by adding learning opportunities that will stimulate student interest and motivation to learn the material. Consider the following:

> *Original outcome statement:*   Students will be able to recite the Bill of Rights.

> *Improved outcome statement:*   Students will work in cooperative groups to plan and perform skits comparing how life in the United States would differ with and without the constitutional amendments known as the Bill of Rights.

Outcome statements are useful guides for educational planning but must be adapted to fit the needs of a particular teacher and class. For this reason, curriculum planning is an evolving process. A curriculum is never a finished product; it is constantly being changed and improved from day to day and year to year.

Examples of Long-Term Curriculum Planning

A Yearlong Plan in Mathematics

We now highlight one subject in the elementary curriculum to provide an example of how curriculum plans are designed. The teaching of mathematics has changed over the years at every grade level. No longer taught by drill and practice, mathematics is now often one of the most highly interactive parts of the elementary school curriculum. Manipulatives that primary children use to demonstrate their understanding of number concepts include beans, beads, and number lines. But many teachers also use such motivating materials as pretzels, fish-shaped crackers, jelly beans, or coated chocolate candies. Recently, a little girl was asked how she knew it was math time and she answered, "That's easy! Math is when we have our snacks."

Kendall and Marzano (1995) provide a summary of recommendations made by the National Council of Teachers of Mathematics and the Mathematics Assessment Framework of the NAEP. These groups stress the importance of teaching mathematics in the context of real-life situations, and they recommend that school curricula should be designed so that the student has these abilities:

1. Effectively uses a variety of strategies in the problem-solving process
2. Understands and applies properties of the concept of number
3. Uses a variety of procedures while performing computation
4. Understands and applies the concept of measurement
5. Understands and applies the concept of geometry
6. Understands and applies concepts of data analysis and distributions
7. Understands and applies concepts of probability and statistics
8. Understands and applies properties of functions and algebra
9. Understands the relationship between mathematics and other disciplines, particularly science and computer technology. (pp. 88–89)

With this emphasis on problem solving and application of mathematical concepts to real-life situations, the curriculum in many elementary schools has changed dramatically from drill and practice to mathematical explorations and investigations. Teachers who try to incorporate these recommendations into their mathematics curricula find that the best way to do it is through the use of projects and multidisciplinary units. A yearlong plan in mathematics will be divided into several strands or concepts with opportunities for reviewing previously learned material from time to time. It may resemble the plan illustrated in Figure 4.1.

Long-Term Planning in Science

As a subject in the curriculum, science consists of a survey of the basic ideas in the academic disciplines of earth and space, life sciences, physical sciences, and environmental studies and the relationship between science and technology. When most of you were in elementary school, you may have learned about science as a collection of facts, laws, principles, and theories that have been found to be important in each of the science disciplines. When this content-oriented approach is used as the basis for curriculum planning in science, students are expected to read, comprehend, discuss, and take tests to demonstrate their mastery of the subject matter. This academic orientation toward science assumes that content is what students must learn to be able to understand science in later schooling.

Project 2061 (an educational study group of the American Association for the Advancement of Science) and the National Committee on Science Education Standards and Assessment are among several national study groups recommending that we

Figure 4.1   A yearlong plan for elementary mathematics.

Outcome Statement
Students will demonstrate the ability to discern mathematical relationships, reason logically and strategically, apply mathematical operations accurately, and use technology to solve mathematical problems.

Assessment Plan
A mathematics portfolio will be initiated and will contain examples of students' work during each month of the school year. Timed tests will be used to demonstrate mastery of math facts in addition, subtraction (primary grades), and multiplication and division (upper elementary grades).

First Month: Patterns in Mathematics
Hands-on activities allow students to discover patterns, relationships, and appreciation for the nature of mathematics. Manipulatives such as beads, geoboards, tangrams, Unifix Cubes, Cuisenaire rods, and attribute blocks are used. When possible, activities will be coordinated with other areas of the curriculum.

Second Month: Numbers and Place Value
Students will learn to compute arithmetic operations: addition, subtraction (primary grades); multiplication and division (upper elementary grades); and use algorithms to solve problems. Place value activities will be stressed. Math facts will be learned and students will demonstrate accuracy and speed in using basic math facts. Students will also solve and create word problems related to other themes being studied in literature, social studies, and science during this month.

Third Month: Measurement
Students will have many opportunities to measure length, weight, and volume in a variety of hands-on experiences. Many of these experiences will be designed to relate to other curricular themes being taught.

Fourth Month: Geometry
Using real objects, students will examine, compare, and analyze one-, two-, and three-dimensional features. They will identify and classify the attributes of various geometric figures. Related activities will be designed to fit the rest of this month's curriculum.

change that approach very significantly. The new recommendations stress the need for students to have realistic, hands-on opportunities to experience the methods and processes scientists use to imagine possibilities, speculate on causes, hypothesize effects, gather and weigh evidence, and reach conclusions.

Reflective teachers who believe in teaching science processes use fewer textbooks and more laboratory experiences. Rather than teach *about* science, they believe that students must learn how to *do* science in order to understand it. They are likely to create a science curriculum that consists of a series of laboratory and experimental situations in which students observe, hypothesize, experiment, and evaluate their results in each topic of science. They may test rocks or create a model of plate tectonics for earth

Figure 4.1   *Continued*

Fifth Month: Logic and Reasoning Strategies

By confronting a variety of real-life problems, students will learn to use logic and problem-solving strategies to make comparisons, decisions, and choices. Many of the problems will be taken from other parts of the curriculum for this month.

Sixth Month: Mathematics and Technology

Students will use calculators, computers, and other technological aids to explore ways to use mathematics to solve real-life problems, conduct business, and keep records. Whenever possible, these activities will relate to other curricular areas.

Seventh Month: Statistics and Probability

Students will work in cooperative groups to do research and use statistics and probability. The results of the research will be displayed for other students to see. These research studies will be coordinated with other curriculum units being taught during this time period.

Eighth Month: Patterns and Functions

Patterns and functions will be examined in a search for understanding the rules that govern mathematical relationships. When possible, these patterns will come from other curricular areas.

Ninth Month: Review of Mathematical Understandings

All aspects of the mathematical curriculum will be reexamined. Individual needs will be addressed to improve understanding and strengthen skills. Portfolio assessments will be reviewed by students, and summaries of students' understandings and needs will be written by students and teacher.

---

science. They may observe the moon or simulate an eclipse for astronomy or collect and classify plants and engage in microscopic examinations of pond water for biology. They may build and test simple machines for physics.

A yearlong plan in science may be presented in a wide variety of sequences. Teachers may decide to offer an earth and space science unit for the first 6 weeks, followed by units on life science, then science and technology, and ending with physical sciences. This order may easily be changed: Many elementary teachers choose to coordinate their science units with other academic subjects. For example, at the same time as a unit on measurement is presented in mathematics, the science unit may emphasize measurement tools and strategies as well. When the social studies curriculum focuses on themes of exploration of new worlds, the science unit may be coordinated to emphasize scientific frontiers in technology.

Long-Term Planning in Social Studies

As in science, development of the social studies curriculum can follow a content-oriented approach or a process-oriented approach. Educators committed to an academic-

or content-oriented view of social studies believe that students need to know and understand the important facts, persons, events, and sequences in the history of our country and the world. Also important to the academic orientation toward social studies are the important concepts that distinguish various cultures and the basic facts about world geography. Recent critics of U.S. schools have decried the lack of knowledge of history and geography among young people. Televised tests and magazine quizzes have demonstrated that many young people lack knowledge about geography. Content-oriented curriculum planners seek to improve this condition by providing history and geography courses that emphasize knowledge and comprehension objectives to teach facts and concepts.

Process-oriented curriculum planners believe that instead of memorizing facts, names, places, and dates, learners should experience the processes of acquiring information on their own. The National Center for History in the Schools (NCHS, 1994) provided benchmarks for teaching students how to think historically, by learning to do their own research in social studies and learning how to use tools such as maps, globes, atlases, charts, graphs, and other resources to enable them to find information when the occasion demands it. The credo of this orientation toward curriculum development can be summed up in the adage "Give a man a fish and he will be hungry the next day; teach him to fish and he'll never go hungry again."

Redesigning the Curriculum to Reflect Multicultural Values

The trend in curriculum development is changing to encourage teachers to create new curricula that teach the basics and, at the same time, encourage students to see the world from points of view different from their own. James Banks, Director of the Center for Multicultural Education at the University of Washington, defines multicultural education as "education for freedom" and recommends that curriculum planners redesign existing curricula to promote "cultural excellence" as well as academic excellence.

Banks (1991–1992) believes that the redesigned curriculum should describe the needs and contributions of all Americans, all their struggles, hopes, and dreams. It should not be an add-on to the existing curriculum, but should become an integral part of every subject we teach. Ask students to reflect, discuss and write about questions such as "Who am I?," "Where have I been?," "What do I hope for?" Banks believes that when students can answer these questions they will be better equipped to function in their own world, as well as in the larger community that may be populated by people who answer the same questions very differently.

To develop a multicultural curriculum for your classroom, no matter what subject you teach, plan learning experiences that reflect the concerns of the diverse cultural groups that make up the class, the school, and the community. Encourage your students to share their different perspectives and opinions and show that you value the different ways in which they solve problems and view the world around them.

Reissman (1994) recommends that as you assign learning tasks, consider how each assignment can be used to strengthen intergroup understandings, respect for each other's cultures, and the development of skills that will later be needed in community, *national, and global citizenship. Her book, entitled The Evolving Multicultural Classroom, may be a very valuable resource for you in your curriculum planning.*

Planning Curriculum for a Multicultural, Bilingual Classroom

Ruth Reyes teaches sixth grade at Washington School in downtown San Diego, California. This school follows a special policy of developing biliteracy among all its students. All classes are taught in both Spanish and English. In her class, Ruth teaches one day in Spanish and the next day in English. Her curriculum is designed to allow students to move from one language to another very flexibly. When she designs a unit of study, she selects resources in both English and Spanish. The students use both or select the ones that fit their own level of language development.

Ruth has chosen to use a yearlong theme that she calls Environment/Survival. This theme grows out of her own special interest in biology. It also ties in with the social studies curriculum and grows out of her belief that sixth-grade students need to be aware of the concept of environment and the relationship between humans and their environment. She wants her students to leave her class with a commitment to saving our natural environment. She also wants them to begin to develop survival skills and strategies to improve their own environment.

Ruth describes how she translates this important goal into daily learning experiences that cover the state- and district-mandated curricula for math, science, social studies, and language arts. Ruth describes the process in this way:

I looked through the course of study provided by the school district and the curriculum guides from the state and the school district. Then I opened up all the teacher's manuals for the textbooks we use in sixth grade. As I looked for a way to organize all this material into meaningful chunks, it was clear to me that I should use the social studies curriculum as the basis for planning. At sixth grade, we focus on the study of World History and Geography. That's a perfect fit with my interest in the environment and its relationship to mankind. I can teach the historic material and at the same time bring in contemporary issues and show how they relate to each other.

But before I plunge into the yearlong thematic curriculum, I spend the first week of school assessing students' interests and needs. My goals are to get to know my students and learn their strengths and interests. For that week, I use a short literature book that really interests me. This year, I used Kurusa's (1981) The Streets Are Free and the Spanish edition, Las calles son libros. This book about the rain forests fits my theme and allows me to introduce the major ideas we'll be studying all year long. The students do a lot of reading, writing, discussion, and group assignments so that I can observe them as they work together. I spend most of my time during that week observing and taking notes on students as they are working in various groupings. I try to identify what each student enjoys, what is easy, and what is a challenge for each of them. As I walk around with my clipboard, I take notes on computer labels (one label per student), which I can then transfer to their portfolios without rewriting. I look for as many positives as possible and also jot down what appears to be challenging for each student. Everyone in my class is learning a new language so I have to be alert when I hear them speak in the unfamiliar language, so that I can encourage them and plan activities that will allow them to be successful.

During the second week of school, we begin our study of the first social studies/literature unit for the year. The topics that are covered in the social studies curriculum include: Early Man, the Beginning of Civilization, Ancient Hebrews and Greeks, India, China, and Rome. For language arts, I locate several literature books that are related in some way to each of these topics. We spend about three weeks on each novel. For example, with the study of Early Man, I use a book about a girl who lived during the Ice Age who has to help her family survive by moving to a winter cave. See, it fits my theme in every way. For math and science, we study the time lines and the ages of prehistoric earth. We also write word problems for math involving the characters in the novel.

I am not rigid in my organization of the whole year, but we spend about three weeks per book. For some historical eras, we read two or three books. I try to get each book in Spanish and in English. When this isn't possible, then I get similar books on the topic so that my students can choose to read in English for one book, Spanish for another.

We begin a new unit by brainstorming what we already know about rain forests. We make a chart of what we know and put it up in the classroom. Then, we make another chart of what we want to learn about rain forests. Based on what we want to know, I create five categories and divide the class up into five groups. Each group focuses on researching one of the categories, such as animals or trees. Each group researches their topic for about three days and then they begin to organize their material into a book. They use the computer to write, edit, and illustrate their books. When they are completed, they teach what they have learned to the rest of their classmates. The books they write become part of the school library's collection for the rest of the year.

When I think of what my students experience during the entire year, I want them to see that every subject is related to the others. When they see the connections between subject matter, I feel that I have been successful. Some children come to school believing that in order to do math, they have to use a math book. I want them to learn that we do math every day of our lives. I also want them to see the relationships between different authors and their style. We concentrate a lot on comparing and analyzing in my room. Whenever we read a new book, we are constantly looking for ways that this book compares to other books we've read or to the social studies book or to some idea in math or science. When I hear my students making these analyses, I feel that my methods of teaching are validated.

Creating Time Lines That Fit Your Goals and Outcome Statements

Time is the scarcest resource in school. Reflective teachers who organize time wisely are more successful in delivering the curriculum they have planned than are teachers who fail to consider it. Teachers who simply start each subject on page one of every textbook and hope to finish the text by June are frequently surprised by the lack of time. In some cases, they finish a text early in the year, but more often the school year ends and students never get to the subjects at the back of the textbook. In mathematics, some classes never get to geometry year after year. In social studies, history after the Civil War is often crammed into a few short lessons at the end of the year.

Will you be satisfied if this happens in your classroom? If not, you can prevent it by preplanning the time you will give to each element or subtopic of each subject area you are going to teach. This may seem like an overwhelming task at first, but it can be less threatening if you understand that you are not required to plan every outcome and objective for every subject before the year begins. You need to give the entire curriculum an overview and determine the number of days or weeks you will allot to each element.

Begin by examining the textbooks in your classroom, looking at the way they are organized. Most books are divided into units, each covering a single topic or collection of related topics within the academic subject. Mathematics books are likely to contain units such as Place Value, Operations, Measuring, and Geometry. History books are divided into units on Exploration, Settling the New Frontier, Creating Government, and others. English books contain units such as Listening, Writing, and Speaking.

Curriculum units are excellent planning devices because they show students how facts, skills, concepts, and application of ideas are all related. The alternative to planning with units is planning a single, continuous, yearlong sequence of experiences or planning unconnected and unrelated daily experiences. Units will be used as the basis for planning throughout the rest of this book.

Decide if the units in your school's textbooks are valuable and important as well as whether you agree with the way they are organized and the quality of learning experiences they contain. Consider whether using the textbook will result in achieving the outcomes in your school curriculum guide. Will it result in achieving the goals and outcomes you have for your class? If the textbook learning experiences match your outcomes, you can plan the year to coincide with the sequence of units in the book. If the textbook does not coincide with your planned outcomes or if you disagree with the quality and/or the organizational pattern of the book, you have several options. You can plan to use the book but present the units in a different order. You can delete units, or you can use some units in the book as they are written but supplement with other materials for additional units not covered or inadequately covered in the book. The most adventuresome and creative teachers may even decide to use the textbook only as a resource and plan original teaching units for the subject.

In any case, you should carefully consider the amount of time you want to allot to each unit you plan to teach. Create a time line, chart, or calendar for each subject and use it as you judge how much time to spend on each subtopic. For time line planning, you can divide the school year into weeks, months, or quarters. For a subject such as mathematics, you may think about the year as a total of 36 weeks and allot varying numbers of weeks to each math topic you want to cover during the year. For a subject such as language arts, you might think of the school year as 8 months long and create eight different units that involve students in listening, speaking, writing, and reading activities. You may divide the year into four quarters for subjects such as science or social studies with four major units planned for the year. These examples are only suggestions. Each subject can be subdivided into any time segment, or you may combine subjects into interdisciplinary units that involve students in mathematics, science, and language arts activities under one combined topic for a time.

Making reasonable and professional judgments about time line planning depends on having information about your students' prior knowledge and their history of success or failure before the year begins. The pace of your curriculum depends to some degree on the skills and knowledge your students have acquired before you meet them. But your own expectation for their success is also important. You want to avoid the trap many teachers fall into of reviewing basic skills all year because a majority of your students have been unsuccessful in the past. If you expect them to succeed in your curriculum and be ready to move on to new challenges, provide them with new challenges and they are likely to respond to your positive expectations.

The time lines you create at the beginning of the year need not be rigid and unchanging. They are guidelines based on the best knowledge you have at the time. As the year progresses, you will undoubtedly have reasons to change your original time line. Students' needs, interests, and success will cause you to alter the pace of the original plan. Current events in the country, your classroom, or your local community may cause you to add a new unit to your plan. Interaction with other faculty members may bring you fresh new insights about how you want to allocate time in your classroom.

Collaborative Long-Term Planning

Long-term planning, either individually or collectively, is an important job for teachers. If you are teaching in a self-contained classroom, you have the freedom to write your own outcomes as long as they relate to the district and state guidelines. If you are working in a team-teaching school, you will need to articulate your vision of student outcomes to your teammates and adjust yours to include their ideas as well as your own. In either case, the outcome statements you create will improve with experience. As you see the effects of your original outcome statements, you will reflect on them and find ways to improve them with each succeeding year.

When you begin teaching, you may be assigned to a curriculum task force or planning committee. In discussions with your colleagues, you are likely to gain new insights and information, but you may also experience frustration with points of view that differ from your own. When this occurs, remember that teachers differ in their curriculum orientations. That may help you see things from a different perspective. Be prepared to speak assertively about your own ideas and beliefs. You may be the one to suggest innovative ways of dividing the curriculum into units. Although your ideas may meet skepticism or resistance from some teachers, it is quite appropriate for you to articulate them, because schools rely on fresh ideas from the faculty members with the most recent college or university training to enhance the curriculum and create positive innovations and change.

Reflective Actions for Your Professional Portfolio

A Sample of Your Long-Term Planning

Use Withitness to Observe and Respond

Observe a classroom in action for a few hours and try to infer what the goals are from what you see taking place. Write what you perceive to be the major affective, cognitive, and psychomotor goals in effect.

Define and Put the Problem into Perspective

Based on your perception of students' needs, what are your highest priority educational goals? Write at least one cognitive, affective, and psychomotor outcome statement that you consider to be extremely important in the elementary curriculum.

Invite Feedback to Help Redefine the Problem

Visit a school and ask to see the mission statement and curriculum goals or outcomes for that site. Ask a classroom teacher to describe his or her goals and show you the long-range plans. Talk with the teacher about how the school's mission statement and goals affected the class curriculum. Do these visits cause you to rewrite your original outcome statements? As with other aspects of teaching, we must always be open and willing to change.

Create an Action Plan

Imagine that you have been hired to teach in the school that you are currently visiting. Create a series of themes for the grade level you would most like to teach. Describe how you would integrate the subject areas into each theme.

Predict Possible Outcomes

Using the themes you selected for your grade level, sketch out a brief yearlong plan using months or quarters of the year as units of planning. What would be the major outcomes in language arts, social studies, math, and science for each month or quarter? How do they relate to the theme?

References

Banks, J. (1991–1992). Multicultural education: For freedom's sake. *Educational Leadership, 49*, 4.

Bell, M. (1990). *Everyday mathematics first grade teacher's manual.* Evanston, IL: Everyday Learning Corp.

Bloom, B., Engelhart, M., Furst, E., Hill, W., & Krathwohl, D. (1956). *Taxonomy of educational objectives: Cognitive domain.* New York: Longman.

Eisner, E. (1994). *Educational imagination* (3rd ed.). Upper Saddle River, NJ: Merrill/Prentice Hall.

Kendall, J., & Marzano, R. (1995). *The systematic identification and articulation of content standards and benchmarks.* Aurora, CO: Mid-continent Regional Educational Laboratory.

Kurusa, D. (1981). *The streets are free (Los calles son libros).* Caracas: Ekare-Banco Del Libro.

National Center for History in the Schools. (1994). *National standards for United States history: Exploring paths to the present.* Los Angeles: Author.

Reissman, R. (1994) *The evolving multicultural classroom.* Alexandria, VA: Association for Supervision and Curriculum Development.

Spady, W. (1994). Choosing outcomes of significance. *Educational Leadership, 51*(6), 18–22.

Tyler, R. (1949). *Basic principles of curriculum and instruction.* Chicago: University of Chicago Press.

Viadero, D. (1993). Standards deviation: Benchmark-setting is marked by diversity. *Education Week,* June 16, 14–17.

Chapter

5

Planning Thematic Units for Authentic Learning

D̲o you have a vision of yourself teaching a roomful of students who are excitedly investigating, experimenting, discussing, and reporting on what they are learning? Beginning teachers and student teachers often report that what they want to do most is create a learning environment that motivates their students to want to come to school and want to learn as much as they can about important matters.

Current national standards and state curriculum guides are also the products of the vision of experienced teachers, working in collaboration to provide all teachers with guidelines for what to teach and how to teach it. These documents encourage teachers to create programs that develop students' deeper understandings of a few important subjects rather than provide them with superficial surveys of data. At the local school district level, teachers are responsible for translating the curricular visions described at the national or state level into practical classroom learning experiences. The word *vision* is carefully chosen in this discussion, because at the local level teachers and principals are often encouraged to develop a common vision and create a mental image of what they want to accomplish with students.

One of the most natural and authentic ways to translate a vision of core curriculum goals into practical classroom experiences is by planning thematic units of study that engage students in actively seeking information on a topic that has meaning in their lives. Many teachers use a series of thematic units for their long-term planning. There is something refreshing and inherently motivating for both teachers and students using this plan.

A unit of study lasts a specified number of days or weeks, during which everyone is motivated to investigate and find out everything they can about the topic. Then, during an exciting culmination, the students proudly display what they have learned. After a brief period devoted to assessment, the unit ends, and a new one begins. When this rhythm is established in a classroom, complaints of boredom or repetition are rare from students or the teacher. The pace is quick, the goals are clear, and the expectations are high when everyone is involved in a thematic unit on an interesting, challenging topic.

How Teachers Plan Thematic Units

No other model of curriculum development involves teachers in a more active and professional capacity than does the planning, teaching, and evaluation of thematic curriculum units. They appeal greatly to reflective teachers who want to be part of the decision-making process and use their own creative ideas and methods. However, the planning of thematic curriculum units also adds greatly to the responsibility of classroom teachers. To create a successful unit, teachers must be willing to gather information and create an excellent knowledge base about the topics they have chosen so that the learning experiences they plan will be based on accurate information. They must also be willing to work with their colleagues to make sure that their curriculum units do not repeat or skip over important material in the elementary curriculum. They must take care to articulate their units with what was covered in earlier grades and what their students will learn in subsequent years.

Even when teachers decide that they want to create their own thematic curriculum units to translate curricular visions into actual classroom experiences, many are not certain about how to create one or what can or should be covered in each unit. In this chapter, we examine how teachers decide what units to teach and how they organize the learning experiences in a curriculum unit to ensure that students learn the knowledge, skills, and processes that are intended when a unit is planned.

Deciding on Unit Topics

A single teacher can work alone or with colleagues to translate state and local curriculum outcomes into units of study. Working alone, a single teacher analyzes state and local outcome statements to be implemented at that grade level in math, science, social studies, language arts, and fine arts. The teacher also examines the curriculum materials supplied by the school district, looking for themes or topics. The teacher may choose to look for topics within a subject, such as a math unit on fractions, a science unit on magnets and electricity, or a social studies unit on the electoral process. Other units may be interdisciplinary—that is, designed to include information and material from several subjects at one time. For example, a theme of "change" may include learning experiences in science, math, social studies, and literature.

Although many teachers choose to work alone, other teachers at the same grade level frequently work together to create units of study. When this occurs, their combined knowledge and ideas are likely to result in a much more comprehensive set of units and greater variety of learning experiences. Whether a teacher works alone or with a team, the first step is to decide on curriculum units that correspond to the major educational goals in a subject or several subjects for that grade level.

Unit topics may be suggested or recommended by the district curriculum guide and the textbooks purchased for the subject area. Teachers can decide to use the suggested topics either in the order presented or in a different order. Teachers may choose to delete recommended units or add others to fulfill the needs of their students.

Teachers may decide not to use units for every subject throughout the year. Instead, they may choose to teach a subject as an unconnected series of lessons. They may use units occasionally to highlight a particular topic in the curriculum. Sometimes teachers are able to plan units that combine more than one subject area, such as language arts and social studies or math and science. No two teachers will use the same units in the same order. Teachers have much discretion in planning units that fit their own strengths and the students' needs.

When a series of units is planned for a subject, each unit within the series is then developed in planning sessions that may begin in the summer before school begins or take place in after-school meetings during the year. Often teachers plan the first unit during the summer so that it is ready for the fall. Later units are then planned during the school year. Once a unit has been planned, it can be reused in subsequent years, although reflective teachers usually review their older units and revise and update them prior to teaching them a second or third time.

Creating a Curriculum Unit Using Reflective Actions

When reflective teachers approach the development of a curriculum unit in a subject area, they first consider their long-term goals for that subject. They may begin with the question "What are my major social studies goals this year, and what should I include in each unit of study to accomplish these goals?" Or they may begin by considering the core outcomes they are expected to achieve during the year and then plan curriculum units that will encourage their students to learn the content and enhance the skills that make up those outcomes.

In the following example, the pictures in the margin represent parts of the reflective action process that we encourage teachers to use as they plan curriculum.

Use Withitness

Teachers who think and plan using the reflective actions described in Chapter 1 are likely to consider the cues they perceive from their students' interests and talents when planning thematic units. As they plan curriculum, they tend to ask themselves, "What do my students need to learn? How do they enjoy working? What learning experiences will motivate my students to become actively engaged in the learning process?"

Define Topics and Put the Curriculum into Perspective

Teachers who use reflective actions begin by using their curriculum guides and state mandates for each subject. They define a topic and sketch a preliminary draft of a curriculum unit. Then they consider some interesting ways to teach it. The first draft may resemble something they have read in a curriculum guide, or perhaps even the type of unit plan they recall from their own school experiences.

Widen Your Perspective

Reflective teachers are also likely to begin to establish some criteria for selecting certain content or methods while omitting others. These decisions are likely to be made on the basis of the teacher's values and moral principles or a philosophy of teaching. As reflective teachers consider what to include and what to exclude, they ask themselves, "What knowledge and skills do I believe that my students need most to succeed in school or in life? How can this curriculum assist them in developing what they need most? What attitudes do I want to instill among my students? How can this unit help them to attain those attitudes? What values do I want to model for my students during this curriculum unit? How can I best model those values for them?"

Invite Feedback

At many points along the way, reflective teachers are likely to do additional research on the subject or on teaching methods they can include in their new unit. They are also likely to talk with other trusted colleagues about how they have taught the subject. Many teachers share their unit plans with others, but most agree that sharing a unit plan is very much like sharing their recipes for making spaghetti sauce. No two sauces or units are identical. Still, a trusted colleague can point out things for the beginning teacher to consider, share strategies for motivating student interest, and suggest new materials to include in the unit.

Redefine the Unit Plan

Reflective teachers consider ideas that arise from interaction with colleagues. They may devise a new and original way to approach the topic or even change basic goals for the unit.

Write an Action Plan

Now, the fun part begins. Teachers who use reflective action tend to enjoy the process of combining all of the content materials and methods they have learned about during planning into an original set of learning experiences that fits their own teaching style and the needs of their students. No two thematic units are ever alike. Even when teachers plan together up to this point, they are likely to interpret the materials they have gathered differently and add their own unique spin to the way they teach the unit.

Throughout the process of planning and teaching the unit, teachers who use reflective action are likely to be asking themselves, "How can I adapt the materials I have available to meet my goals? What new instructional materials shall I create to teach this material effectively? What risks are possible if I try to teach this unit in my own way? Which risks am I willing to take? What gains are possible if I take these risks? Do the possible gains outweigh the risks?"

During a thematic unit, teachers create original bulletin boards, group activities, work or activity sheets, processes for promoting student interaction, methods to assess student accomplishments, and ways to allow their students to perform or display what they have learned. For many reflective teachers, these opportunities for creativity are an important source of pride and are often cited as one of the most significant perks of their careers.

Predict Possible Outcomes

All teachers encounter problems in teaching and managing their classrooms. But teachers who use reflective action are able to prevent some of these because they try to imagine the consequences of their plans before putting them into action. For example, if you are planning to introduce some innovative learning materials to motivate students, you should try to consider what types of behavior management problems might develop.

Teachers who use reflective actions in their thinking and planning expect these kinds of difficulties. Spinning out consequences may prevent some problems, but realistically, others are likely to occur. When they do, the teachers repeat all the reflective action steps again. They use withitness in the midst of the problem to observe what is happening and respond appropriately. Afterward, they talk with the students themselves or with their colleagues in order to reframe the problem and create a new plan.

Putting the Plan into Action and Getting Student Feedback

The day you present your new unit plan to your students is usually an exciting day for you and your class. There is a sense of heightened expectations as you reveal the plan. Students may have a lot of questions. You may be able to answer some but not all of their questions right away. You will use withitness during the initial presentation to get feedback from your most important critics: your students. They will give you cues as they react to the plan with excitement, confusion, fear, or increased motivation to learn. You can also discuss the first day's presentation with your colleagues and get ideas about how to reframe the plan for yourself or for your students. After the first day, you will be even better equipped to spin out the consequences of certain parts of the plan. If your students react with fear or confusion, you can make changes now, before it's too late. If they react with excitement, you can consider adding even more challenging material to the plan.

Reflective teachers are also able to laugh at their own mistakes and learn from their errors in judgment without an overwhelming fear of the consequences or feelings of guilt. As they plan their thematic units, they are likely to encounter difficulties in locating suitable materials. When this happens, they become very good at scrounging for the materials they need or they substitute and go on anyway.

When they begin to teach their units, some of the lessons they planned are likely to turn out quite differently than they expected, but they simply assess, regroup, and reteach as needed. As the unit nears completion, they may discover that, due to their students' choices and actions, some unplanned effects occur. These are simply accounted for and evaluated along with the outcomes that were planned.

Throughout the process of planning, organizing, teaching, and evaluating a thematic unit, good communication skills are necessary. Reflective teachers must often convince or persuade their colleagues or administrators to allow them to take the time, spend money, take certain risks, and establish certain priorities necessary to teach their thematic units the way they want. Assertiveness is a very important trait in curriculum development, especially considering the very different curriculum orientations that various members of the faculty adopt.

Conflicts may arise with students as well. When reflective teachers introduce a creative new way to learn a difficult subject, some students may react by stating their own preferences. When this occurs, teachers who use reflective actions simply begin the cyclical process anew by perceiving what needs the students have that have not been sufficiently addressed in the plan so far and accommodating those needs in a revised version of the unit plan.

Sequencing Learning Experiences in Unit Plans

Practically speaking, the process of developing a curriculum unit also includes the following:

1. Defining the topics and subject matter to be covered in the unit
2. Defining the cognitive psychomotor (process), and affective goals or outcomes that tell what students will gain and be able to do as a result
3. Outlining the major concepts that will be covered
4. Gathering resources that can be used in planning and teaching
5. Brainstorming learning activities and experiences that can be used in the unit
6. Organizing the ideas and activities into a meaningful sequence
7. Planning lesson plans that follow the sequence
8. Planning evaluation processes that will be used to measure student achievement and satisfaction.

Analysis will reveal that these statements correspond to Tyler's four questions. Items 1, 2, and 3 pertain to Tyler's (1949) question "What shall we teach?" Items 4 and 5 relate to the question "How shall we teach it?" Items 6 and 7 respond to the question "How shall we organize it?" Item 8 answers the question "How will we know if we are successful?"

When seen in print, as they are here, these steps appear to depict an orderly process, but curriculum planning is rarely such a linear activity. Instead, teachers find themselves starting at various points in this process. They skip or go back and forth between these steps as ideas occur to them. For example, a team member may begin a discussion by showing a resource book with a particular learning activity that could be taught as part of the new unit. Discussions may skip from activities to goals to concepts to evaluation to organization. Nothing is wrong with this nonlinear process as long as teachers are responsible enough to reflect on the overall plan to determine if all of Tyler's questions have been addressed fully and adequately. When the plan is complete, it is important to review it and ask yourself: "What are the outcomes I expect from this unit? Are the learning experiences directly related to the outcomes? Is my organization of activities going to make it possible for my students to achieve my outcomes? Are the assessment systems I have established going to measure the extent to which the students have accomplished the outcomes?"

Thematic units vary in types of learning experiences and in organization. Some subjects, such as math, are organized very sequentially, and others are not. The types of learning experiences also vary greatly depending on the subject, the resources available, and the creativity or risk taking of the teacher.

Most teachers use the textbook or a district curriculum guide as the basis for planning and as an important resource. *Do not limit yourself, however, to a single textbook as the source of all information in planning your unit or in teaching it.* A good textbook can be a valuable resource for you as you plan and for your students as they learn about the topic, but a rich and motivating unit plan will contain many other elements.

Supplemental reading materials from libraries or bookstores might include biographies, histories, novels, short stories, plays, poems, newspapers, magazines, how-to books, and myriad other printed materials. Other resources to consider are films, videotapes, audiotapes, and computer programs on topics that relate to your unit. Many interesting student-centered computer programs allow your students to have simulated experiences, solve problems, and make decisions as if they were involved in the event themselves. A good example is the computer game called "Oregon Trail," distributed by the Minnesota Educational Computer Consortium, in which the student travels along the Oregon Trail, making decisions about what supplies to buy, when and where to stop along the way, and how to handle emergencies. This program can enrich a unit on westward expansion by providing more problem-solving and critical-thinking experiences than reading and discussion alone.

Many educational games also provide students with simulated experiences. Some are board games that can be purchased in a good toy store or bookstore. Others are more specialized learning games sold by educational publishers or distributors. Your school district probably receives hundreds of catalogs from educational publishers. Locate them and find out about the many manipulative and simulation games available on your topic.

Consider field trips that will provide your students with experiences beyond the four walls of the classroom. Which museums have exhibits related to your topic? A simple walk through a neighborhood to look for evidence of pollution or to view variations in architecture can add depth to your unit. If you cannot travel, consider inviting a guest to speak to your students about the topic. Sometimes parents are excellent resources and are willing to talk about their careers or other interests.

In thinking about how to organize a unit, many reflective teachers prefer to begin with a highly motivating activity such as a field trip, a guest speaker, a simulation game, a hands-on experiment, or a film. They know that when the students' initial experience with a topic is stimulating and involving, interest and curiosity are aroused. The next several lessons in the unit are frequently planned at the knowledge and comprehension levels of Bloom's taxonomy to provide students with basic facts and concepts so that they can build a substantial knowledge base and understanding of the topic. After establishing the knowledge base, further learning experiences can be designed at the application, analysis, synthesis, and evaluation levels to ensure that the students are able to think critically and creatively about the subject. This model of unit planning is not universal, nor is it the only logical sequence, but it can be adapted to fit many topics and subjects with excellent results.

Examples of Thematic Units

The following sections illustrate the processes teachers use as they select, order, and create unit plans in several subjects from the elementary curriculum. Because each teacher has a personal curriculum orientation and philosophy, the process of decision making is more complex when teachers plan together than when they plan alone. The following examples demonstrate how teachers create their own curriculum units and what they put down on paper to record their plans for teaching. You will notice many variations in the way units are created and what they contain depending on their purposes and the philosophies and values of the teachers who create them.

Creating a Multidisciplinary Primary Unit

Some units of study cross the boundaries between subjects or disciplines such as math, science, language arts, and social studies. For instance, a unit on Ancient Rome could incorporate many communication and language arts skills in what might be considered primarily a social studies unit. Curriculum plans that include learning experiences from more than one subject area are called *multidisciplinary* or *interdisciplinary* units.

To create such units, teachers frequently choose themes or topics and plan learning experiences that involve students in reading, writing, speaking, science investigations, mathematical problem solving, music, and art. A single teacher can certainly plan and teach a multidisciplinary unit, but we have found that the units planned by two to four teachers are often more exciting because they incorporate each teacher's different perspectives and strengths. For example, at Woodland School in Carpentersville, Illinois, three first-grade teachers often plan their whole language thematic units together. Virginia Bailey, Judy Yount, and Sandra Krakow recently planned an interdisciplinary unit on "change," highlighting the changes of butterflies and moths.

Bailey, Yount, and Krakow know that teachers often have difficulty fitting in all the subjects of their busy curricula. They find that by using a thematic unit, they can teach several subjects simultaneously. To plan a unit, these teachers use a graphic organizer known as a *planning web*. They sit down with a large piece of paper and write the thematic topic in the middle of the page. They write the various disciplines they want to cover at different positions on the paper and then brainstorm learning experiences that fit the topic under the appropriate subject areas. An example of their planning webs is shown in Figure 5.1.

Through their observations of the students they teach, the three teachers learned that, in the minds of first-grade students, reading and writing are very closely related. Their interdisciplinary thematic units allow students to read, write, and investigate interesting topics such as caterpillars, cookies, and planets. In each unit they select appropriate topic-specific children's books of fiction, nonfiction, and poetry. They locate songs on the topics when possible. Skill teaching is embedded in the unit, within the context of the literature, poetry, or music. The science and social studies facts and concepts are easily mastered by students when they are presented in the context of hands-on experiments and are reinforced by illustrated stories, poems, and songs. Math concepts are introduced by counting, measuring, sequencing, and patterning games and activities appropriate to each unit. Figure 5.2 shows a written plan for the unit "Changes," describing some of the specific learning experiences and how the unit is evaluated.

Developing a Mathematics Unit

Mathematics is generally thought of as a subject that does not lend itself to multidisciplinary planning, but recently, many teachers have been experimenting with ways to

Figure 5.1   Planning web for a thematic unit.

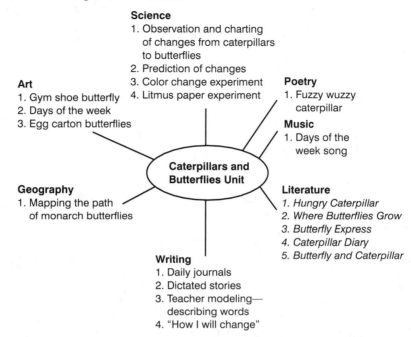

Source: Virginia Bailey, Judy Yount, and Sandra Krakow, Woodland School, Carpentersville, Illinois.

connect mathematics to other subject areas and life experiences. As Piaget demonstrated, mathematics is a subject that requires early experiences with concrete examples and hands-on experiences allowing students to manipulate materials to understand mathematical relationships. Later, upper intermediate grade students can be expected to understand these same relationships at a more abstract level without the need to "see" them in a concrete way. Many teachers like to plan their mathematics curriculum using thematic units so that students have many opportunities to experience and investigate the mathematical relationships they are learning.

Mathematics is also a subject that requires lateral thinking, reasoning, and problem-solving strategies that cannot be taught in a sequential series of lessons. Current mathematics units encourage students to explore mathematical relationships and select from a variety of strategies to set up and solve problems. Skillful computation is no longer sufficient as an outcome or performance expectation; it is also important that students be able to apply mathematical operations to real-life problems and tasks.

Based on these organizational principles, an effective curriculum unit in math is likely to (1) present new skills and concepts in order of difficulty; (2) initiate new learning with concrete, manipulative experiences so that students can understand the concepts involved; (3) teach students a variety of problem-solving strategies; and (4) provide examples, tasks, and problems that call on students to apply their newly learned skills and strategies in lifelike situations to problems they can relate to and want to solve.

Figure 5.2   A multidisciplinary primary unit on "Changes: Butterflies and Moths." This first-grade unit plan was created by Virginia Bailey, Judy Yount, and Sandra Krakow, Woodland School, Carpentersville, Illinois.

Description

This primary learning unit was planned to provide students with a set of varied learning experiences to understand the concept of change, with an emphasis on changes in the life cycle of living things.

- **Cognitive goal:** Students will understand that all living things change over time.
- **Affective goal:** Students will accept change as a natural part of their own lives and environment.
- **Psychomotor goals:** Students will use observation skills to identify changes. They will use writing and speaking skills to report what they have learned through observation.

Activities

Nature Walk: Before the nature walk, students are asked to imagine what they might find out about caterpillars and butterflies on their walk. During the walk, they look especially for cocoons. When they return to the classroom, they discuss their findings. They predict whether the cocoons they found will become butterflies or moths. Then they write about what they saw on their nature walk.

Observing Caterpillars: Caterpillars ordered from a science supply dealer arrive in plastic jars. Students observe them climb to the top of the jar preparing to form a chrysalis. In just a few days, they begin to spin their chrysalis. They remain in this form for three or four days and then emerge as butterflies or moths.

   As a follow-up activity, students are asked to illustrate the various changes they observe. A strip of 18-inch by 6-inch paper is prepared for each child. Children fold the paper into fourths and draw each stage of a butterfly's development: (1) egg on a leaf, (2) caterpillar, (3) chrysalis or cocoon, and (4) butterfly or moth.

   In groups of four, children evaluate their products and check the proper sequence. Each child can then tell the other children a story about his or her butterfly.

Color Changes: In a learning center, students experiment to discover how colors change. Working with diluted red, blue, and yellow food color, the children use an empty cup and an eye dropper to mix colors and experiment on their own to create new colors from the original primary colors.

Children's Literature: The teacher collects a variety of picture books for use in this unit. Some books will be read aloud by the teacher and used as a focus for discussion. Others will be selected by the children to read on their own.

Caterpillar/Butterfly Art Activity: Students create a wiggly caterpillar by cutting 12 cups from an egg carton and turning them upside down. They make a small hole in the bottom of each cup, tie a knot at one end of a piece of yarn, and string the 12 cups together. Then they add paper eyes and decorate the caterpillars with crayons or paint.

   They create a butterfly by cutting out 3 of the 12 cups from an egg carton for the body. Then they add wings and pipe-cleaner antennae.

Gym Shoe Butterfly: Each child places his or her gym shoes on a large piece of pastel paper (arches facing out) and traces the shoes into a butterfly shape. The child then cuts out the shape and adds antennae. The child can write a poem inside the butterfly shape.

Figure 5.2   *Continued*

Days of the Week: Students create a caterpillar with seven circles cut from construction paper. They then copy the name of a different day of the week on each circle and glue them onto a background paper in the correct order. Afterward, they add a face, legs, and antennae. Students learn a song about the days of the week.

How People Change: Students bring in pictures of themselves as babies and put them on a bulletin board. Current school pictures are also arranged on the bulletin board. Students have to try to match the baby pictures with the current pictures of their classmates. Discussions focus on how people change (observing differences in size, hair, and other physical features) and what people are able to do at different ages. As a follow-up, students write in their journals about how they have changed.

Growth Charts: Charts on the students' current heights and weights are initiated during this unit. Each student measures and weighs a partner. The data are recorded on a wall graph. The charts are updated three times during the year.

Poetry about Change: Poems about caterpillars and butterflies, seasons, and other changes are distributed frequently during the unit. Students read them, memorize and recite them, discuss them, and illustrate them. The poems are also used to teach language structure and vocabulary skills. A poem is projected onto a screen using an overhead projector. Students also have copies of the poem on their desks. We teach skills such as these:

1. Reading from left to right
2. Finding and reading individual words
3. Using the context of the poem to decode words
4. Learning specific phonics skills (such as beginning sounds, endings, rhyming words)

Art/Nutrition: Create a caterpillar out of fruit, vegetables, and peanut butter. Eat it for a snack and discuss its nutritional value.

Unit Evaluation Activity

Provide students with a paper that has the beginning of three paragraphs (shown below). Use a copy on the overhead projector and clarify for students how to begin and what is expected.

Because primary students are unable to write all that they know and have observed, this evaluation can be extended by asking children from an upper elementary grade to interview the primary children and write the younger students' responses for them.

This week, I learned about butterflies and moths. First, I learned _____
_____
_____

Next, I learned _____
_____
_____

Finally, I learned _____
_____
_____

Mathematics is an example of a *spiral curriculum*. This means that certain concepts and skills are taught every year but in an upward spiral of difficulty. Each year begins with a review of skills from previous years, then an introduction of new skills and concepts. For this reason, the topics of mathematics units are likely to be similar from year to year, but the way these topics are addressed and the complexity of the concepts vary greatly. Mathematics education now emphasizes problem solving and investigation as a means of developing mathematical power. Whenever possible, real situations and problems are becoming the basis for the curriculum.

A good example of a mathematics unit that involves students in realistic investigations and problem solving is presented in Figure 5.3. Pam Knight created this unit, entitled "Television Viewing Habits," for her sixth-grade students. She uses it during the first week of school to engage her students' interest in mathematics, help to develop a sense of confidence in their mathematical power, and show them how useful and important mathematics can be in their everyday lives.

Creating a Science Unit

Godwin Higa is a fifth-grade teacher and a mentor teacher for new teachers in his district. He enjoys teaching science at this stage in his career, although he recalls having misgivings about his ability to teach science when he began. He overcame his fears by taking hands-on workshops in which he got to experiment with science himself. He has learned to ask for help when he needs it. He goes to visit other teachers to see what they are doing and continues to take workshops and classes to keep himself fresh.

A few years ago he visited another teacher's class and watched his students launch hot air balloons. Godwin adapted the ideas of this teacher and got additional ideas from an article about teaching science. The result is a 4-week science unit that he offers each year in the fall or winter.

When I ask students to draw a picture of a scientist, they almost always draw a picture of a man in a white lab coat working alone in a science lab. But I want them to know that scientists can work out of doors, can be men and women or even children. I want them to know that science is trial and error and that scientists get to create ideas and things and test their ideas in a variety of ways. I want students to see science as very lively. I want them to work together, learn together, and teach each other what they have learned. I believe that the best way to retain knowledge is by teaching it to someone else.

Godwin's science unit on creating and launching hot air balloons is described in Figure 5.4.

Like the teachers we have cited in this chapter, you may want to explore the world of curriculum planning by using hands-on experiences, conferring with colleagues, and creating original units of study. When you complete your first unit and present it to your students, you will understand firsthand why thematic, integrated teaching is an important part of a relational teacher's work.

Figure 5.3   A mathematics unit on "Television Viewing Habits," created by Pam Knight, Garden Road Elementary School, Poway, California.

Description
This unit functions both as a personal exploration of how students use their free time and as a mathematics investigation. Students keep a log of all the time they spend watching TV every day for a week. With parental permission, students may also log the TV viewing habits of their parents. After a week of data gathering, students carry out a variety of mathematical calculations and interpret the data they collected.

Cognitive and Skill Outcome Statements
- Students will be able to collect and record data accurately and efficiently.
- Students will be able to calculate percentages of time spent watching television and compare those with percentages of time spent doing other activities.
- Students will be able to create bar and circle graphs based on the data they collected and the percentages they calculated.
- Individually, students will interpret the data they collected about their own television-viewing habits.
- As a class, students will combine their data with that collected by other members of the class to make interpretations and generalizations regarding TV-viewing habits of their age group.
- Individually, students will write articles describing the conclusions and generalizations they reached from this study.
- In small groups, students will make oral presentations on the findings of their group.

Affective Outcome Statement
Students will become aware of the amount of time they and their classmates spend watching television and will make value judgments about whether they want to continue spending their time in this way.

Calendar of Events
I plan this investigation for the first week of school. It gives me insight into the students' incoming work habits and mathematical power.

First Week of School
Friday: Introduce unit and distribute data collection materials. Assign students the task of collecting data, beginning Sunday, on the amount of time they watch television. Because video games are played on a TV screen, my students also decided to count the time spent playing video games. I ask students to be as honest as possible and to keep track to the nearest quarter of an hour.

Figure 5.3   *Continued*

Second Week of School

Monday–Friday: Data collection continues. Discussions in class focus on data collection problems and techniques.

Third Week of School

Monday: Bar Graphs. Individually, students create bar graphs demonstrating the amount of time they watched TV each day of the preceding week.

Tuesday: Calculating Percentages and Circle Graphs. Individually, students calculate the amount and percentage of time they spent sleeping, in school, in after-school or weekend activities, and watching television, as well as extra time not spent watching television. They create circle graphs showing these percentages.

Wednesday–Friday: Group Data Interpretation. Cooperative groups combine class data in order to answer these questions:

1. Which grade level watches more television? Explain how you came to this conclusion.
2. Which day of the week do people watch the most television? Explain how you came to this conclusion.
3. Who watches more television in general—boys or girls? Does any particular age group watch more television? How did you come to your conclusions?
4. By using data about parent viewing habits, have you discovered any relationship between the television-viewing habits of a parent and the habits of a child?

Fourth Week of School

Monday: Writing Articles. Individuals are assigned to write an article about their conclusions about the television-viewing habits of fifth and sixth graders. They must answer the questions "Who? What? When? Where? and Why?" in the articles.

Tuesday–Wednesday: Oral Presentation Planning. Cooperative groups plan presentations on the findings of their groups. They create visual displays to show the data they collected.

Thursday: Oral Presentations. Cooperative groups present their findings to the rest of the class.

Friday: Unit Evaluation. Students evaluate their accomplishments in this unit. Individuals participate in a teacher-student conference to discuss the points each student earned in the unit. Cooperative groups discuss the processes they used in their group planning sessions, the visual displays they made, and the effectiveness of their oral presentations.

Figure 5.4 "Hot Air Balloons: A Science Unit on Energy, Heat, and Density," created by Godwin Higa, Dingeman Elementary School, San Diego, California.

Description
Students work in teams to create and launch a huge tissue paper balloon and send it into the air. They conduct various experiments to gain understanding of air volume, mass, density, and the effects of temperature.

Outcome Statements
- Students will acquire knowledge about the relationship between volumes of air at different temperatures and the gravity of Earth. They will see that a balloon with hot air is pushed up from Earth by the descending cold air that surrounds it.
- Students will experience working together as a scientific team and will learn to share their ideas with colleagues.
- Students will experience the feelings of real scientists as they test and retest their ideas and look for the effects of each attempt to launch their balloons.

Materials
Tissue paper, oak tag paper, glue sticks, tar buckets, charcoal briquettes, water, fire extinguisher, scotch tape to repair holes in tissue paper, staples and pennies to add weight.

Schedule of Events
This unit takes place over a period of about four weeks and is best offered during cool fall or winter months so that the temperature differential is greatest. We do this project during our science lab time of about one-and-one-half hours per session two times a week.

Week One
Day One: We talk about the concepts of air volume, gravity, and climate. We do preliminary experiments to illustrate floating and sinking in liquid. For example, we observe bananas floating in a sea of cornflakes and a small piece of wood in a glass of water.

Day Two: We use protractors to measure a 30 degree angle and rulers to draw a pattern for the hot air balloon out of oak tag paper. It is a 20- by 60-inch pattern piece. Working in pairs, students select any color tissue paper they want and create a pattern for their own hot air balloon. Parents come in and help teams glue the pieces together to create the balloon panels.

Figure 5.4   *Continued*

Week Two
Day One and Two: Students begin to glue together the panels they have made into hot air balloons. It takes six panels to make one balloon. The team works together to create a name and design for the base for the balloon out of oak tag paper. They staple the base to the panels. Through experimentation, they learn how many staples add the appropriate amount of weight to their balloon for flight to occur.

Week Three
Day One: Guest speakers from the Aerospace Museum or parents with knowledge about flight principles are invited to speak to the class. Students are encouraged to ask specific questions to assist their team to make a successful launch.

Day Two: We write letters to parents to invite them to our balloon launch. We make posters to announce our event to other classes.

Fourth Week
Day One: Prepare for launch by getting together our materials for creating hot air. I bring in two tar buckets and charcoal briquettes. We punch holes in the tar buckets to create ventilation. We inform the media and the fire department of our event. We create danger zone flags and orange patrol cones to set up an off-limits viewing area for classmates and parents who will come to see our launch.

Day Two (launch day): We start early in the morning to get the coolest air. Using garden mittens, we place a metal funnel upside down over the bucket filled with heated charcoal. Teams of students come forward with their balloon and fill it with hot air. When they feel it begin to pull away from the ground, the team lets go and we all watch the balloon ascend. Some go as high as 100 feet into the air. Teams retrieve their own balloons and are allowed to launch as often as possible. If a balloon does not ascend, students must make repairs or remove weight to get the balloon to fly.

During their attempts to launch balloons, they begin to experiment with other hypotheses. Just before the balloon takes off, they may tape pennies onto the tag board to determine just how much weight their balloon can carry. Using this data, we can calculate the volume and mass of a balloon needed to carry each child's own weight.

Assessment Method
In a class discussion, we talk about the event. We talk about the process, comparing their plans with the outcomes. We talk about various trials and ways they learned to improve their flights. Individual students write about their experiments and place their reflective writings in their portfolios with pictures of their balloons.

Reflective Actions for Your Professional Portfolio

A Sample Thematic Unit Plan

Use Withitness: Observe a Curriculum Unit in Action

Visit a class and talk with the teacher about unit plans. Ask to see samples of unit plans used in the class. Then, ask to observe the students at work on their unit study.

Put the Plan into Perspective

Brainstorm and make a list of possible unit topics that interest you. We always advise that you create your first unit plan around a strength or long-standing interest of yours. You will then be highly motivated to seek information on the topic and will have much to share with your students when you teach it.

Widen Your Perspective

How do your interests coincide with the elementary curriculum at the district near you? By reflecting on your interests and looking for a good match with the curriculum, you may be able to decide what grade levels you will enjoy teaching.

Invite Feedback About Your Unit Plan

Ask to see the school district's curriculum guides and the state guidelines for curriculum planning for the subject matter of your unit. If you are considering creating a multidisciplinary unit, you should examine the curriculum guides for all subjects that will be included. Also, visit a school library or media center. Locate resources that you could use in the thematic units you are considering. Interview the librarian to ask for suggestions for other resources on that topic. Include these materials in your unit resource list.

Show your initial plan to the classroom teacher or to other trusted colleagues. Brainstorm and share ideas for the unit topic together. Ask your colleague to predict possible roadblocks or other sources of difficulty standing in the way of implementing your unit plan successfully. Ask for advice about the types of materials you need to gather or create. Ask for suggestions about teaching strategies and assessment strategies that are appropriate for your unit.

Redefine the Scope of Your Plan

Select one unit theme and brainstorm ideas for the cognitive, affective, and psychomotor outcomes that are possible for your students. Select another interesting theme and do the same thing. Now compare the outcomes possible with each theme and decide which one best fits the needs of the students and also the principles that guide your teaching philosophy. Sketch an initial plan for the theme you choose.

Write Your Unit Plan

Write the final version of your unit to include in your professional portfolio. Give your thematic unit an interesting, motivating title. Make a folder for the paper copy of your unit plan so that you can file it for safekeeping. Keep another copy on your computer.

Predict Possible Outcomes

Using your cognitive, affective, and psychomotor outcomes as a place to begin, allow yourself to envision your students accomplishing these outcomes. Sketch out a planning web as you brainstorm learning experiences that will allow your students to achieve these outcomes. What are the likely consequences of each step of your plan? Which outcomes will be easy to achieve and which will be difficult? Use a calendar to plan the sequence of learning events for your unit. Create a time line of events for your students and a complementary one for yourself so that your teaching plans coincide with the events in the unit.

Now begin to plan a way to assess the outcomes for your unit. What types of products or tests will you use to evaluate the degree to which your students achieve success on each of the outcomes you have for the unit? Show your assessment plan to a colleague and get feedback on making this important part of your unit a meaningful and accurate representation of what students have learned.

Reference

Tyler, R. (1949). *Basic principles of curriculum and instruction*. Chicago: University of Chicago Press.

Chapter
6

Lesson Planning and Sequencing

When you think of lesson plans, what comes to mind? Have you been required to write lesson plans? How did the experience go? If you have not yet written any lesson plans, what do you think preparing them will be like?

Debra asked a group of teachers enrolled in a master's program to reflect on their first experiences with lesson plans and student teaching. Some of the teachers had taught a year or two; others were veterans. Interestingly, all agreed on several issues. Here are some of the comments they e-mailed to one another during an on-line discussion:

> *When I first began my methods courses, I felt that writing objectives got in the way of my lesson plans. The professors were all very rigid in their requirements concerning objectives. A certain number of objectives had to be typed out and most of them began "The students will. . . . " Initially it was very hard for me to see the point of writing them all out. However, when I began student teaching I realized the importance of objectives. Without them, your lessons become unfocused and watered down. Now, before I decide what and how I am going to teach something, I look at the goal that I want my students (and myself) to reach, and then I decide how to get there most effectively and efficiently*
> *—Third-year fifth-grade teacher*
>
> *I think that it is crucial to have objectives set when planning a lesson, especially when you are student teaching. When you plan a lesson you need to have a reason for teaching it. I know when I was student teaching I almost always wrote down my objectives. This allowed me to then reflect on my lesson when it was over to see if it was a success. If I was not able to meet my objectives then I knew I needed to change something I did or did not do.*
> *—Second-year first-grade teacher*
>
> *I have found that I really need to have solid, concrete objectives in mind as I plan my lessons. I owe it to my students to let them in on what we are working to achieve. Even with objectives, my lessons don't always go as planned. I see that as a positive thing. I continually assess and make adjustments to my lessons according to student needs. It horrifies me to think of teachers who have their whole year scripted day by day. I have never had two classes that were alike, much less two students! I don't mind making changes as necessary if it is best for my students. Isn't that the point?*
> *—Third-year sixth-grade teacher*

As these teachers have described, educational goals, learning outcomes, and unit plans are important elements in educating students. But they are meaningless words on paper unless they are translated into a practical set of logically ordered day-to-day learning events. Goals, outcome statements, and unit plans are a reflective teacher's guides for real-life classroom events. Teaching without those guides can become an overwhelming and discouraging task for both the teacher and the students. You may have noticed, as you read the preceding comments, that teachers often use the same term (*objective*) to refer to a number of different ideas. For the sake of clarity, we will define some of these terms so that you and your colleagues will be able to communicate clearly with one another. Most lesson plans include four very important aspects: (1) articulating goals and outcomes, (2) setting clear objectives, (3) modeling tasks at the physical and mental level, and (4) considering contingencies. Let's look at each of these in some detail.

Writing Effective Objectives to Fit Goals and Outcomes

As you may recall from Chapter 5, goals are the broad, long-term descriptions of how you want your students to grow and develop; outcome statements refer to what you want students to know, understand, and be able to do during a given time. As you try to visualize your students accomplishing these goals and outcomes, it is useful to envision a sequence of events that will lead to successful accomplishment of the goal. Teachers often find it useful to write down these sequential steps as a series of objectives that work together to accomplish the goal or outcome. Reflective teachers rarely plan a lesson in isolation. Rather, they consider each lesson in relation to what students already know as well as what they hope students will be able to do at a later time. This type of "big picture" thinking characterizes reflective teachers, who realize that larger goals guide the selection of small daily tasks.

Educational Objectives

Educational objectives are short-term, specific descriptions of what teachers are expected to teach and/or what students are expected to learn. As described by Bloom and colleagues in the *Taxonomy of Educational Objectives* (1956), they are intended to be used as an organizational framework for selecting and sequencing learning experiences. Embedded in any large goal (such as teaching children to read) are hundreds of possible specific objectives. One teacher may have an objective of teaching students how to decode an unfamiliar word using phonics and another objective of teaching students how to decode an unfamiliar word using context clues. Another teacher may select and emphasize the objectives of decoding unfamiliar words by using syllabification or linguistic patterns in order to meet the same overall goal.

Objectives are also used to describe the sequence of learning events a teacher feels will help students achieve a given outcome. As the teachers mentioned in their e-mails at the beginning of this chapter, objectives also allow teachers to assess and chart group or individual progress. Teachers can ascertain students' needs more accurately if they have established a guideline of normal progress with which to compare each student's achievement.

Teachers who prefer to be very specific about their lesson planning choose to write behavioral objectives. These include (1) the conditions under which the learning will take place, (2) the action or behavior that will provide evidence of the learning, and (3) the criteria for success (how well a task must be completed or how often the behavior will occur). For example, a behavioral objective could be written as follows:

> After practice-writing the spelling words five times each, the student will write the words when dictated by the teacher, spelling 18 of the 20 words correctly.

This statement includes a description of the conditions for learning ("after practice-writing the spelling words five times each"), the behavior ("write the words when dictated by the teacher"), and the criterion for success ("spelling 18 of 20 words correctly").

Behavioral objectives can have a very positive effect on teaching effectiveness; teachers who use them become better organized and more efficient in teaching and in measuring the growth of students' basic skills. When following a planned sequence of behavioral objectives, the teacher knows what to do and how to judge students' success. This system of planning also allows the teacher to better explain to students exactly what is expected of them and how to succeed.

As with any educational practice, however, there are positive and negative aspects to planning this way. Critics of behavioral objectives believe that when curriculum planning is reduced to rigid behavioral prescriptions, much of what is important to teaching and learning can be overlooked or lost. Thus, reflective teachers use behavioral objectives in their lesson planning for those learning events and activities that warrant them and rely on other less rigid objectives when appropriate.

As an alternative form for learning that cannot be predicted and calibrated, Eisner (1994) suggests the problem-solving objective:

> In a problem-solving objective, students are given a problem to solve—say, to find out how deterrents to smoking might be made more effective, how to design a paper structure that will hold two bricks 16 inches above a table, or how the variety and quality of the food served in the cafeteria could be increased within the existing budget. In each of these examples, the problem is posed and the criteria necessary to resolve the problem are clear. But the forms of its solution are virtually infinite. (pp. 117–118)

Eisner points out that behavioral objectives have "both the form and the content defined in advance. There is, after all, only one way to spell aardvark." The teacher using behavioral objectives is successful if all the children display identical behavior at the end of the instructional period. "This is not the case with problem-solving objectives. The solutions individual students or groups of students reach may be just as much a surprise for the teacher as they are for the students who created them" (p. 119).

As an example, a problem-solving objective might be written:

> When given a battery, a light bulb, and a piece of copper wire, the student will figure out how to make the bulb light.

This objective describes the conditions and the problem that is to be solved, but does not specify the actual behaviors the student is to use. The criterion for success is straightforward but is not quantifiable; in fact, some of the most important results of this experience are only implied. The teacher's primary aim is to cause the student to experiment, hypothesize, and test methods of solving the problem. This cannot be quantified and reported as a percentage. Problem-solving objectives, then, are appropriate when teachers are planning learning events that allow and encourage students to think, make decisions, and create solutions. For that reason they are frequently employed when teachers plan lessons that are designed to develop critical, creative thinking. They are especially valuable when teachers are planning learning events at the higher levels of Bloom's taxonomy (1956).

Bloom's Taxonomy

Many teachers use Bloom's *Taxonomy of Educational Objectives* (1956) as the basis for organizing instructional objectives into coherent, connected learning experiences. The term *Bloom's taxonomy* (as commonly used by teachers) refers to the six levels of the cognitive domain described here. Any curriculum project—a yearlong plan, a unit, or a lesson plan—can be enriched by the conscious planning of learning events at all six levels of the taxonomy:

Higher Level Objectives	Level 6	Evaluation
	Level 5	Synthesis
	Level 4	Analysis
	Level 3	Application
Lower Level Objectives	Level 2	Comprehension
	Level 1	Knowledge

Knowledge-level objectives can be planned to ensure that students have a knowledge base of facts, concepts, and other important data on any topic or subject. *Comprehension-level objectives* cause students to clarify and articulate the main idea of what they are learning. Behavioral objectives are very useful and appropriate at the knowledge and comprehension levels.

At the *application level,* problem-solving objectives can be written that ask students to apply what they have learned to other cases or to their own lives, thereby causing them to transfer what they have learned in the classroom to other arenas. *Analysis-level* objectives and outcomes call on students to look for motives, assumptions, and relationships such as cause and effect, differences and similarities, hypotheses, and conclusions. When analysis outcomes are planned, the students are likely to be engaged in critical thinking about the subject matter. Because the *synthesis level* implies an original response, open-ended outcomes are very appropriate. They offer students opportunities to use creative thinking as they combine elements in new ways, plan original experiments, and create original solutions to problems. At the *evaluation level,* students again engage in critical thinking as they make judgments using internal or external criteria and evidence. For these levels, problem-solving objectives are likely to be the most appropriate planning devices.

For example, in planning a series of learning events on metric measurement, the teacher may formulate the following objectives and outcome statements:

> *Knowledge-level behavioral objective:*   When given a meter stick, students will point to the length of a meter, a decimeter, and a centimeter with no errors.

Comprehension-level behavioral objective: When asked to state a purpose or use for each of the following units of measure, the student will write a short response for meter, centimeter, liter, milliliter, gram, and kilogram, with no more than one error.

Application-level problem-solving objective: Using a unit of measure of their choice, students will measure the length and width of the classroom and compute the area.

Analysis-level problem-solving objective: Students will create a chart showing five logical uses or purposes for each measuring unit in the metric family.

Synthesis-level open-ended outcome: A group of four students will hide a "treasure" on the playground and create a set of instructions using metric measures that will enable another group to locate the treasure.

Evaluation-level open-ended outcome: Students will debate their preference for metric or nonmetric measurement as a standard form of measurement.

In reviewing the six objectives and outcomes for metric measurement, it is clear that the first two differ from the others in that they specify exactly what students will do or write to get a correct answer. In addition, the criteria for success are not ambiguous. These two qualities are useful to ensure successful teaching and learning at the knowledge and comprehension levels. After successfully completing these first two objectives, students will have developed a knowledge base for metric measurement that they will need to do the higher level activities. In the problem-solving objectives, students are given greater discretion in determining the methods they use and the form of their final product. In the open-ended outcome statements, discretionary power is necessary if students are to be empowered to think critically and creatively so they can solve problems for themselves.

Although the taxonomy was originally envisioned as a hierarchy, and although it was believed that students should be introduced to a topic beginning with level 1 and working upward through level 6, most educators have found that the objectives and learning experiences can be successfully taught in any order. For example, a teacher may introduce the topic of nutrition and health by asking students to discuss their opinions or attitudes about smoking (an evaluation-level objective). The teacher may then provide the students with knowledge-level data about the contents of tobacco smoke and work back up to the evaluation level. When students are asked their opinions again, at the end of the lesson, their judgments are likely to be stronger and better informed.

As in the example about smoking and health, it is often desirable to begin with objectives that call on students to do, think, find, question, or create something and thereby instill in them a desire to know more about the topic. Knowledge- and comprehension-level objectives can then be designed to provide the students with the facts, data, and main ideas they need to know to further apply, analyze, synthesize, and evaluate the ideas that interest them. Figure 6.1 shows a planning device offering teachers ideas for learning events that correspond to each level of the taxonomy.

Figure 6.1. Curriculum planning using Bloom's taxonomy.

Learning objectives can be planned at all levels of Bloom's taxonomy. Behavioral objectives are best suited for knowledge and comprehension levels; problem solving and expressive objectives are best suited for application, analysis, synthesis and evaluation levels.

Examples of Objectives

Appropriate Action Verbs

Knowledge Level

Can recognize and recall specific terms, facts, and symbols

Knowledge Level

Find, locate, identify, list, recite, memorize, recognize, name, repeat, point to, match, pick, choose, state, select, record, spell, say, show, circle or underline.

Comprehension Level

Can understand the main idea of material heard, viewed, or read. Is able to interpret or summarize the ideas in their own words.

Comprehension Level

Explain, define, translate, relate, demonstrate, calculate, discuss, express in own words, write, review, report, paraphrase, summarize.

Application Level

Is able to apply an abstract idea in a concrete situation, to solve a problem or relate it to prior experiences.

Application Level

Change, adapt, employ, use, make, construct, demonstrate, compute, calculate, illustrate, modify, prepare, put into action, solve, do.

Analysis Level

Can break down a concept or idea into its constituent parts. Is able to identify relationships among elements, cause and effect, similarities and differences.

Analysis Level

Classify, distinguish, categorize, deduce, dissect, examine, compare, contrast, divide, catalog, inventory, question, outline, chart, survey.

Synthesis Level

Is able to put together elements in new and original ways. Creates patterns or structures that were not there before.

Synthesis Level

Combine, create, develop, design, construct, build, arrange, assemble, collect, concoct, connect, devise, hypothesize, invent, imagine, plan, generate, revise, organize, produce.

Evaluation Level

Makes informed judgments about the value of ideas or materials. Uses standards and criteria to support opinions and views.

Evaluation Level

Appraise, critique, consider, decide, judge, editorialize, give opinion, grade, rank, prioritize, value.

Source: From *Taxonomy of Educational Objectives: The Classification of Educational Goals: Handbook I: Cognitive Domain*. By Benjamin S. Bloom et al. Copyright 1956. By Longman Publishing Group. Reprinted by permission of Longman Publishing Group.

Clarifying Objectives by Verbal, Physical, and Mental Modeling

Remember how we described teaching as a relational experience in Chapter 1? Teaching a lesson to students is very much a relational experience. Teachers must use withitness throughout the process as they try to anticipate what their students need, what they can do easily, and where they will need the most guidance and positive feedback.

Relational teachers recognize that students learn best by knowing what it is they are supposed to learn and why this learning is important. They also benefit from seeing an example of the desired behavior, being helped to approximate the behavior, and then undertaking the task on their own. Explain to your students the goals and purposes of each lesson and then model the desired behaviors so that students clearly understand what is expected of them. When explaining your goals, use terms students themselves might use rather than reading a formally phrased behavioral objective. For example, during a spelling lesson, a reflective teacher might say:

> We are doing this activity today to help you become better spellers. Many good spellers know that by copying their spelling words and paying attention to the patterns in words, they learn their spelling words better. After you write each word five times today, I expect you will be able to spell correctly at least 18 of the 20 words on our list.

In our experience, students are much more willing to undertake an activity when its purpose and value are clearly explained in terms they understand. To make learning tasks even more inviting, caring, reflective teachers model physical behaviors (such as how to write a capital letter), and provide concrete examples for the students that clearly show how they can achieve the particular objective.

In addition, the most effective teachers model internal behaviors (such as critical thinking) by thinking aloud for students. By doing an example for the students and telling the students verbally what their thinking might sound like when they are trying to work on this problem, teachers provide real-life examples of how learning occurs. This think-aloud procedure is particularly helpful when asking students to comprehend an unfamiliar text. Thinking aloud while reading a paragraph, the teacher demonstrates how students can learn to process the meaning of words.

Some of Debra's students use a three-step mantra to help them consider the relational aspects of lesson planning. The three steps are:

1. I do (What I will do myself to model a desired action for my student).
2. We do (How I will set up a learning activity so my students can attempt the action with my help).
3. You do (What the students will do to practice the action on their own).

During each of the three modeling periods, reflective teachers carefully observe and interact with their students—learning what students already know and where they need extra help. This observation and assessment period is critical to the success of any given lesson, as well as to the planning and sequencing of future lessons. It also helps to think again about this three-step process when things happen during a lesson that surprise you or upset your plans.

Considering Contingencies: Expecting the Unexpected

When you are first learning to plan lessons, it is natural to follow a linear format. In other words, you imagine what you want to teach, the steps you will take to arrive at your goal, and how those steps should be sequenced. You enter the classroom, ready to implement your plan. And then, horror of horrors, nothing goes as planned and you are left with no idea of what to do. Most veteran teachers have experienced this scenario more than once! Even the best plans can go wrong! Indeed, part of the nervousness many teachers feel before teaching a lesson comes from this very realization: It is hard to prepare for the unexpected!

Debra helps beginning teachers address this concern ahead of time by thinking about and planning for three types of contingencies: (1) what to do if students do not seem to understand, (2) what to do if students already know the material planned, and (3) what to do if you cannot decide whether students understand a concept or not.

If Students Do Not Understand.   Most teachers quickly learn to plan for this contingency in teaching, because it is almost a given that in any lesson, some students will require different experiences or explanations to arrive at the desired knowledge. Some teachers can think on their feet and address student confusion on the spot, but this can be a challenge for a new teacher. We suggest that you consistently plan a second way of introducing or extending any given concept just in case you need it! We think you will often be glad you did. Relational teachers are aware that students learn differently and that some may need a second strategy to achieve the lesson objective.

If Students Master the Lesson Quickly.   As we observe new teachers presenting lessons, one thing we have noticed is that discipline and management problems rarely occur when the lesson content is focused slightly above students' current knowledge base. This is probably due to the fact that students feel challenged, but not overwhelmed by the experience, so they are engaged in learning and feel happy to cooperate. In contrast, problems seem to arise when a teacher prepares a lesson that covers content the students already know. They act restless and may become disruptive when they feel that the teacher is babying them or talking down to them. What should you do when you arrive in a setting, materials in hand, and find out the students have already mastered the content you planned to teach? Should you press bravely on, working your way through the lesson because it is what you worked so hard to prepare? To do so is to ignore the relational aspect of teaching. We have often seen this, and believe that the biggest reason for this choice is a simple one—the teacher has nothing else prepared.

Caring teachers realize that in any classroom, there is likely to be at least one student (and probably several) who already knows the concepts being taught. Planning for ways to extend the knowledge of these students is just as important to the success of your lesson as is planning for ways to help students who do not understand the concept right away. When you enter a classroom with a plan for extending a lesson's concepts and content, you will feel more confident and you will enhance the learning experiences of more of your students.

If Students Appear Neutral or Nonresponsive to the Lesson.   Even with your withitness tuned to a highly receptive mode, some students appear to be *nonresponsive* or neutral during a lesson. They give no readable cues as to whether they understand or do not understand the lesson concepts. Nonresponsive students may remain silent or refuse to try the learning task you have assigned to them. They may do something vastly different from what you expected, confusing you as to their intent.

Relational teachers accept that there are many reasons students may fail to respond in the ways we hope and plan for. For example, a student may be hungry, tired, or preoccupied with a concern (outside or inside of school) that is more compelling than this lesson. The student may doubt his or her ability to succeed at the task outlined and, therefore, avoid it in an attempt to save face, or the student may feel the task is far too easy and therefore not worth the effort to complete.

If you consider reasons a student may appear nonresponsive to your lesson, you can also brainstorm ways you might invite a more informative response. For example, if you realize students may feel threatened by a particular task (e.g., reciting part of a poem aloud), you can plan for alternate tasks, such as allowing students to work in pairs and recite the poem with a peer. By having a backup plan for the neutral student, you will know what to do when a student stares blankly instead of working. By planning for this contingency, you can avoid these uncomfortable responses, maintain the flow of the lesson, and involve all your students more productively.

Writing a Well-Organized Lesson Plan

When teachers plan for day-to-day learning experiences, they are creating lesson plans. Usually a lesson plan is created for a single subject or topic for one day, although some experiential, hands-on lessons may continue for several days in a row. Teachers in self-contained classrooms must devise several different lesson plans each day, one for each subject they teach, unless they choose to use multidisciplinary units. Teachers in the upper grades who work in departmentalized settings where students travel from class to class for various subjects must still create different lesson plans for each grade or group of students they teach.

In the university or college courses designed to prepare teachers, the lesson plan is an important teaching/learning device. The professor and experienced classroom teachers can provide the aspiring teacher with models of good lesson plans. As students create their own plans, they are able to demonstrate the extent to which they understand and can apply the theories and principles they have learned about reflective thinking and planning.

For that reason, many university and college programs require students to create a number of precise and detailed lesson plans. Sometimes students observe that the classroom teachers they know do not write such extensive plans for every lesson. Instead, these teachers write their lesson plans in large weekly planning books, and a single lesson plan may consist of cryptic notations such as "Math: p. 108" or "Social Studies: Review Ch. 7" or "Science: Continue Nutrition." Although experienced teachers may record their lesson plans with such brief notes, novice teachers need to write lessons in great detail to know which resources to gather for a lesson. Writing detailed lesson plans also enables novice teachers to communicate their plans to the professor or mentor teacher, who can provide feedback on the plan before the lesson is taught.

Well-written lesson plans have additional value: They can be shared. A teacher's shorthand notes that serve as a personal reminder can rarely be interpreted by an outsider. If a substitute teacher is called to replace a classroom teacher for a day or longer, the substitute needs to see the daily plans in language he or she can understand and use. Teams of teachers often write lesson plans together or for one another. In this case, they need to have a common understanding of the lesson objectives, procedures, evaluation, and resources.

The form may vary, but most lesson plans share a number of common elements. Three essential features of a complete, well-organized lesson plan are the *objectives*, *procedures*, and *evaluation*. These correspond to the four questions of curriculum planning formulated by Tyler (1949). Lesson objectives specify the "educational purposes" of the lesson. The procedures section describes both "what educational experiences can be provided" and the way they can be "effectively organized." The evaluation section describes the way the teacher has planned in advance to determine "whether these purposes are being attained" (Tyler, 1949, p. 1).

The description, another feature in a lesson plan, is used to identify it and give the reader a quick overview of its purpose. Also, a lesson plan often contains information about the resources teachers need as background preparation for teaching the lesson as well as any materials necessary for actual execution of the lesson.

A suggestion for teachers in this age of computers is to create a basic outline of a lesson plan on a word processor and save it on a disk. Then, whenever you wish to write a lesson plan, you can put the outline on the screen and fill in the spaces. You may also want to take some time to access the Internet and look at various lesson plans posted there. Many sites are available through commercial publishers, as well as through groups of teachers at local and state levels.

The Relational Lesson Plan Model

Including all of the ideas discussed in this chapter in one lesson plan can sound pretty daunting, but it is something that will become second nature to you with experience. To help you remember the important aspects of a lesson, we offer you a model of a lesson plan in Figure 6.2 that is based on the work Debra does with her students. Take some time to review it now, and see if you can describe the reason each part has been included. This outline can be copied on your computer disk for use in college and the rest of your teaching career.

After you have put in the title, subject, grade level, and lesson duration, you can describe what you want students to gain from this lesson. Debra suggests that you also rephrase your description in words that students might use. By thinking about this as you plan your lesson, you will be considering the lesson from the students' point of view and that will help you clarify exactly what students should learn from this experience. It is also useful to use later as a postassessment to see if students can describe what they learned in their own words. You may want to model this sentence for your

Figure 6.2　The Relational Lesson Plan model.

Title of Lesson:

Subject Area:

Grade Level:　　　　　　　　　　　　　**Approximate Lesson Duration:**

Teacher's Description (What will students ideally know and/or feel as a result of this lesson?):

Students' Summary of Lesson (What will students be able to say in their own words at the end of the lesson?):

Objectives (What will students do and what do those behaviors indicate?):

1.

2.

3.

Materials and Resources Needed (What do I need to teach this lesson? What do students need to participate?):

students at the beginning of the lesson. For example, in a metric measurement lesson, you might say, "Today I learned that a meter is the same as 100 centimeters or 10 decimeters."

We suggest using from one to three objectives for each lesson to help you maintain focus and avoid overwhelming students with too many ideas at once. By listing the

Figure 6.2 *Continued*

I-We-You Procedures (What will I do? What will we do together? What will the students do on their own?):

1. *Presassessment* (What do students already know about this topic? How will I find out?):

2. *Motivation* (What will I do to make a connection between students and this topic?):

3. *Statement of Purpose* (What will I say to explain the importance of learning this lesson?):

4. *Teacher Modeling or Demonstration* (What will I do to show students what is expected?):

5. *Guided Practice* (What will we do together as they learn how to succeed at the new task?):

6. *Check for Understanding* (What will I do to see if students understand so far?):

7. *Contingencies*
   What will I do if my students:

Don't understand?	Appear neutral or nonresponsive?	Have already mastered the concept?

8. *Independent Practice or Activity* (What will students do on their own to internalize the knowledge?):

9. *Postassessment and Closure* (What do I want students to be able to say or do to show that they learned the concept?):
   "Today I learned that …"

materials you need ahead of time, you avoid getting partway through the lesson and finding out that something you need is missing.

The procedures that teachers use for teaching a lesson vary, but we suggest that you think of the procedures using the I–We–You strategy. Each step of the procedures in our model should help you think through what you will do to prepare for and teach the lesson. The preassessment step refers to the process of finding out what your students already know prior to teaching a new lesson. Reflective teachers use this strategy to avoid behavior problems from bored students as well as from those who do not have a clue as to what you are talking about. This strategy also helps you build the background for the day's lesson. For example, to preassess students' knowledge of metric measurement, you might want to show a meter stick to your students and ask if they know what it is and what it is used for.

The contingencies section of the lesson plan model was explained earlier. Here you think through what you will do if students do not understand, seem nonresponsive, or appear to be bored because they have already mastered the concept. You can see that contingency planning is linked to preassessment. The rest of the steps in the lesson plan are explained on the form itself. In a following section, you will see two examples of lesson plans using this format.

Sequencing Objectives in School Subjects

Teaching is a relational activity and it is also often a highly sequential activity. Preschool lessons are designed to help students build background for academic subjects. Many primary lessons, especially those known as the basic skills in math, letter recognition, and letter formation, are taught first so that more complex learning activities can follow. Some subjects are more sequentially ordered than others, but most academic disciplines have some parts that are sequential in nature. Each lesson plan you create should fit into a series of lessons that allows students to use what they already know to solve unknown problems or comprehend unfamiliar material.

Sequencing Objectives in Mathematics

Some subjects are very sequential in nature. Mathematics is the best example in the elementary curriculum because many of its concepts and operations can be ordered from simple to complex quite readily. Teachers can organize effectively the teaching of computational skills in the basic operations of addition, subtraction, multiplication, and division. For example, outcome statement 1 describes a possible sequence for teaching an essential understanding about the concept of numbers:

> *Mathematics outcome statement 1:*   Primary students will be able to show how addition and subtraction are related to one another.

To accomplish this outcome, primary teachers introduce the students to the concept of numbers and give them concrete, manipulative experiences in adding and subtracting one-digit numbers. Students may act out stories in which children are added and subtracted from a group. They may make up stories about animals or objects that are taken away and then brought back to demonstrate subtraction and addition.

Math textbooks offer a sequence of learning activities and practice of math facts, but reflective teachers find that the math textbook must be used flexibly and supplemented with other learning experiences. Prior to planning math lessons for a particular group of students, the teacher must assess their entry-level knowledge and skills. Pretests or other assessment techniques can reveal that some children have already mastered some of the skills in the sequence and do not need to spend valuable time redoing what they already know. They need enriched math activities to allow them to progress. Other children may not have the conceptual understanding of number relationships to succeed on the first step. For them, preliminary concrete experiences with manipulative materials are essential for success. An example of a set of sequential activities in mathematics follows.

The sample math objectives to fit outcome statement 1:

Students will be able to:
1. Use blocks to show addition of two single-digit integers.
2. Use blocks to show subtraction of two single-digit integers.
3. Use pennies and dimes to show place value of 1s and 10s.
4. Subtract pennies without regrouping.
5. Add pennies and exchange 10 pennies for a dime.
6. Subtract pennies by making change for a dime to show regrouping.
7. Tell how subtraction is related to addition using coins as an example.

These sample objectives are representative of the basic knowledge- and comprehension-level skills needed to accomplish outcome statement 1. They can be written in the behavioral objective form, specifying what percentage of correct answers must be attained to demonstrate mastery.

These objectives emphasize the basic computational skills that all students need to learn. However, in keeping with the National Council of Teachers of Mathematics' recommendations to also emphasize problem-solving over computation, reflective teachers are likely to plan lessons that allow students to explore the relationships between addition and subtraction. They are also likely to include many additional math outcomes and objectives at the higher levels of Bloom's taxonomy (1956) to teach students how to apply the math facts and computation skills they are learning to actual problem-solving situations. However, this example does illustrate the importance of matching objectives to outcome statements in a logical sequence. Each of the objectives builds on the one before it. As students master each objective, they are continually progressing toward mastering the outcome statement.

Sequencing Objectives in Language Arts

Not all subjects in the elementary curriculum are as sequential as mathematics. Language arts consists of knowledge, skills, and abilities that develop children's understanding and use of language. Reading, writing, speaking, and listening are all part of the language arts curriculum, and each one can and should have its own outcome statement(s). Outcome statement 2 suggests one illustration of how the language arts curriculum is designed:

> *Language arts outcome statement 2:*   Students will be able to write standard English with correct spelling, accurate grammar, and well-organized meaning and form.

This outcome statement will take years to accomplish, but teachers at every grade level are responsible for providing learning experiences that build toward the ultimate goal. The objectives to reach this goal may be similar each year for several years, but written in increasing levels of difficulty. This is known as a *spiral curriculum,* and often looks like the following example.

Sample language arts objectives to fit outcome statement 2:

By the end of grade 2, students will be able to:
1. Write a sentence containing a subject and verb.
2. Use a capital letter at the beginning of a sentence.
3. Use a period or question mark at the end of a sentence.
4. Review and edit sentences for complete meaning.

By the end of grade 4, students will be able to:
1. Write a paragraph that focuses on one central idea.
2. Spell common words correctly in writing samples.
3. Use capitalization and sentence-end punctuation correctly.
4. Review and edit a paragraph to improve the organization of ideas.

By the end of grade 6, students will be able to:
1. Write several paragraphs that explain one concept or theme.
2. Use a dictionary to spell all words in a paper correctly.
3. Use correct punctuation, including end marks, comma, apostrophe, quotation marks, and colon.
4. Review and edit papers to correct spelling, punctuation, grammar, and organization of ideas.

When teachers have curriculum guidelines such as these, they must still translate the outcome statements and objectives into actual learning experiences that are appropriate and motivating for their students. To assess how well your students can use written language when they enter your classroom, plan a writing experience in the first week. Analyzing these writing samples will allow you to plan suitably challenging activities for your students. In this example, the second-grade teacher must decide what topics to have students write about and when to provide teacher-made examples and when to have them generate their own sentences. The fourth-grade teacher knows that students will not learn all of these skills in just one writing lesson. It is necessary to provide many interesting classroom experiences so that students will have ideas to express in their writing.

The sixth-grade teacher has to plan a series of research and writing experiences so that students will have ample opportunities to synthesize all of the skills required at that grade level.

Curriculum planning of subjects such as language arts is a complex undertaking because it contains so many varied outcomes and objectives. The previous example illustrates only a single outcome for teaching students how to write. Teachers must also plan outcome statements and objectives for reading, listening, and speaking.

Sequencing Objectives in Science

As discussed in Chapter 4, the science curriculum should inform students of the basic facts and concepts of science topics, but it should also allow students to experience how scientists work. These dual goals of the science curriculum are often expressed as teaching both content and process. An example of an outcome statement in science that covers both content and process follows:

> *Science outcome statement 3:*   Students will demonstrate the properties of electricity and magnetism, and show how their energy can be used to benefit mankind.

If Judy was planning a series of lesson plans to accomplish this outcome, she would use a sequence of process-oriented learning experiences that allow students to discover some important properties of electricity and magnetism, followed by a few content-oriented lessons to review and articulate what they discovered. As a culmination, she would ask students to apply what they have learned and synthesize their own inventions using the energy from batteries and magnets. The order of these learning experiences would be as follows:

By the end of the unit on electricity and magnetism, students will be able to:
1. Demonstrate how electricity travels in a closed circuit.
2. Demonstrate how magnetism attracts and repels certain metals.
3. Investigate the basic properties of electricity and magnetism.
4. Be able to compare and contrast electricity and magnetism and identify key properties of each.
5. Invent some beneficial ways to use electricity and magnetism.

Using this approach, the first lesson plan would involve hands-on experiences using batteries, copper wire, and light bulbs so that students can demonstrate to themselves how electricity travels in a closed circuit. On subsequent days, lessons would be planned to allow students to investigate the properties of magnets and electricity. Then, Judy would plan a lesson in which students created charts comparing the two, and there would be a lesson in which students discussed the properties and learned to use terminology correctly. We might then have a written, individual test on these properties and terms. Finally, students would take several days to work on their inventions and present them to classmates and parents.

Sequencing Objectives in Social Studies

Reflective elementary teachers can also see the need for both content and process in their social studies curriculum. They attempt to help their students build a knowledge base in history and geography, but they also give attention and time to teaching students how to acquire information on their own.

An example of an outcome statement in social studies that covers both content and process follows:

> *Social studies outcome statement 4:*   Students will be able to use a map and globe to find place names and locations. They will then create a chart listing the countries, capital cities, rivers, and mountain ranges in each continent.

Sample social studies objectives to meet outcome statement 4:

At the end of the map and globe unit, students will be able to:
1. Identify the seven continents on a world map and globe.
2. Interpret the country boundaries with a map legend.
3. List the countries in each continent.
4. Interpret the symbol for rivers on the map legend.
5. List the major rivers in each continent.
6. Interpret the symbol for mountain ranges on the map legend.
7. List the major mountain ranges in each continent.
8. Create a chart showing the countries, capitals, and major rivers and mountain ranges in each continent.

In this example, the teacher has planned a set of learning activities that will add to the students' knowledge base about world geography. This set of activities also equips the student to be able to find and interpret information on maps and globes. This social studies curriculum is an example of one in which students are able to learn both content (geography facts and locations) and processes (research and chart-making skills) simultaneously and that they are active rather than passive learners throughout the entire set of activities. An oral or written preassessment might consist of having students name or point to certain geographical locations and read and interpret a map legend. The information from the pretest is valuable in planning lessons that use students' existing knowledge and add to it.

Sequencing Objectives in Interdisciplinary Units

Whenever possible, many teachers enjoy enriching the curriculum units they plan by incorporating fine arts experiences into the academic subjects. Primary children are often asked to illustrate math examples by drawing one pumpkin plus two pumpkins or to create 10 different pictures containing a rectangle. Songs and rhymes frequently accompany learning about historical events and people. Many such events are dramatized as well. Stories and films are often used to augment many aspects of the curriculum.

In later years, emphasis on the fine arts may decline except in special art and music classes or on special occasions and holidays. This is due, in part, to the crowded curriculum that teachers are required to deliver. Given the prevailing culture of the late 20th century, the fine arts often take a backseat to academic and social subjects. But each teacher must consider the place of fine arts in the curriculum. Reflective teachers are likely to consider the importance of the arts in enhancing the joy of living and to make them an integral part of every learning experience. This has the effect of increasing children's active involvement, creative thinking, and inventiveness.

An example of an outcome statement that includes fine arts with an academic subject follows:

> *Fine arts/social studies outcome statement 5:* Students will be able to distinguish the important contributions made by various world cultures in sports, art, music, literature, and drama.

Sample objectives to meet outcome statement 5:

Each learning team of students will be able to:
1. Select one country of the world to study.
2. Locate at least three sources of information about that country.
3. Draw a map of the country's geographical boundaries and features.
4. Describe the country's contributions to sports.
5. Play or sing an example of the country's music.
6. Draw examples of the country's treasures of art and architecture.
7. Read aloud a story or poem from that country.
8. Work with other learning teams to create a dramatic event featuring the stories, poems, art, and music of all of the countries.

This ambitious set of learning experiences demonstrates how well the fine arts can be incorporated into an academic subject. Cognitively, children who take part in this series of experiences will learn a knowledge base of facts, ideas, and concepts about the world. They will also gain understanding and use of such processes as communication and problem-solving skills. Affectively, they will learn to appreciate and understand differences and similarities among people by sharing the cultural arts of each country.

Planning Assessments That Fit Your Objectives

How does a teacher measure success? Chapters 11 and 12 cover the topic of assessing students' needs and accomplishments in detail, with a focus on creating authentic assessment systems that describe students' progress over time. In designing lesson plans, however, it is useful to consider some options for assessing students' accomplishments on a single lesson.

Traditionally, the methods used to assess individual achievement are written or oral quizzes, tests, and essays. When elementary teachers want to determine whether the class as a whole has understood what was taught in a lesson, they frequently use oral responses to questions that usually begin "Who can tell me . . . ?" These are useful and efficient ways to assess student achievement at the knowledge and comprehension levels of Bloom's taxonomy, but reflective teachers are seldom satisfied with these measures alone. They seek other methods that are less frequently used but more appropriate in evaluating learning at the higher levels.

Knowledge-level objectives are tested by determining if the student can remember or recognize accurate statements or facts. Bloom et al. (1956) observed: "Probably the art of testing has been developed to the greatest extent in the measurement of knowledge. This type of behavior can be measured with great efficiency and economy" (p. 78). Multiple-choice and matching tests are the most frequently used measuring devices.

Comprehension-level objectives are often tested by asking students to define terms in their own words (only knowledge would be tested if the students were asked to write a definition from memory). Another frequently used testing device is a question requiring a short-answer response, either oral or written, showing that the student understands the main idea. Essays that ask students to summarize or interpret are also appropriate. Multiple-choice tests are also used as a test of comprehension, but the questions call on the students to do more than recall a fact from memory; they ask students to read a selection and choose the best response from among several choices.

Knowledge- and comprehension-level objectives are very frequently written as behavioral objectives that specify the criteria for success in a measurable form. If the observable behavior is writing an essay, the teacher may need to describe the length, form, and content of a paper that is acceptable. For example, the criteria may be specified as follows:

> . . . with a minimum of five paragraphs, each describing a geographical feature of the country being studied . . .

At the application level, students are usually asked to apply what was learned in a classroom to a new situation. For that reason, application-level objectives are usually assessed by presenting an unfamiliar problem that requires the student to transfer what has been learned to the unfamiliar situation. Assessment of student success cannot be quantified into minimums, maximums, or percentages. Instead, success is measured by the extent to which the problem is solved and the means employed to solve it.

To assess application, then, teachers must provide students with challenging problems to solve and a format for tendering their solutions. Essays in which the students describe what they would do to solve an unfamiliar problem can be used. In classrooms where students are encouraged to use manipulative materials and experiment with methods to solve problems, teachers can assess the processes used by the student and the end product such as a hand-drawn or computer-generated design of a new device, a written plan for solving a problem, or a model of a new product. These products may or may not be graded, depending on the teacher's need to quantify or qualify students' success.

Analysis-level objectives may also require that the teacher present unfamiliar material and ask the student to analyze it according to some specified criteria. "The material given for analysis in a test may be a literary passage, a description of a scientific experiment or a social situation, a set of data, an argument, a picture, or a musical selection" (Bloom et al., 1956, p. 149). In these situations, students may be asked to analyze various elements, relationships, or organizational principles, such as the way elements are categorized, differences and similarities, cause and effect, logical conclusions, or relevant and irrelevant data.

Again, essays may be used to assess analytical behavior, but the essays must do more than tell the main idea (comprehension) and describe how the student would apply previously learned knowledge. Analytical essays must clarify relationships, compare and contrast, show cause and effect, and provide evidence for conclusions. Other student products that are appropriate for assessing analysis are time lines; charts that compare, contrast, or categorize data; and a variety of graphs that show relationships.

Bloom et al. (1956) noted that there were special problems in the assessment of synthesis-level objectives:

> A major problem in testing for synthesis objectives is that of providing conditions favorable to creative work. Perhaps the most important condition is that of freedom. This should include freedom from excessive tension and from pressures to adopt a particular viewpoint. The student should be made to believe that the product of his efforts need not conform to the views of the instructor. Time is another important condition. Many synthesis tasks require far more time than an hour or two; the product is likely to emerge only after the student spends considerable time familiarizing himself with the task, exploring different approaches, interpreting and analyzing relevant materials, and trying out various schemes of organization. (p. 173)

The types of student products that demonstrate synthesis are infinitely variable. Written work such as creative essays, stories, poems, plays, books, and articles are certainly appropriate for assessing language arts objectives. Performances are just as useful, including original speeches, drama, poems, and musical compositions. Student-created products may include original plans, blueprints, artwork, computer programs, and models of proposed inventions. Student work may be collected in portfolios to demonstrate growth and achievement in a subject area.

Evaluating the relative success of synthesis products is very difficult. No objective criteria may exist for judging the value or worth of a student's original product. When student products are entered in a contest or submitted for publication, outside judges with expertise in the subject area can provide feedback and may even make judgments that the classroom teacher cannot make. "Checklists and rating scales should be especially useful here, but the examiner ought to insure that they do not emphasize elements of the product to the neglect of global qualities which, after all, may be more fundamental in any synthesis" (Bloom et al., 1956, p. 174). Many elementary teachers simply record whether a finished product was turned in by the student, rather than attempt to evaluate or grade it.

Bloom and his colleagues (1956) describe two quite different forms of evaluation-level objectives. One type calls on students to make a judgment based on internal evidence. In this case, all of the facts and data needed to make the judgment are provided in the test situation and the student simply selects and applies them. To test a student's ability to make this type of judgment, the teacher must provide all of the needed data, perhaps in the form of charts or graphs, and ask the student to draw certain conclusions from these data.

Another form of evaluation is to make judgments based on external criteria, such as rules and standards by which such works are generally judged. In this case, teachers may use assessment strategies in which the student is given a situation, makes a judgment, and justifies that judgment by applying the appropriate criteria. For example, students may be asked to make and justify aesthetic judgments of a work of art or to judge the validity of a political theory, stating the appropriate criteria used in making the evaluation. The types of products that students create at this level are critical essays, discussions, speeches, letters to the editor, debates, dramatizations, videotapes, and other forms that allow students to express their points of view.

As with synthesis outcomes, evaluation outcomes and objectives are also difficult to grade. A teacher who offers students an opportunity to express their own views usually places high value on independent thinking and freedom of expression. Therefore, the teacher cannot grade a student response "right" or "wrong." But the teacher can assess whether the student has used accurate, sufficient, and appropriate criteria in defending a personal opinion. Student work that has cited inaccurate, insufficient, or inappropriate evidence should probably be returned to the student with suggestions for revision.

Affective outcomes may be assessed by teacher observation as students work on various projects. It is also useful to involve students in self-evaluation to monitor their own affective growth in areas such as self-confidence, independence, cooperation, or creativity.

In summary, evaluation of student accomplishment should be directly linked to the lesson's objectives. To assess basic knowledge and skills, behavioral objectives are useful because they state exactly what the student will be able to do and specify the criteria for success. For higher level objectives, problem-solving objectives may be less precise but still should describe the type of student behavior or product expected and give some general criteria for success. To assess the growth in the affective domain, open-ended outcomes are planned and students can state orally or in writing what they have gained from a certain experience.

When teachers plan by writing clear behavioral, problem-solving, and open-ended objectives for their lessons, they are, in effect, clarifying their expectations regarding what students will gain from the lesson and their criteria for success. The evaluation section of a lesson plan is then usually a restatement of the criteria expressed in the objectives. You will see an example of this in the sample lesson plans discussed next in this chapter.

Sample Lesson Plans

Sample Lesson Plan in Mathematics

Students like to explore their own world. A large portion of time in the middle-school student's world is devoted to watching television. Figure 6.3 shows a lesson plan from Pam Knight's unit on television-viewing habits (see discussion in Chapter 5 and Figure 5.3). On the surface, this appears to be a mathematics lesson. However, after analyzing the objectives and activities in it, you will see that it involves the social sciences and language arts as well.

Figure 6.3 Mathematics/social studies lesson plan by Pam Knight, Poway School District, Poway, California.

Title of Lesson: Television-Viewing Habits of Students

Subject Area: Mathematics/Social Sciences

Grade Level: 5th–6th Grades

Approximate Lesson Duration: Two 60–minute lessons 1 week apart

Teacher's Description: Students will keep records of the amount of television they watch and present this information using graphs.

Students' Summary of the Lesson: I learned that comparing television watching is easier to do with bar graphs.

Objectives:
1. *(application level)* Students will construct bar graphs using data collected on television-viewing habits.
2. *(analysis level)* Students will interpret and make inferences based on the analysis of the data by writing a statement that describes the data on the graph.
3. *(evaluation level)* Students will evaluate their television-viewing habits and the television-viewing habits of the class as a whole.

Materials Needed: Graph paper, rulers and pencils.

Procedures:
1. *Preassessment:* I ask students how we can compare the amount of time each student watches television. What could we do if we wanted to know who watches the most TV?
2. *Motivation:* Students discuss their own television-viewing habits. This is an open-ended discussion, and students may talk about types of shows seen (MTV, movies, sports contests, etc.). Ask students: Do students watch too much television and play too many video games? How much TV do students really watch? Are there methods by which students can gather data on their television-viewing habits?

Figure 6.3   *Continued*

3. *Statement of Purpose:* We will learn how to gather information and data to make informed decisions about important matters in our lives.

4. *Teacher Modeling and Demonstration:* Teacher models data collection by surveying students on their favorite TV show. Teacher tallies these data and, with class participation, creates a bar graph of the data at the chalkboard.

5. *Guided Practice:* Students duplicate the teacher's tally and bar graph at their desks.

6. *Check for Understanding:* Ask questions to determine whether the students know the processes of recording data and constructing a bar graph.

7. *Contingencies:*

   What will I do if my students:

Don't understand?	Appear neutral or nonresponsive?	Have already mastered the concept?
Assign radio listening if they can't watch TV at home	Provide a sample graph	Create web page to gather data on-line

8. *Independent Study/Activity:* Students gather data for 1 week. In Lesson 2, students choose ways to display their data using bar graphs. Examples of displaying the data could be the amount of television boys watched compared with the amount girls watched, the amount of television watched on different days of the week, or the types of programs watched. In groups of three, students construct the graph and identify an inference they could make based on their graph. They share their graphs and display them on a bulletin board.

9. *Postassessment and Closure:* Students discuss what they have learned about their television-viewing habits. They discuss what the results mean to them. For example, do they think they watch too much television? Do they watch more or less television than they expected? Is the bar graph an effective way to display the data they gathered?

This lesson plan requires more than one class period. One day is needed to prepare for data collection; a week is needed to collect and record the data; and 1 or 2 days are required for constructing the bar graphs and describing the findings.

Pam's lesson demonstrates how students can use mathematics in their lives. They become researchers who collect and organize data. For the data to be relevant, they must be able to analyze them and explain what they found. Finally, the students are expected to make inferences and evaluate an important factor in their lives.

Sample Primary Bilingual Lesson Plan Using Learning Centers

Conchita Encinas teaches in a bilingual first-grade classroom in Chula Vista, California. To encourage her students to interact and use oral language in small groups, she likes to plan many of her lessons using learning centers. For each topic that she wants to teach, she designs four different activities that students can do independently or in a small group. For example, her spring curriculum includes a unit on plants and growing things. For the lesson on plants and seeds she designs four different learning center activities.

She begins the lesson with all of the children sitting in a circle. She provides students with some general information in both Spanish and English about plants and seeds. She encourages her students to learn and use new English words related to the topic being studied. Then she introduces the four different activities they will be able to explore in the centers. She divides the class into four groups and each group travels from one center to another for 20-minute intervals. At the end of the morning, the students gather in a circle again to share what they have done and learned about seeds and plants. Conchita reads aloud the stories the children have written at the first center. Figure 6.4 shows Conchita's lesson plan for the exploration of seeds and plants.

Figure 6.4 *Seeds and plants lesson plan. A hands-on science lesson designed for learning centers by Conchita Encinas for a first-grade bilingual class, Chula Vista, California.*

Title of Lesson: Seeds and Plants

Subject Area: Science and Language Development

Grade Level: K–1

Teacher's Description: Students will explore how seeds grow into plants and compare the seeds in various fruits and vegetables.

Students' Summary of the Lesson: Each student will state one observation, such as "The apple has the most seeds."

Objectives:
1. Students will observe that seeds are different sizes, shapes, and colors.
2. Students will be able to describe how seeds grow into plants.
3. Students will analyze the variation in number and type of seeds among several different fruits and vegetables.

Procedures:
1. *Preassessment:* Begin in a circle. Review concepts students have already learned about plants. Have students give thumbs-up signal if they agree, thumbs-down signal if they disagree with statements such as "Flowers are plants." "Plants need water to grow." "Plants need milk to grow."
2. *Motivation:* Show some fruits and vegetables to the class.
3. *Statement of Purpose:* Today we will be scientists and examine the inside of these fruits and vegetables. We will find out what their seeds look like and how each type of seed is special.
4. *Teacher Demonstration* and 5. *Guided Practice:* Teacher cuts open one fruit and counts the seeds inside with the class. Students describe the color, size, and shape of the seeds together.

Figure 6.4   *Continued*

6. *Check for Understanding:* Review with the whole group directions for the activities at the four centers. Divide class into four groups. Assign rotation schedule so that each group goes to all four centers.

7. *Contingencies:*

Don't understand?	Appear neutral or nonresponsive?	Have already mastered the concept?
Can't understand English	Are quiet, don't participate	Do the tasks quickly
Use a vocablulary chart in Spanish and English	Rotate or have another adult go around and help quiet ones	Give additional fruits and vegetables

8. *Independent Study/Activity:*

   Center 1: Students cut out parts of a plant, glue them on a piece of paper and write a story about it.

   Center 2: Students examine and count seeds in a variety of vegetables and fruits, including apple, cantaloupe, peapod, green pepper. They graph the number of seeds in each.

   Center 3: Students plant rye seeds in a paper cup and discuss what happens to seeds under the ground.

   Center 4: Students identify various vegetables, cut them up, and taste them. They list words about the way each vegetable tastes.

9. *Postassessment and Closure:* Story boards and stories from Center 1 are read aloud at the closing circle. Graphs from Center 2 are displayed on the bulletin board. Seeds in cups from Center 3 are placed near a window to grow. Students discuss the tastes of different vegetables during the closing circle.

Teachers write lesson plans to create a well-organized set of learning experiences for their students. The objectives of the lesson specify the teacher's expectations for what the students will learn or be able to do as a result of the lesson. When teachers plan objectives that specify the criteria for success, they are clarifying for themselves what the students must be able to do to demonstrate mastery of the skill or understanding of the lesson's concepts.

To plan the procedures of a lesson in advance, many reflective teachers visualize themselves teaching the lesson. They write what they must do to teach the lesson successfully and what the students must do to learn the material. Teachers who can visualize the entire process of teaching and learning can write richly detailed lesson plans. When they begin to teach the lesson, they can pay more attention to their students' responses because the lesson activities are familiar to them.

As teachers become more proficient and experienced at planning and teaching, their written lesson plans are likely to become less detailed. But for beginning teachers, a thorough, richly detailed plan is an essential element for a successful lesson.

Reflective Actions for Your Professional Portfolio

Three Sample Lesson Plans

At the end of Chapter 5, you chose a topic for a curriculum unit and wrote the unit plan to include in your portfolio. Now you will write three sample lesson plans to fit your unit topic. When they are included in your professional portfolio, the unit plan and the three sample lesson plans will be important evidence of your original teaching style and will demonstrate your ability to be a reflective, caring teacher.

Use Withitness: Examine Other Lesson Plans

Ask an experienced teacher to show you his or her lesson plans. How do these plans differ from the ones in this chapter? Observe a lesson in action and try to perceive the teacher's objectives, procedures, and assessment strategies.

Define and Put Problem into Perspective: Choose a Topic

Choose a subject or topic for your three demonstration lesson plans. Write an initial description of what you want to accomplish by the end of these three lessons.

Widen Your Perspective: Imagine the Lessons in Action

Picture yourself teaching these three lessons. Consider the contingencies you may encounter. What will you do if students do not understand the lessons? What will you do if they seem nonresponsive or neutral? What will you do if they already know this material?

Invite Feedback: Talk About Teaching This Subject

Talk with experienced teachers about what they encountered when they taught the subject or topic you have chosen. Ask them to share their good and bad experiences. Ask them for ideas to use if students do not understand the subject the first time. Ask for ideas to extend your lessons to meet the needs of students who easily master the subject.

Redefine the Problem: Write Well-Sequenced Objectives

Now write three lesson objectives for each of three lessons on your topic. You will have nine objectives in all, each one building on the basis of the previous ones.

Create an Action Plan: Write Your Three Lesson Plans

Write three sample lesson plans to fit the unit plan you have created. You may wish to use very different types of lessons to demonstrate your flexibility and creativity.

Predict Possible Outcomes: Revise Your Lessons Based on Feedback

Show your lesson plans to a knowledgeable teacher and get feedback that will help you to improve them. Make the revisions that you agree with and explain your rationale for elements that you retain. If possible, teach the lessons and then make further revisions. Describe the changes that you made as a result of teaching the lessons.

References

Bloom, B., Engelhart, M., Furst, E., Hill, W., & Krathwohl, D. (1956). *Taxonomy of educational objectives: Cognitive domain.* New York: Longman.

Eisner, E. (1994). *Educational imagination* (3rd ed.). Upper Saddle River, NJ: Merrill/Prentice Hall.

Tyler, R. (1949). *Basic principles of curriculum and instruction.* Chicago: University of Chicago Press.

7

Authentic Teaching and Learning

Your units and lesson plans are ready to go. You have taken the time and effort to create a safe, encouraging, and stimulating classroom environment. You have clarified your expectations for student behavior and involved your students in the process of creating classroom rules. You have rehearsed the procedures for coming in and going out of the classroom and you know the names of each student and something about their background and needs. Now, you can begin to focus on developing instructional strategies that will promote authentic learning.

The term *authentic learning* is used to distinguish between the achievement of significant, meaningful, and useful knowledge and skills from that which is trivial and unrelated to students' lives. The Wisconsin Center on Organizing and Restructuring of Schools has concentrated on defining standards of authentic instruction (Newman and Wehlage, 1993). Their studies have led them to conclude that many conventional instructional methods do not allow students to use their minds well and result in learning that has little or no intrinsic meaning or value to students beyond achieving success in school.

These studies recommend establishing standards for teachers to use as guidelines in selecting and learning to use teaching strategies that promote authentic learning. According to their research, the standards for authentic instructional methods should emphasize higher order thinking, depth of knowledge, connectedness to the world, and substantive conversation and should also provide social support for student achievement (Newman and Wehlage, 1993).

As a learner, you may have had teachers who used teaching strategies that stimulated you to use your higher level thinking and problem-solving skills. You may recall learning experiences that encouraged you to delve deeply into a subject that had real meaning to your life. You may recall class discussions that sparkled with enthusiastic exchanges of ideas and opinions within a learning community that encouraged you to challenge yourself to make more and more meaningful accomplishments. If you recall school experiences such as these, you have experienced authentic learning.

Unfortunately, it is likely that you had other teachers who relied on very conventional methods that required rote memorization of meaningless material. You may recall learning a lot about little and boring recitations in which students were expected to parrot what they had memorized. You may recall competitive social systems that encouraged only those students who were able to memorize and recite quickly and those who were able to figure out what the teacher wanted to hear. If you recall school experiences such as these, you will need to overcome the natural tendency to repeat learned patterns and challenge yourself to learn to use many new and exciting instructional strategies.

Your personal conception of the teaching–learning process is drawn from your own experiences as a learner, but for reflective teachers, it is also drawn from the values and beliefs you hold about what students need to know and how students ought to behave and from your perceptions and reflections about the theories and practices of other classroom teachers that you observe.

To become a reflective teacher, you must make yourself aware of the emerging research and knowledge base about teaching and learning. Gathering information from research is an important attribute of a reflective thinker and teacher.

Retrieval Processes

Schema Theory

The retrieval process is obviously a critical factor in being able to use stored information. Knowledge, concepts, and skills that are learned must be stored in the brain until they are needed. According to *schema theory*, each subset of knowledge is stored in a *schema*, an outline or organized network of knowledge about a single concept or subject. It is believed that young children develop *schemata* (the plural form of schema) made up of visual or other sensory images, and as language increases, verbal imagery replaces the sensory images (Anderson, 1989a).

For example, an infant stores sensory images in the schemata for mother, bottle, bed, and bath. Later, the verbal labels are added. A schema grows, expands, or otherwise changes due to new experiences. If the infant sees and touches a large, round, blue ball, he or she can store sensory images of its size, color, rubbery feel, and softness. At a later encounter, the infant may experience it bounce and he can store these images in the same schema. A year later, when the child learns to say the word *ball*, the label is activated in working memory and then stored in long-term memory within the schema for ball.

Students come to school with varied schemata. Some students who have had many experiences at home, in parks, at zoos, in museums, and in other circumstances may enter kindergarten with complex schemata for hundreds of topics and experiences. Other students, whose experiences have been severely limited by poverty or other circumstances, are likely to have very different schemata, and some of these may not match the prevailing culture's values or verbal labels. Similarly, if students come from highly verbal homes where parents talk with them frequently, their schemata are likely to contain accurate verbal labels for many stored sensory experiences and phenomena. But students raised in less verbal homes may have fewer verbal components to their schemata. This theory complements Piaget's observations of stages of development and helps us to understand how a child's vocabulary develops.

Schemata also vary according to their organizational patterns. As children mature, each schema expands to include many more facts, ideas, and examples. In cases of healthy development, the schemata are frequently clarified and reorganized. Learning new information or observing unfamiliar examples often causes a schema to be renamed or otherwise altered. For example, very young children have a schema labeled *doggy* that includes all four-legged, furry creatures. As they see new examples of animals and hear the appropriate labels for each type, the original schema of doggy is reorganized to become simply a subset of the schema *animal*. New patterns and relationships among schemata are formed every day of a child's life when the environment is full of unfamiliar concepts and experiences.

At the elementary grade levels, teachers recognize that one of their most important responsibilities is to aid students in attaching accurate verbal labels to appropriate schemata. At the earliest grades (especially kindergarten), teachers emphasize spoken labels, teaching students to recognize and be able to name objects and concepts such as numbers, letters of the alphabet, and colors. At the primary grades, teachers emphasize the recognition and decoding of written labels as an integral part of the reading program. When students exhibit difficulties in learning to read, the caring and reflective teacher is likely to plan learning experiences that assist these students in developing schemata related to classroom reading materials.

Students who have been raised in environments characterized by few experiences with books are likely to have an underdeveloped schema for reading and books. Reflective teachers who consider the needs of the whole individual are likely to provide their students with many opportunities to hear stories read aloud, to choose from a tempting array of books, and to write their own stories as a means of developing a rich and positive schema for the concept of reading.

Advance Organizers

When teachers want to assist students in retrieving information from their schemata, they provide verbal cues that help the students access the appropriate information efficiently. Teachers can also provide cues to assist students in accurately and efficiently processing and storing what they read, see, or hear. Ausubel (1960) proposed that learners can comprehend new material better when, in advance of the lesson, the teacher provides a clear statement about the purpose of the lesson and the type of information they should look or listen for. This introductory statement is known as an *advance organizer*.

It is apparent that the advance organizer provides the learner with an important cue as to which schema will incorporate this new knowledge. The learner can be more efficient in processing the information in working memory and transferring it to the appropriate schema in long-term memory than if no advance information were presented.

For example, consider what is likely to happen when a third-grade teacher introduces a lesson on long division with no advance organizer. Some students may simply reject the new knowledge as incomprehensible. But what if the teacher tells students to listen for how division is similar to subtraction and how it is the opposite of multiplication? The teacher is providing students with the cues they need to retrieve their subtraction and multiplication schema in advance of the new learning. In the second case, students are more likely to route the new facts into working memory, where they can be processed using the subtraction and multiplication schemata as a framework.

In follow-up studies of Ausubel's hypothesis, many educational researchers designed experiments that showed the same effects. Therefore, this knowledge has been added to our growing common knowledge base about teaching and learning. In fact, this particular study demonstrates the way the knowledge base grows. The original hypothesis and study conducted by Ausubel (1960) led others to apply the principle to different types of students and environments. As the hypothesis was confirmed in subsequent studies, the knowledge was gradually accepted as a reliable principle of effective teaching. You probably experience the beneficial effects of advance organizers when your teachers tell you in advance what to listen for in a lecture or what to study for an exam. Now you can learn how to use this principle in your teaching career for the benefit of your students.

Presentation Skills That Increase Clarity and Motivation

Teaching is more than telling. You have been on the receiving end of teachers' lectures, discussions, and other forms of lessons for many years. You know from your own experience that the way teachers teach or present material has an effect on student interest and motivation, which are both integral aspects of the classroom climate. You may have been unable to understand the beginning of a lesson taught by a teacher who failed to get the full attention of a class before speaking. You have probably experienced sinking feelings when a teacher droned on in a monotonous voice during a lecture. You may have experienced frustration when a teacher explained a concept once and hurried on, ignoring questions or comments from the class. Reflective teachers are not likely to be satisfied with a dull, repetitive, or unresponsive presentation style. Most of them are anxious to improve their presentation skills to stimulate interest and motivate student achievement.

Getting Students' Attention

To consider systematically the way you present a lesson, think about the beginning. The introduction to a lesson is very important, whether it is the first lesson of the day or a transition from one lesson to another. As Kounin (1977) found in his study of well-functioning classrooms, transitions and lesson beginnings start with a clear, straightforward message or cue signaling that the teacher is ready to begin teaching and stating exactly what students should do to prepare themselves for the lesson. To accomplish this when you teach, you need to tell your students to get ready for a certain lesson and to give you their full attention. Some teachers use a visual cue for this purpose, such as a finger on the lips or a raised arm. Others may strike a chime or turn off the lights to cue the students that it is time to listen.

It is unlikely that students will become quiet instantly. It will probably take a few moments to get the attention of every student in the class. While you are waiting, stand up straight and direct your eye contact toward those who are slow to respond. Watch quietly as the students get their desks, pencils, books, and other needed materials ready for the lesson. The waiting may seem uncomfortable at first. You will be tempted to begin before they are ready because you will think that time is being wasted. Do not give in to this feeling. Wait until every voice is quiet, every chair stops scraping, every desk top stops banging, and every pencil stops tapping. Wait for a moment of pure, undisturbed silence. Then quietly begin your lesson. You will have the attention of every student.

Some teachers use a bit of drama to begin a lesson. They may pose a question or describe a condition that will interest their students. Richard Klein, a teacher at the Ericson School on the west side of Chicago, begins teaching a unit on aviation by asking students what they know about the Wright brothers. The students' replies are seldom very enthusiastic, so he unexpectedly asks them, "Then what do you know about the Wrong brothers?" They show a bit more interest but are still unable to provide many informed responses. So Mr. Klein turns off the lights and turns on a videotape of the Three Stooges in a skit called "The Wrong Brothers." Afterward, partly in appreciation of Mr. Klein's humor, the students show a greater willingness to learn about the real historical events.

Often teachers begin with a statement of purpose, describing how this particular lesson will help their students make important gains in skills or knowledge. Still others begin by doing a demonstration or distributing some interesting manipulative materials. Our relational lesson plan model (Chapter 6) has a step called "motivation" that is designed to gain attention and make a connection between the students and the subject of the lesson. Teachers are encouraged to use a variety of opening activities appropriate to the lesson content and objective.

In contrast, less reflective teachers begin almost every lesson with: "Open your books to page ___. David, read the first paragraph aloud." This example employs limited presentation skills. This nonmethod relies on the material itself to whet the students' interest in the topic. Although some materials may be stimulating and appealing, most are not. The message the teacher gives to the students is "I don't care much about this; let's just get through it." The students' motivation to learn drops to the same level as this message and can best be expressed as "Why bother?"

Teachers often display a greater degree of excitement and interest for material they themselves enjoyed learning, and they pass that excitement about learning on to the students. A teacher who reads aloud with enthusiasm conveys the message that reading is fun. A teacher who plunges into a science investigation with delight causes students to look forward to science.

After you gain your students' attention and inspire them to want to know more, you move on to the lesson itself. Presentation skills that you can learn to use systematically in your lessons include enthusiasm, clarity, smooth transitions, timing, variation, interaction, active learning, and closure. Each of these skills is discussed next in turn.

Enthusiasm

Animation is the outward sign of a teacher's interest in the students and the subject. Enthusiasm is the inner experience. "There are at least two major aspects of enthusiasm. The first is conveying sincere interest in the subject. The other aspect is vigor and dynamics," and both are related to getting and maintaining student attention (Good & Brophy, 1987, p. 479). Outwardly, the teacher displays enthusiasm by using a bright, lively voice; open, expansive gestures; and facial expressions that show interest and pleasure. Salespeople who use animated, enthusiastic behavior could sell beach umbrellas in the Yukon in January. Why shouldn't teachers employ these techniques as well? You can "sell" long division better with an enthusiastic voice. You can convince your students that recycling is important with a look of commitment on your own face. You can encourage students' participation in a discussion with welcoming gestures and a warm smile.

Is animation something you can control? Absolutely. You can practice presenting information on a topic with your classmates, using an animated voice and gestures. They can give you feedback, which you can use to improve your presentation. Have yourself videotaped as you make a presentation. When you view yourself, you can be your own best teacher. Redo your presentation with new gestures and a different voice. Repeat this procedure several times, if necessary. Gradually, you will notice a change in your presentation style. You will add these techniques to your growing repertoire of effective presentation skills.

Clarity

The clarity of the teacher's presentation of lesson directions and content is a critical factor in student success. Brophy and Good (1986) listed the importance of teacher *clarity* as a consistent finding in studies of teacher effectiveness. Their review of research on teacher clarity describes negative teacher behaviors that detract from clarity. These include using vague terms, mazes, discontinuity, and saying "uhh" repeatedly.

As an example of *vague terms*, Brophy and Good (1986) present the following, with ambiguous language in italics:

> This mathematics lesson *might* enable you to understand *a little more* about *some of the things* we *usually* call number patterns. *Maybe* before we get to *probably* the main idea of the lesson, you should review *a few* prerequisite concepts. (p. 355)

The vague terms in this example have the effect of making the teacher sound tentative and unsure of the content. As an introduction to a lesson, it is not likely to capture students' attention or interest. Clarity can be improved, in this example, by exchanging the vague terms for specific ones, resulting in a simple, straightforward statement: "This mathematics lesson will enable you to understand the concept of number patterns. Before we get to the main idea of the lesson, we will review four prerequisite concepts."

Clarity also suffers from what Brophy and Good (1986) call *mazes*: false starts or halts in the teacher's speech, redundancy, and tangled words. For example:

> This mathematics lesson *will enab*—will get you to understand *number, uhh,* number patterns. Before we get to the *main idea of the,* main idea of the lesson, you need to review *four conc*—four prerequisite concepts. (p. 355)

Even when students attempt to pay attention, they may be unable to decipher the meaning of the teacher's words if the presentation is characterized by the false starts in this example. It is quite obvious that the way to improve this statement is to eliminate the redundant words. This example is a very simple one. Clarity is also reduced when the teacher has begun to present a lesson, is interrupted by a student's misbehavior or a knock at the door, then begins the lesson again.

Kounin (1977) observed that the most effective teachers are able to *overlap* teaching with other classroom management actions. That is, they are able to continue with the primary task, presenting the lesson to the class, while at the same time opening the classroom door or stopping misbehavior with a glance or a touch on the shoulder. When teachers can overlap their presentations, the clarity of their lessons is greatly enhanced.

The third teacher behavior that detracts from clarity is discontinuity, "in which the teacher interrupts the flow of the lesson by interjecting irrelevant content" (Brophy & Good, 1986, p. 355). This is why lesson planning is so important. Without a plan, teachers may simply begin a lesson by reading from a textbook. As they or the students are reading, the teacher (or a student) may be reminded of something they find interesting.

They may discuss the related topic for quite some time before returning to the original lesson. This side discussion may or may not be interesting or important, but it is likely to detract from the clarity of the original lesson.

The fourth detractor from teacher clarity noted by Brophy and Good (1986) is repeatedly saying "uhh." It is also likely that other repetitive speech patterns are just as annoying, such as "you know." For the beginning teacher, some of these teacher behaviors are likely to occur simply as a result of nervousness or unfamiliarity with the content being taught. It would be interesting to study the hypothesis that these four detracting behaviors decrease as a result of teaching experience—in other words, as a teacher gains experience, the four detracting behaviors subside and clarity increases. Two teacher behaviors found to enhance clarity were an "emphasis on key aspects of the content to be learned and clear signaling of transitions between parts of lessons" (p. 355).

Smooth Transitions

Just as lesson introductions are important to gain students' attention, *smooth transitions* are essential to maintaining that attention and making the classroom a productive working environment. Transitions occur within a lesson, as the teacher guides students from one activity to another. They also occur between lessons, as students put away what they were working on in one lesson and get ready for a different subject.

Good and Brophy (1987) also note that knowing when to terminate a lesson is an important element of teacher withitness:

> When the group is having difficulty maintaining attention, it is better to end the lesson early than to doggedly continue. This is especially important for younger students, whose attention span for even the best lesson is limited. When lessons go on after the point where they should have been terminated, more of the teacher's time is spent compelling attention and less of the students' time is spent thinking about the material. (p. 245)

In addition to going to another classroom, transitions between activities and lessons may require that students move from place to place in the room, such as having one group come to the reading circle while another group returns to their seats. Usually students are required to exchange one set of books and materials for another. These movements and exchanges have high potential for noise in the form of banging desk tops, scraping chairs, dropped equipment, and students' voices as they move from lesson to lesson.

Jerky, chaotic transitions are often caused by incomplete directions or vague expectations about student behavior from the teacher. "Take out your math books" is incomplete in that the teacher does not first specify that the students should put away other materials with which they have been working. The result may be that the students begin to work on desks cluttered with unnecessary materials.

Often, inexperienced teachers begin to give directions for a transition, and the students start to get up and move around while the teacher is speaking. When this happens, teachers may attempt to talk louder so that they can be heard over the din. A way to prevent this from occurring is to clearly inform students that they are to wait until all directions have been given before they begin to move.

Smooth transitions are characterized by clear directions from the teacher about what is to be put away and what is to be taken out, who is to move, and where they are to go. Clear statements of behavioral expectations are also important. The same techniques for getting attention that were described previously apply to the beginning of each new lesson. After a noisy transition between lessons, it is essential for the teacher to have the students' complete attention before beginning the new lesson. The teacher should wait until all students move into their new positions and get all their materials ready before trying to introduce the lesson.

The teacher can use a signal to indicate that the new lesson is about to begin. A raised hand, lights turned off and then on again, or a simple verbal statement such as "I am ready to begin," will signal to the students that they should be ready for the next lesson. After giving the signal, the teacher should wait until the students have all complied and are silent before beginning the new lesson.

In considering strategies that result in smooth transitions, teachers do well to reflect on the students' needs for physical activity. In a junior high or high school, students can move between periods. At the elementary school or in a block period of time in the middle school, it is unrealistic to expect students to be able to sit still through one lesson after another. Some teachers take 5 to 10 minutes to lead students in singing or movement games between two working periods. Other teachers allow students to have a few moments of free time in which they may talk to friends, go to the washroom or get a drink of water. Some transitions are good opportunities for teachers to read aloud from a story book or challenge students to solve a brain teaser or puzzling mathematics problem. Reflective teachers find that when they allow students a respite and a change of pace during a brief transition period, the work periods are more productive and motivation to learn is enhanced.

Timing

Actors, speakers, and comedians give considerable attention to improving the timing of their presentations. Good use of timing engages the attention of an audience, is used for emphasis of major points, and sometimes creates a laugh. Teachers also work in front of an audience, and class presentations can be improved by considering timing and pacing as a means of getting attention and keeping it. Pausing for a moment of complete silence before you begin teaching is a good example of a way to incorporate timing into your presentation.

In most instances, students respond best to teachers who use a brisk pace when delivering information and instructions. Kounin's (1977) research on the most effective classroom managers demonstrated that students are best able to focus on the subject when the lesson has continuity and momentum. Interruptions result in confusion. When teachers forget to bring a prop, pause to consult a teacher's manual, or backtrack to present material that should have been presented earlier, inattention and disruptive behavior are likely to occur (Kounin, 1977). Jones (1987) found that students' attention improved when teachers gave them efficient help, allocating *20 seconds or less* to each request for individual help or reteaching. When this time was lengthened, the result was restlessness and dependency on the part of students.

However, there are times when a pause in instruction can improve your presentation. Researchers have found that it is important to present new information in small steps, with a pause after the initial explanation to check for understanding. Students may not respond immediately during this pause because they need a moment to put their thoughts into words. Wait for them to do so. Encourage questions and comments. Ask for examples or illustrations of the fact or concept being discussed. This pause lets your students reflect on the material and allows you to test their understanding.

Variation

Lesson variation is an essential presentation skill for teachers who want to develop a healthy, vital classroom climate. In analyzing classroom videotapes, Kounin (1977) noticed that satiation results in boredom and inattentiveness. If presentations are monotonous, students will find a way to introduce their own variation by daydreaming, sleeping, fiddling with objects, doodling, or poking their neighbors.

Planning for variation is important whenever you plan a lesson of 30 minutes or longer. Divide your lesson into several segments. Use lecture for only a part of the time. For example, include segments of discussion, independent practice, small-group interaction, and application activities. If you cannot break a single lesson into segments, plan to use a variety of strategies during the course of a day. Use quiet, independent work for one subject, group interaction for another, lecture for a third, and hands-on activities for a fourth. In this way, your students will always be expectant and eager for each new lesson of the day. They will feel fresh and highly motivated to learn because of the variations in the way you choose to present material. If teachers attempt to address different ways of learning in each lesson, they cannot help but provide variation in the classroom. All lessons should be checked for activities that address different intelligences, or ways of knowing. This is discussed in more detail later in this chapter.

Interaction

Students thrive on interaction with the teacher and with their classmates. Rather than employing a traditional teacher-to-student, student-to-teacher communication pattern, open your classroom to a variety of interactive experiences. Pushing the desks into a large circle encourages open-ended discussion from all students. Arranging the desks in small groups encourages highly interactive problem solving. Moving the desks aside leaves a lot of space in the middle of the room for activities. Pairing the desks provides opportunities for peer teaching or partnerships of other kinds. Your presentations can include all of these types of activities, and you will find them motivating not only to your students, but to you as well. You will feel a sense of expectant excitement as you say, "All right, students, let's rearrange the desks."

The need for interaction derives from the powerful motivational need for belonging described by Maslow (1954) and Glasser (1986). When these needs are frustrated or denied, disruptive behavior is likely to occur as a means of satisfying them. When teachers consciously plan interactive learning experiences, they allow students to satisfy their important drive for belonging and thereby prevent unnecessary discipline problems.

Active, Authentic Learning Experiences

Teachers who value authentic learning present material in ways that engage their students in active, rather than passive learning, by including many verbal, visual, or hands-on activities. Consider a lecture on a topic such as the closed circuit in electricity. Ho-hum. Add a visual aid—a poster or an overhead projection. Students sit up in their seats to see better. Now add a demonstration. Turn off the lights. Hold up a battery, some copper wire, and a light bulb. Your students watch expectantly with a new sense of interest.

All of these techniques are adequate to teach the students a concept, but none is as valuable as a hands-on experience for in-depth learning and understanding. Picture this scene instead. After lunch the students come into their classroom to find a battery, a flashlight bulb, and a piece of copper wire on each desk. After getting their attention, the teacher simply says, "Working independently, try to get your bulb to light up." Lights go on all over the room—in children's eyes and in their minds as they struggle with this problem. The motivation to succeed is intense and it is intrinsic, not tied to any exterior reward. Each individual has a sense of power and a need to know.

The key to authentic learning is in allowing your students to encounter and master situations that resemble real life. Simulated experiences are often just as valuable as real life for elementary school students and are much safer and more manageable for the beginning teacher. While your students may never invent a marketable product, you can simulate this type of exploration by inventing products that are needed in your classroom. You can simulate the debate and communication skills necessary to solve international crises by creating a mini United Nations in your room, in which each student studies one country in depth and engages in substantive conversations about the varied needs and strengths of each country.

Closure

In the active learning experience example, the teacher can aid the students in comprehending what they have learned by having them share what they did that worked and what did not work. Concepts can be developed by articulating and generalizing what they learned about electricity. Such a teacher-led discussion is an essential part of active, hands-on learning. It provides a sense of closure.

Every lesson or presentation can benefit from some thoughtful consideration to its ending. It is important to allow time for closure. You may use this time to ask questions that check for understanding so that you will know what to plan for the lesson that follows. You may allow the students to close the lesson with their own conclusions and new insights. A few moments spent summarizing what was learned is valuable in any form. If insight is to occur, it will probably occur in this period. At the close of one lesson, you can also indicate what will follow in the next lesson so that your students know what to expect and how to prepare for it.

Systematic Classroom Instruction

Direct Instruction of New Knowledge and Skills

The curriculum contains a high proportion of basic knowledge and skills that learners must master thoroughly to succeed in the upper grades. Language concepts such as letter recognition, phonics, word decoding, letter and word writing, and the conventions of sentence and paragraph construction must be mastered. Mathematical concepts such as number recognition, quantity, order, measurement, and the operations used in computation must be learned.

Many models of direct instruction are appropriate for teaching this type of material. They are known as five-step or seven-step lessons because they include a chronological sequence of steps for getting students' attention; reviewing what has been learned up to the current lesson; systematically teaching, modeling, and practicing the new material; and then demonstrating individual and independent mastery of what was taught.

The direct instruction model includes the following steps:

1. Create an anticipatory set to interest your students in the lesson by asking a thought-provoking question or providing an interesting visual aid or using a puzzling and intriguing opening statement about the topic.
2. Connect this lesson with what has come before by providing a short review of previous, prerequisite learning or otherwise describing relationships between the current lesson with other subjects being studied by the class.
3. A short statement of the purpose of learning this new information is likely to convince your students that this lesson has a meaning to their lives beyond just achieving well in school. Tell them what they are going to learn and why it is important.
4. Present new, unfamiliar, and complex material in small steps, modeling each step by doing an example yourself. Give clear and detailed instructions and explanations as you model each process.
5. Provide a high level of active practice for all students. After you model a step, allow every student to practice the example on his or her own or with a learning partner.
6. Monitor students as they practice each new step. Walk around and look at their work as they do their sample problems. Ask a large number of questions to check for student understanding. Try to obtain responses from many different students so that you know the concept is being clearly understood by the entire class. Provide systematic feedback and corrections as you see the needs arise.

7. At the end of each practice session, provide an opportunity for independent student work that synthesizes the many steps they have practiced during the lesson. This may be assigned as seatwork or homework. It is important to check this work and return it to students quickly with assistance for those who have not demonstrated independent mastery of the new material.

When these seven strategies are reviewed quickly, many readers may respond with reactions such as "But isn't that what all teachers do? What is new about these methods?"

It is true that many teachers have used these strategies throughout the history of education. Unfortunately, many other teachers have not. We have all observed classroom teachers who take a much less active role than these systematic procedures call for. Some teachers use only two steps: assigning workbook pages and correcting them the next day.

In selecting appropriate teaching methods and strategies, reflective teachers are likely to look for and discover relationships among various theories of learning and methods of teaching. One such relationship exists between this direct instruction model of systematic teaching and the process of thinking and learning known as *information processing.*

The first step—b*egin a lesson with a short review of previous, prerequisite learning*—is a signal to the learner to call up an existing schema that will be expanded on and altered in the new lesson. Beginning a lesson with a short statement of goals provides the student with an advance organizer that allows more efficient processing. In practice, these first two steps are often presented together and can be interchangeable with no ill effects.

Current information processing theories suggest that there are limits to the amount of new information that a learner can process effectively at one time (Gagné, 1985). When too much information is presented at one time, the working memory becomes overloaded, causing the learner to become confused, to omit data, or to process new data incorrectly. This overload can be eliminated when teachers *present new material in small steps, with student practice after each step.* This allows learners to concentrate their somewhat limited attention on processing manageable pieces of information or skills.

Teachers who *model new skills and give clear and detailed instructions and explanations* are likely to provide students with the support they need while they are processing new information in their working memories.

Providing students with a *high level of active practice* after each step and again at the conclusion of a series of steps is important because the practice enhances the likelihood that the new information will be transferred from working memory to long-term memory, where it can be stored for future use. Each time a new skill is practiced, its position in long-term memory is strengthened.

As teachers *guide students during initial practice and ask a large number of questions, check for student understanding, and obtain responses from all students,* they are also encouraging their students to process the information accurately. Learning occurs when schemata stored in long-term memory are expanded, enriched, and reorganized. Effective teacher questions and checks for understanding cause students to think about new ideas from a variety of perspectives and to update their existing schemata accordingly.

Providing systematic feedback and corrections and monitoring students during seatwork also increases the likelihood that students will process the important points and practice the new skills in the most efficient manner.

Teacher Modeling and Demonstration

When teachers present new information to students, they must carefully consider the method they will use to introduce it. For students, it is rarely sufficient for teachers to simply talk about a new idea or skill. A much more powerful method of instruction is to model or demonstrate it first, and then give students an opportunity to practice the new learning themselves.

A simple example of this technique occurs at the primary grades when teachers say, "First, I will say the word; then you will say it with me." In the middle grades, the teacher may first demonstrate the procedures used in measuring with a metric ruler and then ask students to repeat them. In the upper grades, teachers may write an outline of a paragraph and then ask students to outline the next one.

Teacher demonstration and modeling is an effective instructional technique for almost every area of the curriculum. It is useful in teaching music: "Clap the same rhythm that I do." It is vital in teaching mathematics: "Watch as I do the first problem on the chalkboard." It can be easily applied to the teaching of creative writing: "I'll read you the poem that I wrote about this topic, and then you will write your own."

When teachers circulate throughout the classroom to monitor students as they practice or create their own work, it is efficient to use modeling and demonstration on a one-to-one basis to assist students in getting started or in correcting mistakes.

Scaffolding

Scaffolding is a variation on the technique of teaching that involves modeling and demonstrating a new skill. It requires a highly interactive relationship between the teacher and the student while the new learning occurs. Anderson (1989b) cites Jerome Bruner's work with mothers and children as the first reference to scaffolding. As a mother reads aloud to a toddler, she may simplify the book to meet the attention span and interests of her child, calling the child's attention to material that is appropriate and eliminating material that is beyond the child's present capacity. She is also likely to allow the child to interact with her as they read and discuss the words and pictures on each page. This flexible and simplified interaction between child and parent allows the child to connect new ideas to existing schemata at his or her own level.

Teachers can apply scaffolding in the classroom by reducing complex tasks to manageable steps, helping students concentrate on one task at a time, being explicit about what is expected and interpreting the task for the student, and coaching the student using familiar, supportive words and actions. When a teacher coaches the student through a difficult task, it is important to provide sufficient scaffolding through the use of hints and cues so that the student can succeed. As students become more skillful, the scaffolding can be reduced and finally eliminated entirely.

Scaffolding is an especially valuable technique for the primary teacher, because most young students require supportive interaction and accommodation to their existing vocabularies to learn new skills. But scaffolding is also appropriate for upper-level students when the tasks are complex or the students have difficulty with the language.

Some teachers do not use scaffolding techniques at any level.

Instead of seeing themselves as supporters of students' constructions of knowledge, many teachers see themselves only as presenters of content, especially facts and skills. This style of teaching is known as the recitation mode of instruction, in which the teacher asks a question, and students raise their hands to answer out loud. Teachers such as these spend little time in the classroom encouraging students to explain how and what they are thinking, elements that are necessary for scaffolded dialogues.

For some beginning teachers, scaffolding may not come naturally, because they may not have experienced scaffolded learning in their own school experiences. This technique can be learned only by reflecting on the needs of students, gathering the latest information on such techniques from reading and talking to experienced teachers who have used the techniques successfully, and gradually adding such strategies to personal repertoires.

Structuring Tasks for Success

Researchers have found that the degree of success students have on school tasks correlates highly with achievement in the subject area. This supports the widely known maxim that "success breeds success." Both formal research and informal discussions with students reveal that when students experience success on a given task, they are motivated to continue working at it or to tackle another one. The number and type of successful learning experiences students have affect their self-knowledge, leading them to have expectations regarding probable success or failure in future tasks.

To structure tasks for success, there must be a good fit between the teacher's expectations, student ability, and the difficulty of the task. Rimm (1986), who has specialized in assisting underachieving students reach their potential, describes it this way:

> Children must learn early that there is a relationship between their effort and the outcome. If their schoolwork is too hard, their efforts do not lead to successful outcomes but only to failures. If their work is too easy, they learn that it takes very little to succeed. Either is inappropriate and provides a pattern which fosters underachievement. (p. 92)

When teachers select and present academic tasks to their students, they need to reflect continuously on how well the task fits the students' present needs and capacities.

Glasser (1986) has been committed to improving schools throughout his career. As a psychiatrist, he strongly believes that a person cannot be successful in life until he can in some way first experience success in one important part of his life. Glasser recognizes that children have only two places in which to experience success: home and school. If they are lucky enough to experience success in both settings, they are likely to be successful in their adult lives. If they achieve success at home, they succeed despite a lackluster school experience. But many students come from homes and neighborhoods where failure is pervasive. For these students especially, it is critical that they experience success in school.

Multiple Intelligences

For students to experience success in school, it is necessary for teachers to understand that each individual perceives the world differently and that there is not just one way to learn or one way to teach. Prior to the emergence of this theory, most people were convinced that there was just one type of intelligence and that all human beings had an intelligence quotient (IQ) that ranged from zero to approximately 200, with the great majority of individuals in the average range near 100, plus or minus 16 points.

Gardner's (1993) emerging theory of multiple intelligences disputes that old belief system. He proposed the alternate theory that humans have more than one type of intelligence. He originally described seven different intelligences: verbal/linguistic (word smart), logical-mathematical (logic and math smart), visual/spatial (art smart), musical (music smart), bodily-kinesthetic (body and movement smart), interpersonal (people smart), and intrapersonal (self-awareness smart). Later, he added another intelligence known as the naturalist, describing people who are very smart about nature and natural phenomena. Other researchers have suggested that there are additional intelligences as well. In her teaching and curriculum planning, Judy Eby proposed that there is an intelligence related to mechanical and technical inventiveness. She created curriculum projects that encouraged students to be inventive and expand their technical and mechanical skills.

Teachers who wish to acknowledge and support the varied intelligences of their students try to provide learning experiences that allow students to use their special strengths in learning a subject or skill. For example, when teachers present new material to a class, they are likely to describe it in words and ask for verbal feedback for linguistically talented students. They attempt to provide problem-solving activities related to the subject for logical-mathematically oriented students. They give spatially talented students visual cues and allow them to react to the new material with drawings or diagrams. They may encourage musically talented students to commit the new material to memory via a song or allow them to create a musical response to what they have learned. They set aside time and space for bodily-kinesthetically gifted students to learn with their bodies by modeling, acting out, or pantomiming the material they are learning. For students with a special facility for interpersonal communication, teachers plan stimulating classroom discussions, and for students who are especially good at intrapersonal examination, they provide opportunities for written or oral responses related to how the new material relates to their own sense of self.

Kagan and Kagan (1998) provide a teacher's guide to using the multiple intelligences (MI) in their classrooms, entitled *Multiple Intelligences: The Complete MI Book*. This resource suggests three MI visions: matching, stretching, and celebrating. The first vision describes methods teachers can use to match instructional strategies with their students' varied intelligences. The second vision encourages teachers to stretch each student's capacities in their nondominant as well as their dominant intelligence. The third vision suggests ways of celebrating and respecting one another's differences and unique patterns of learning.

Reflective, caring teachers are likely to believe that students must be active learners rather than passive recipients of knowledge. With this philosophy, reflective teachers attempt to plan varied and interesting lessons, which their students view as authentic, meaningful learning experiences.

In this chapter, we have discussed some general presentation skills that can engage the learner's interest in the lesson being taught. We have also focused on the strategies that teachers use to instruct a large group of students in the basic skills of a subject. Because the techniques of direct instruction are used frequently in classrooms, it is important for the beginning teacher to become proficient in planning and teaching lessons of this type.

Although some teachers may rely on direct instruction of the entire class as their major or only teaching strategy, reflective teachers are likely to want to be able to choose from a variety of strategies. The next three chapters offer the beginning teacher a glimpse at a range of teaching methods. From these, you may begin to build a repertoire of teaching strategies to expand your own teaching skills and increase your students' motivation for learning.

Reflective Actions for Your Professional Portfolio

Presentation Skills

Withitness: Observe Your Own Teaching

To perceive your own teaching performance, it is important to see yourself in action. Have someone videotape a lesson as you teach. As you observe the videotape of your own teaching, observe your presentation skills and rate your enthusiasm, clarity, smooth transitions, timing, variation, interaction, active learning, and closure. If possible, teach the lesson again, making improvements according to your perceptions.

Define Your Strengths and Put Them into Perspective

As you observe your videotape, allow yourself to see your own strengths and weaknesses. What does your body language say? How does your voice sound? Do you make false starts in your phrasing, such as "Here is an example ... I mean ... Look at this.... " Do you have eye contact with your students? What facial expressions and gestures are strong and attractive? Which do you want to work on?

Widen Your Perspective

Decide which are your strongest presentation skills at this point in time. Make a new videotape demonstrating these strengths to include in your professional portfolio.

Invite Feedback

Choose one of the presentation skills described in this chapter that you want to improve in your own teaching. For example, you may choose *enthusiasm* if you feel that your presentation style is too low key. For the next four occasions that you have to work with students, focus on the chosen skill and attempt to improve it. Ask the classroom teacher for feedback and work to refine and master this skill to your own satisfaction.

Redefine Your Best Presentation Skills

Videotape a lesson again to see if the presentation skill you worked on has improved. If it has improved, redo your videotape for the portfolio to take advantage of this growth. Plan to review and retape your presentation video frequently as your presentation skills develop and become even stronger. As with every part of your portfolio, improvements and new accomplishments need to be updated every year.

Create an Action Plan for Your Portfolio

Create a section of your portfolio on teaching strategies and presentation skills. Write a 1-page description of the videotape so that people looking at your portfolio will know what is on the videotape.

Predict the Possible Outcomes

Think honestly again about the strengths and weaknesses you observed in your videotaped presentation. What are the possible consequences that may occur when you are teaching a whole class? What is the next presentation skill you want to work on to improve?

References

Anderson, L. (1989a). Learners and learning. In M. Reynolds (Ed.), *Knowledge base for the beginning teacher* (pp. 85–89). Elmsford, NY: Pergamon.

Anderson, L. (1989b). Classroom instruction. In M. Reynolds (Ed.), *Knowledge base for the beginning teacher* (pp. 101–115). Elmsford, NY: Pergamon.

Ausubel, D. P. (1960). The use of advance organizers in the learning and retention of meaningful verbal material. *Journal of Educational Psychology, 51*, 267–272.

Brophy, J., & Good, T. (1986). Teacher behavior and student achievement. In M. Wittrock (Ed.), *Handbook of research on teaching* (3rd ed., pp. 328–375). New York: Macmillan.

Gagné, E. (1985). *The cognitive psychology of school learning.* Boston: Little, Brown.

Gardner, H. (1993). *Multiple intelligences: The theory in practice.* New York: Basic Books.

Glasser, W. (1986). *Control theory in the classroom.* New York: Harper & Row.

Good, T., & Brophy, J. (1987). *Looking in classrooms* (4th ed.). New York: Harper & Row.

Jones, F. (1987). *Positive classroom discipline.* New York: McGraw-Hill.

Kagan, S., & Kagan, M. (1998). *Multiple intelligences: The complete MI book.* San Clemente, CA: Kagan Cooperative Learning.

Kounin, J. (1977). *Discipline and group management in classrooms.* New York: Robert E. Kreiger.

Maslow, A. (1954). *Motivation and personality.* New York: Harper & Row.

Newman, F., & Wehlage, G. (1993). Five standards of authentic instruction. *Educational Leadership, 50*(7), 8–12.

Rimm, S. (1986). *Underachievement syndrome: Causes and cures.* Watertown, WI: Apple.

8

Discussion and Questioning Strategies

W hen students become actively and enthusiastically interested in thinking about and discussing an idea, they are experiencing cognitive engagement, a powerful new concept for teachers to aim for when they select teaching strategies for their classrooms.

Cognitive engagement results in the opposite of a passive class-room environment in which students attend listlessly to the lessons and carry out their seatwork and homework with limited effort or interest. When students are fully engaged in reading, listening, discussion, or creation, the classroom climate is likely to be lively and stimulating. When teachers structure classroom discussions to engage their students fully in substantive, meaningful, and highly interactive exchanges of information and ideas, authentic learning is likely to occur, even without the use of hands-on manipulatives.

Can you recall a classroom learning experience so powerful that you have almost total recall of it many years later? When you recall the event, do you feel as if you are reliving it because the memory is still so vividly etched in your mind? Do you think of this event as life changing? Perhaps it altered the way you think about an issue or caused you to change your career goal or provoked you into making a lifestyle change. Bloom (1981) calls these relatively rare classroom events "peak experiences."

For many students, peak learning experiences occur during especially stimulating classroom discussions in which all members of the classroom community are expressing ideas, opinions, and points of view. Students experience these discussions as authentic, substantive, and valuable. Teachers also have a sense of exhilaration and pride when they are able to create the environment and structure needed for such powerful exchanges. In this chapter, we examine some of the strategies you can use to stimulate and guide substantive and satisfying classroom discussions.

Asking Questions That Stimulate Higher Level Thinking

Imagine you are observing a classroom discussion after the students have read a biography of Dr. Martin Luther King, Jr. The teacher asks the following questions:

When and where was Dr. King born?

Who were the other members of his family?

How did King's father and mother earn a living?

What career did Dr. King choose?

What does the term *ghetto* mean?

What does *prejudice* mean?

What did Dr. King accomplish that earned him the Nobel Peace Prize?

As you watch and listen to this discussion, you might reflect on the way you would lead it and the questions you would like to ask the students. Perhaps you believe that there are other, very different types of questions that the teacher could use to stimulate more higher level thinking and engage the students in a discussion that connects what they have read to their own lives.

Many reflective teachers use Bloom's taxonomy (Bloom, Engelhart, Furst, Hill, & Krathwohl, 1956) to think of discussion questions that promote the use of higher level thinking processes. Discussion questions can be readily planned at every level of the taxonomy, just as other learning experiences are planned. The term *higher level* refers to the top four levels of the hierarchy:

Higher Level Thinking Processes
> Evaluation
>
> Synthesis
>
> Analysis
>
> Application

Lower Level Thinking Processes
> Comprehension
>
> Knowledge

In the previous example, the teacher has asked only lower level (knowledge and comprehension) questions. But you can plan your discussions to highlight the thinking processes of application, analysis, synthesis, and evaluation. Although this system can be used at any grade level and with any topic, the following examples are taken from the discussion of Dr. King's biography.

Knowledge Level.   At this level, the learners are asked to recall specific bits of information, such as terminology, facts, and details:

> When and where was King born?
>
> Who were the other members of his family?
>
> What were the jobs King's father did to earn a living?
>
> What jobs did his mother do?
>
> What career did Dr. King choose?

Comprehension Level.   At this level, the learners are asked to summarize and describe the main ideas of the subject matter in their own words:

> What does the term *ghetto* mean?
>
> What does *prejudice* mean?
>
> How did the church affect his life?
>
> What did Dr. King accomplish that earned him the Nobel Peace Prize?

While the teacher in the previous example stopped here, a reflective teacher is likely to use those questions only as a beginning to establish the basic facts and ideas so that the class can then begin to engage in a spirited discussion of how Dr. King's life and accomplishments have affected their own lives.

Application Level.   At this level, learners are asked to apply what they have learned to their own lives or to other situations:

Are there ghettos in this community? What are they and who is affected by them?

Give an example of prejudice that has affected you.

If Dr. King were alive today, what do you think he would be most concerned about? What do you think he would do about it?

Analysis Level.   At this level, the learners are asked to describe patterns, cause-and-effect relationships, comparisons, and contrasts:

How did Rosa Parks's decision to sit in the front of the bus change King's life? How did her decision change history?

In what ways was Dr. King a minister, a politician, and a teacher?

If Dr. King had never been born, how would your life be different today?

Synthesis Level.   At this level, the learners are asked to contribute a new and original idea on the topic:

Complete this phrase: I have a dream that one day. . . .

If there were suddenly a strong new prejudice against people that look just like you, what would you do about it?

How can we, as a class, put some of Dr. King's dreams into action?

Evaluation Level.   At this level, the learners are asked to express their own opinions or make judgments about some aspect of the topic:

What do you believe was Dr. King's greatest contribution? Why?

Which promotes greater social change: nonviolence or violence? Give a rationale or example to defend your answer.

What social problem do you most want to change in your life? Why?

Some teachers find that Bloom's taxonomy is a useful and comprehensive guide for planning classroom discussion questions as well as other classroom activities. Others find that the taxonomy is more complex than they desire and that it is difficult to discriminate among some of the levels, such as comprehension and analysis or application and synthesis. Other systems of classifying thinking processes are available. Doyle (1986) proposes that teachers plan classroom tasks in four categories that are readily applicable to classroom discussions: (1) memory tasks, (2) procedural or routine tasks, (3) comprehension tasks, and (4) opinion tasks.

Classroom questions and discussion starters can be created to fit these four task levels, as follows:

Memory Questions.   Learners are asked to reproduce information they have read or heard before:

When and where was Dr. King born?

Who were the other members of his family?

Procedural or Routine Questions.   Learners are asked to supply simple answers with only one correct response:

What jobs did King's father and mother do to earn a living?

What career did Dr. King choose?

Comprehension Questions.   Learners are asked to consider known data and apply it to a new and unfamiliar context:

What does the term *ghetto* mean? What ghettos exist in our town?

What does *prejudice* mean? How is prejudice manifested today?

How did the church affect Dr. King's life?

What did Dr. King accomplish that earned him the Nobel Peace Prize?

How did Rosa Parks's decision to sit in the front of the bus change King's life? How did her decision change history?

In what ways was Dr. King a minister, a politician, a teacher?

Opinion Questions.   Learners are asked to express their own point of view on an issue, with no correct answer expected:

Are there ghettos in this community? What are they and who is affected by them?

Give an example of prejudice that has affected you.

If Dr. King were alive today, what do you think he would be most concerned about? What do you think he would do about it?

Complete this phrase: I have a dream that one day. . . .

If there were suddenly a strong new prejudice against people who look just like you, what would you do about it?

What do you believe was Dr. King's greatest contribution?

What can we, as a class, do to carry out some of Dr. King's dream?

Which promotes more social change: nonviolence or violence? Give a rationale or example to defend your answer.

What social problem do you most want to change in your life? Why?

You will notice that the questions in Doyle's four categories are very similar to those listed in the taxonomy's six levels. Questions at the comprehension and analysis levels are both contained in Doyle's comprehension category, and questions at the application, synthesis, and evaluation levels are contained in the opinion category. Both of these systems offer teachers a comprehensive framework for planning a range of thought-provoking questions. You may choose to write out the questions you ask ahead of time or you may just remind yourself as you participate in a discussion that you need to include questions from the higher level thinking categories.

Strategies for Authentic Discussions

Some classrooms are dominated by mundane question-and-answer periods rather than true discussion. Some teachers may simply read aloud a list of questions from the teachers' manual of the textbook and call on students to recite the answers. As you probably recall from your own school experiences, when this type of "discussion" occurs, many students disengage entirely. They read ahead, doodle, or do homework surreptitiously. They seldom listen to their classmates' responses and when it is their turn to recite, they frequently cannot find their place in the list of questions.

Reflective teachers value the process of considering alternatives and debating opinions and ideas. That is how reflective teachers approach the world themselves, and they are likely to want to stimulate the same types of behavior among their students.

Authentic learning experiences depend heavily on the promotion of high-quality and actively engaged thinking. Teachers who are committed to creating authentic learning for their students do so by planning discussions that stimulate *higher level thinking processes, problem-solving skills, critical thinking,* and *creative thinking.* They also acknowledge the *multiple intelligences* of their students.

These terms and concepts can be confusing and overwhelming for the beginning teacher, who may think it is necessary to establish separate programs for each of them. That is not the case, however. It is possible to plan classroom discussions and other experiences that promote higher-level thinking, problem-solving skills, and critical and creative thinking and draw from all of the multiple intelligences at the same time. One question may pose a problem; another may call for a creative response; a third may be analytical; and a fourth may ask students to evaluate a situation and make a critical judgment. The best (which is to say, the most highly engaging) classroom discussions do all of these in a spontaneous, nonregimented way.

The following sections describe various thinking processes along with alternatives for planning classroom discussions to promote these processes. As you read these sections, reflect on the similarities and differences; look for patterns and sequences; and consider how you would use, modify, and adapt these systems in your classroom.

Although these processes can be applied to both academic and nonacademic areas of the curriculum, we will illustrate how classroom discussions are created and managed, using the topic of racial discrimination as a common theme. In this example, the operational goal is to promote understanding of how racial discrimination affects the lives of human beings and to generate a sense of respect for individuals who differ from oneself.

Problem-Solving Discussions

Much is written about the need for developing students' problem-solving and decision-making abilities. This can be done by presenting students with a complex problem and providing adequate scaffolding support for them to learn how to solve problems. Although some solutions require paper and pencil or a hands-on experimental approach, classroom discussion can solve other problems.

To create productive problem-solving discussions, the teacher must understand the processes involved in problem solving and then structure the questions to guide students through that process. A problem is said to exist when "one has a goal and has not yet identified a means for reaching that goal. The problem may be wanting to answer a question, to prove a theorem, to be accepted or to get a job" (Gagné, 1985, p. 138).

According to cognitive psychologists, the framework for solving a problem consists of identifying a goal, a starting place, and all possible solution paths from the starting place to the goal. Some individuals are efficient and productive problem solvers; others are not. An excellent classroom goal for the beginning teacher is to help students become more efficient and more productive problem solvers.

Nonproductive problem solvers are likely to have difficulty identifying or defining the problem. They may simply feel that a puzzling situation exists, but they may not be aware of the real nature of the problem. Students who are poor problem solvers need experience in facing puzzling situations and defining problems. They also need experience in identifying and selecting worthwhile goals.

When a problem has been defined and a goal established, it is still possible to be either efficient or inefficient in reaching the goal. Efficiency in problem solving can be increased when students learn how to identify alternative strategies to reach a chosen goal and recognize which ones are likely to provide the best and quickest routes to success. This can be done by helping students visualize the probable effects of each alternative and applying criteria to help them choose the most valuable means of solving the problem they have defined.

As in the teaching of higher level thinking processes, several useful systems are available to teachers who want to teach students to become better problem-solvers. Osborne (1963) proposed the technique known as *brainstorming*, which includes four basic steps:

1. Define the problem.
2. Generate, without criticism or evaluation, as many solutions as possible.
3. Decide on criteria for judging the solutions generated.
4. Use these criteria to select the best possible solution.

Brainstorming is an excellent way to generate classroom discussion about a puzzling issue. Rather than formulating a series of questions, the teacher supplies a dilemma or puzzle, teaches the students the steps involved in brainstorming, and then leads them through the process itself.

In discussing the life of Martin Luther King, and helping students to understand the effects of racial discrimination, the teacher might use a portion of the classroom discussion to brainstorm answers to one of the most perplexing questions. For example, the teacher might choose to use brainstorming to expand discussion of the following question:

If Dr. King were alive today, what do you think he would be most concerned about? What do you think he would do about it?

The techniques of brainstorming call for the teacher to pose the question or problem in such a way that it engages students' interest and motivates them to take it seriously. Because students may not be proficient at discussion of this sort, it is frequently necessary for the teacher to give additional cues and suggestions as a scaffold. In this instance, the teacher might need to pose the original question and then follow it up with prompts such as these:

What do you think he'd be concerned about in our community?

What has been in the news lately that might alarm him?

Who are the people in the world who are presently in need?

What about threats to our environment?

Open-ended questions such as these will generate many more responses than if they were not used. After recording all of the student responses on the chalkboard, the teacher leads the students through a process of selecting the most important items for further consideration. This may be done by a vote or a general consensus. When the list has been narrowed to several very important issues, the teacher must then lead the students through the process of establishing criteria for judging the items.

Because the question is related to Martin Luther King, Jr.'s values, one possible criterion is to judge whether King showed concern for the issue in his lifetime. Another criterion might be the number of people who are threatened or hurt by the problem. After judging the items by these criteria, the class makes a judgment about which items would most concern King. Then the process of brainstorming begins again, but this time the class is considering what King would be likely to do to help solve the problem. Generating responses to the first question—"If Dr. King were alive today, what would he be most concerned about?"—will help students understand the many aspects of racial discrimination that exist today. By selecting one of these as the main concern and generating responses to the question "What do you think he would do about it?" the students will reflect on their own responsibilities to other human beings and on ways to increase tolerance and caring in their own community.

To moderate a brainstorming discussion, the teacher faithfully records every response generated by the students, no matter how trivial or impossible it sounds. The teacher then leads students through the process of eliminating the least important items and finally works through a process of establishing criteria to use in evaluating the best possible solutions.

Brainstorming alone does not solve problems. It merely trains students in thinking productively about problems and in considering many alternative solutions. In some classrooms, teachers may wish to extend the hypothetical discussion of possible solutions to an actual attempt to solve a problem or at least contribute to a solution.

Group Investigations

Occasionally, a crisis or unusual event will excite students' interest and concern. When the topic is appropriate, and especially if it relates to the curriculum for that grade level, teachers allow students to participate in an investigation of the puzzling event to learn as much as they can about the subject and, in the process, learn research and communication skills. Often teachers create puzzling situations or present unusual stimuli as a means of causing students to become curious and learn how to inquire and investigate to gather information that leads to accurate assessments and judgments.

Perhaps there is a change in local government or a national election that students want to know more about. Perhaps a change occurs in the way their own school is managed, or a community event that affects their lives unfolds around them. The first hint of student interest may occur in a classroom discussion. To the extent that reflective teachers are sensitive to their students' concerns, they may wish to allow students time to talk about the event.

The first discussion of the event may simply be time to air students' early opinions and express their feelings about the event. If the teacher decides that the event is a worthwhile issue, the class may be encouraged to read about it, ask questions, or interview other members of the community and bring back their findings for more expanded discussions. These, in turn, may lead students to form small investigative groups that attempt to discover as much as they can about the event and even suggest solutions to the problems or issues under discussion.

The teacher's role in this type of investigative discussion is to encourage students to find out more about the subject and to allow them opportunities to express their opinions and share their findings. The discussion may continue for a few days or a few weeks, depending on the seriousness of the event and its impact on the students' lives. Under the guidance of a caring, reflective teacher, this type of discussion is authentic learning at its very best.

When teachers want to stimulate curiosity and discussion, they may present a social dilemma or demonstrate a strange event. For example, the teacher may drop a number of different fruits and vegetables into a large, clear bowl of water, asking students to predict and observe which will sink and which will float. Students are encouraged to ask the teacher questions and to formulate hypotheses about floating and sinking objects. As the discussion progresses, the large group discussion may be adjourned to allow small groups to make investigations of their own, reaching their own conclusions. After small group investigations are completed, class members reconvene to share their hypotheses, demonstrate their investigations, and present their conclusions.

Discussions That Promote Critical Thinking

The term *critical thinking* is not a separate and distinct concept that is different from higher level thinking processes and problem solving. It overlaps both of them. It is presented here in a separate section because during the past few years, it has become a field of study with its own research base and suggested classroom processes.

The field of study known as *critical thinking* grew out of the philosophical study of logic, which was a staple in the secondary curriculum in the 20th century. The principles of logical thinking were meant to train people to think about a single hypothesis deductively to arrive at a rational conclusion. But in the late 1960s, deBono (1967) observed that although logical thinkers were prepared to deal with a single issue in depth, they were not prepared to deal with unexpected evidence or ideas.

Using the analogy of digging for treasure, deBono (1967) suggested that in thinking about a hypothesis, a logical thinker might dig a deeper and bigger hole, but if the hole is not in the right place, then no amount of digging would improve the solution. In contrast, deBono believed that a critical thinker would be more flexible than a logical thinker, and after considering a problem or issue, the critical thinker would be able to select from a toolbox of thinking skills that allows the individual to clarify where to dig, select from alternative digging methods, use a variety of procedures to analyze the contents of the hole, and judge the worth of what is excavated.

Critical thinking, then, is partially defined as a complex set of thinking skills and processes that are believed to lead to fair and useful judgments. Lipman (1988) points out the strong association between the words *criteria* and *critical thinking*. Through the use of problem-solving discussions, students learn the technique of brainstorming and applying criteria to select the best solution.

But critical thinking is a much more multifaceted concept than problem solving. Critical thinking involves much more than simply training students to use a set of strategies or procedures. It also involves establishing some affective goals for students to support them in becoming more independent and open minded. Paul (1988), director of the Center of Critical Thinking at Sonoma State University in Rohnert Park, California, proposes that some of the affective attributes of critical thinking include independence, avoidance of egocentricity and stereotyping, and suspending judgment until appropriate evidence has been gathered.

Paul (1988) recommends that school curricula should be designed to teach students cognitive strategies such as observation, focusing on a question, distinguishing facts from opinions, distinguishing relevant from irrelevant information, judging credibility of sources, recognizing contradictions, making inferences, and drawing conclusions. Because almost every specialist in critical thinking proposes a slightly different set of thinking processes and skills that comprise critical thinking, reflective teachers need to judge for themselves which of the strategies to stress in their own classrooms.

Raths, Wasserman, Jonas, and Rothstein (1986) describe a set of thinking operations that they believe comprise critical thinking, and then provide a wealth of practical classroom applications at both the elementary and secondary levels. The operations they emphasize are comparing, summarizing, observing, classifying, interpreting, criticizing, looking for assumptions, imagining, collecting and organizing data, applying facts and principles in new situations, and decision making.

To systematically train students to become better thinkers, Raths et al. (1986) suggest that teachers select one thinking operation at a time and tell the class that they will be focusing on improving this thinking skill. The teacher then proposes a discussion topic, listens attentively to students' responses, and records them if appropriate. In the following sections, some of their specific suggestions are paraphrased.

Discussions That Improve Observation Skills

Whenever possible in your curriculum, bring in photos or objects related to the subject you are studying. Invite students to read their stories, essays, or poems aloud for other students to listen to and respond. You may even be able to stage an event to elicit student observation skills. For example, as you study the concept of community, ask some students to role play a disagreement, then ask them to describe what they observed, using as many details as they can. Call on as many students as possible and encourage each of them to make his or her own response to the situation. If they seem to be making impetuous or repetitive observations, guide their thinking with questions that ask them to explain or support their observations.

Show your students that they can observe with all five senses, not just sight. As you study nutrition, for example, allow students to taste a variety of foods and describe their taste observations. During a study of sound waves, provide a variety of different sounds and ask students to identify the objects they have heard. The more students use their five senses and discuss what they observe, the likelier they are to develop accurate, detailed schemata for the subject matter they are studying.

Discussions That Enhance Comparing Skills

In classroom discussions, compare two or more objects, stories, characters, or events by asking students first to articulate ways in which the two subjects are the same. Take as many responses as possible. Then ask students to tell how the two are different. This type of discussion can occur in any subject area. You may ask them to compare fractions with percentages in math; George Washington and Abraham Lincoln in history; Somalia and the United States in geography; electric- and gasoline-powered engines in science; or compare the wording and effects of two different classroom rules in a classroom meeting.

Discussions That Guide Classification Skills

Introduce a collection of words or, for young children, a set of manipulative materials appropriate to their grade level. For example, you may use a collection of buttons, small toys, macaroni shapes, or shells. When possible, conduct this type of discussion using cooperative groups. Ask each group to examine the collection, look for distinguishing attributes, and create a system for classifying the objects into groups. During follow-up discussions, a spokesperson for each group can describe the attributes they observed and present a rationale for the classification system they used.

Older children can classify the words on their spelling lists, books or stories they have read, foods, games, clothing, famous people, or television programs. The best results occur when the teacher has no preestablished criteria or notion of right or wrong classification systems. As children discuss the characteristics of the shells or television programs they are classifying, they may discover some of the same attributes that adults have already described or they may discover a completely original rationale on which to base their categories. The object of the discussion is not to get the most "right" answers, but to participate in the open-ended process of sharing their observations and making critical judgments they can defend with evidence.

Discussions That Identify Assumptions

Use advertisements for products your students want to buy as a means of stimulating a discussion to identify assumptions people make. Show a newspaper ad for a product and ask students to describe what they believe the product will be like based on the advertisement alone. Then discuss the actual product and compare the students' prior assumptions with the real item.

Talk about assumptions human beings make about each other. Ask students to examine the meaning of clothing fads in their lives. Whenever a subject arises that illustrates the effects of making decisions based on assumptions, take the time to discuss these events with your class. For example, ask students to discuss what assumptions are being made when they hear someone say, "He's wrong," or "She's the smartest girl in the class."

Socratic Dialogues

One form of discussion that reveals individual assumptions to the speaker and the listeners at the same time is the technique known as *Socratic dialogue* in which the teacher probes to stimulate more in-depth thinking among students. Teachers who use this method believe that individuals have many legitimate differences in opinion and values. They want to encourage their students to listen to each other to learn different points of view.

To conduct a Socratic dialogue, the teacher presents an interesting issue to the class and asks an individual to state an opinion on the case. With each participant, the teacher probes by asking the student to identify the assumptions and values that led to this opinion. Further questions may be posed to the same student to encourage clarification of the consequences of the students' opinion or the relative importance it has in the students' priorities.

This type of exchange between the teacher and one student may take several minutes and from 3 to 10 questions. While the teacher conducts the discussion with one student, the others are expected to listen carefully, comparing what they believe to what is being said by their classmate. Another student with a different opinion is likely to be the next subject of the Socratic dialogue. When the teacher believes that the most important issues have been raised by the dialogues, then a general class discussion can be used to express how opinions may have been changed by listening or participating in the Socratic dialogues.

Discussions That Enhance Creative Thinking

Can individuals learn to be creative? Perhaps the more important question is, do individuals learn to be uncreative? A century ago, William James (1890) stated his belief that education trains students to become "old fogies" in the early grades by training them to adopt habits of convergent, conformist thinking.

Divergent thinking is the opposite of convergent thinking in that it deviates from common understanding and accepted patterns. Guilford (1967) contributed a definition of divergent thinking that is still well accepted and has become the basis for E. Paul Torrance's (1966–1984) well-known tests for creativity. Guilford describes (and Torrance's test measures) four attributes of divergent thinking: *fluency, flexibility, originality,* and *elaboration.* In other words, a divergent thinker is one who generates many ideas (fluency), is able to break with conformist or set ideas (flexibility), suggests ideas that are new in the present context (originality), and contributes details that extend or support the idea beyond a single thought (elaboration).

Classroom discussions can be designed to help students develop these four attributes of creativity. In a technique similar to brainstorming, the teacher can ask students to generate many responses to a single question as a means of helping them to become more fluent in their thinking. For example, given our topic of King's "I Have a Dream" speech, the teacher may begin the process with the unfinished sentence, "I have a dream that someday. . . ."

Students may be asked to write their own responses for several minutes before the actual discussion begins. This allows each student to work for fluency individually. Then the ideas on paper are shared, and other new ideas are created as a result of the discussion. To promote flexibility, the teacher may ask students to imagine making their dreams come true and suggest ways that they could do this, using flexible and original strategies rather than rigid and ordinary methods. Finally, to extend the students' elaborative thought, the teacher may select one dream and ask the entire class to focus on it and create a more detailed vision and a more in-depth plan to accomplish it.

Einstein and Infeld (1938) add a further dimension to our understanding of creative thinking:

> The formulation of a problem is often more essential than its solution, which may be merely a matter of mathematical or experimental skill. To raise new questions, new possibilities, to regard old problems from a new angle, requires creative imagination and marks real advance in science. (p. 92)

Problem solving, then, is related to creative thinking. It is readily apparent that the methods described for improving problem solving involve critical thinking and that both involve the use of higher level thinking processes. Whatever we call it, the goal of aiding students in developing better thinking skills is an integral part of any classroom discussion.

Just as we respect Einstein's ability to pose new problems, we should respect and develop our own and our students' capacity to ask questions and suggest new ways of solving age-old problems. Certainly, the teaching profession needs people with the capability of regarding old educational problems from a new angle. Often it is the newest and youngest members of a faculty who see things from a helpful new perspective and suggest new ways of dealing with difficult school issues.

Another dimension of creativity involves the production of something useful, interesting, or otherwise valued by at least a small segment of society. In synthesis, a creative thinker is one who poses new problems, raises new questions, and then suggests solutions that are characterized by fluency, flexibility, originality, and elaboration. The solutions result in a product unique for that individual in those circumstances.

Discussions That Encourage Imagination and Inventiveness

In the process of discussing almost any type of subject, teachers always have opportunities to ask students to consider "What if . . . ?" "Imagine living on an island with no electricity; what would your life be like? How would it be different than it is now?" "What could we do to make our school better?" "What would you do if you were the main character in the story? How would your actions change the ending of the book?" For many reflective teachers, these questions are as important as those that test student recall of information or understanding of the main idea. While it is seldom necessary to plan a discussion with the sole intent of stimulating children's imagination, it is a worthy goal to include these types of questions in any classroom discussion.

Another technique is to assign a group of students a certain task that requires them to discuss strategies and invent a method to carry it out. For example, give students a single dollar bill and ask them to discover how high a stack of one million dollar bills would be. Give them a few pieces of cloth and some string and ask them to make an effective parachute. Have each group work together to design one map of the school property. Such real-life and simulated tasks provide incentives for authentic discussions on substantive and meaningful topics.

Prewriting Discussions

Another method teachers may use is to focus on images, analogies, and metaphors in creative discussions. These are very effective discussions before students begin writing, encouraging students to use these word pictures in their writing as well. Gordon and Poze (1975) suggest that analogies allow us to make the strange familiar and the familiar strange. In discussions, teachers can present an unfamiliar idea or object and assist students in describing it using sensory images, or comparing it with another, more familiar concept. For example, when presented with a rusty old lawnmower engine, students may be led to describe it according to its size, shape, imaginary sounds, or uses. They can compare it to other, more familiar objects. The teacher may ask students what the machine reminds them of. This may generate responses such as "the machine is like my old shoes." Then, the teacher probes by asking the child to tell why the machine and the old shoes are alike. "Because they are both old and muddy." Another child may see the machine in a whole different context. "The machine is like a kangaroo because it has a lot of secret compartments." Discussions like this can begin to have a life of their own and can lead to fresh new ways to express one's ideas.

Do schools enhance or undermine the conditions and processes that encourage creativity? Do textbooks, curriculum guides, rules, regulations, and expectations support the development of creative thinking and the process needed to create a unique product? Caring and reflective teachers do. They work very hard to create stimulating classroom discussions that assist students in learning to become critical and creative thinkers.

Discussions That Address Multiple Intelligences

Thomas Armstrong (1994) was asked by a Wisconsin school district to create a format for teaching children to tell time, using all seven of the multiple intelligences described by Gardner (1983) in *Frames of Mind*. To create this set of learning experiences, he linked his instructional objective to "words, numbers or logic, pictures, music, the body, social interaction, and/or personal experience" (Armstrong, 1994, p. 26).

Armstrong told a story about a land of No Time and how confusing it was for people who lived there. The king and queen sent a group of explorers in quest of time that was rumored to exist beyond their horizons. The explorers met with a family named the O'Clocks, who had 12 children: one, two, three, . . . , twelve.

After telling the story, Armstrong engaged the students in verbal experiences of retelling and restating what they had learned. He asked questions that engaged students in logical and mathematical problem solving to figure out the relationships among the O'Clocks. He used visual aids such as clock faces for spatially talented learners and allowed bodily-kinesthetic learners to act out the times while musically oriented youngsters sang special rhyming songs for each hour:

> *My name's One O'clock*
> *I tell time*
> *Listen while I sing*
> *My timely little chime*
> *BONG!*
>
> *(Armstrong, 1994, p. 26)*

Everyone danced to the tune of Bill Haley's "Rock Around the Clock," and students wrote stories illustrated with clock faces showing different times. In a subsequent discussion, they read aloud and shared their pictures and stories.

As Armstrong (1994) plans classroom discussions, he asks himself the following questions to guide himself through the planning process:

Linguistic: How can I use the spoken or written word?

Logical-mathematical: How can I bring in numbers, calculations, logic, classifications, or critical thinking?

Visual/spatial: How can I use visual aids, visualization, color, art, metaphor, or visual organizers?

Musical: How can I bring in music or environmental sounds, or set key points in a rhythm or melody?

Bodily-kinesthetic: How can I involve the whole body, or hands-on experiences?

Interpersonal: How can I engage students in peer or cross-age sharing, cooperative learning, or large group simulation?

Intrapersonal: How can I evoke personal feelings or memories, or give students choices?
(p. 29)

Role of the Teacher in Leading Discussions

Discussions that promote the use of critical thinking can be exciting classroom events for both students and teachers, but beginning teachers may find it difficult to elicit responses from students who are not used to taking part in such activities. Raths et al. (1986) asks:

> "What if you ask a wonderful question and the pupils don't respond?"
> There is nothing quite so demoralizing for a teacher as a lack of response from students.
> "Now boys and girls, how do you think the sound got onto this tape?"
> No response. Interminable silence. Finally the teacher leaps in to break the tension and gives the answer. Everybody, including the teacher, visibly relaxes. Whew! Let's not try that again. (p. 183)

This example of a nondiscussion is more common than is desirable. Students in your classroom may not have been encouraged to think creatively and express their own ideas. Thus, they may be very reluctant to do so at first. They may believe that you expect one right answer as some of their teachers did in the past. Because they do not know the one right answer, they may prefer to remain quiet rather than embarrass themselves by giving a wrong answer. Your response to their silence will tell them a great deal. If you jump in with your own response, they may conclude that their own responses were not really wanted after all.

Scaffolding is a necessary component of teaching critical thinking and discussion strategies to students. Be explicit about what you expect from them in a discussion. Tell them that there are no wrong answers and that all opinions are valued. If they still hesitate, provide cues and prompts without providing answers. Simplify or rephrase the question so that they are able to answer it. If the question "How do you think the sound got on this tape?" gets no response, rephrase it. "What sounds do you hear on this tape?" "Can you imagine how those sounds were captured on a piece of plastic like this?" "Do you think machinery was used?" "What kinds of machines are able to copy sounds?" These supporting questions provide scaffolds for thinking and talking about unknown and unfamiliar ideas.

Another consideration in leading discussions is to *value* silence rather than fear it. Silence can indicate that students are truly engaged in reflection. Allowing a few moments of silence can result in much more creative and productive discussions. Students need time to process the question. They need time to bring forward the necessary schema to their working memories and to consider the question in light of what they already know about the topic. Some students need more time than others to see connections between new ideas and already stored information and to generate a response of their own.

Some teachers consciously use *wait time*, requiring a short period of silence after each significant question is asked. Students are taught to listen quietly, then think quietly for several seconds and not raise their hands to respond until the wait time has passed. Rowe (1974) found that when teachers used a wait time of 3 to 5 seconds, more students were able to generate a response to the question. Without a planned wait time, the same group of fast-thinking students is likely to dominate all discussions. With the wait time, even slower thinking students will have an opportunity to consider what it is they do believe before hearing the opinions of others.

Lyman (1989) recommends that teachers employ a system called *listen, think, pair, share* to improve both the quantity and the quality of discussion responses. This technique employs a structured wait time at two different points in the discussion. When a question is asked, wait time goes into effect while students jot down ideas and think about their responses. Students are then expected to discuss their ideas in pairs for a minute. Then a general discussion takes place. After each student makes a contribution, other members of the class are expected to employ a second wait time of 3 to 5 seconds to process what their classmate has said before they raise their hands to respond.

The quantity and quality of students' responses may be improved by introducing the questions early in the class period, followed by reading, a lecture, or another type of presentation and actual discussion of the questions themselves. This strategy follows the principle of using the question as an advance organizer. Giving students the question prior to presentation of new material alerts them to what to listen or read for and allows sufficient time for them to process the information they receive in terms of the question. When teachers use this technique, they rarely experience a silent response.

Another strategy that promotes highly interactive discussions involves the physical setup in the classroom. To facilitate critical and creative thinking, students must be able to hear and see one another during the discussion. Arranging the chairs in a circle, rectangle, U-shape, or semicircle will help ensure that each student feels like a contributing member of a group.

Meyers (1986) notes that a hospitable classroom environment is the most important factor in engaging students' attention and interest and promoting their creative responses during discussion:

> Much of the success in teaching critical thinking rests with the tone that teachers set in their classrooms. Students must be led gently into the active roles of discussing, dialoguing, and problem-solving. They will watch very carefully to see how respectfully teachers field comments and will quickly pick up nonverbal cues that show how open teachers really are to student questions and contributions. (p. 67)

Reflective teachers are critical and creative thinkers themselves. They welcome opportunities to model their own thinking strategies for their students and plan experiences that encourage the development of their students' higher level thinking processes. They are likely to make even the simplest discussion an exercise in problem solving, reasoning, logic, and creative and independent thinking. They examine the subjects taught in the curriculum in search of ways to allow their students to learn to think and communicate their ideas. They plan discussions involving the creation and testing of hypotheses in science. They promote thinking that avoids stereotypes and egocentricity in social studies. They teach their students to suspend judgment when they lack sufficient evidence in discussions of math problems. They promote flexible, original thinking in discussions of literature. Discussions in every part of the curriculum can be crafted in ways that teach individuals to think reflectively, critically, and creatively.

Reflective Actions for Your Professional Portfolio

Videotape and Reflection of Your Class Discussion

Withitness: Observe Other Discussion Leaders

Observe a classroom and record the amount of time spent on teacher talk and on authentic student discussions. What amount of time do you want to set aside each day for students to express their ideas in discussion?

Put Discussions into Perspective

Write about your own experiences as a participant in discussions. Do you enjoy contributing ideas? What type of support do you need from a teacher or discussion leader to encourage you to take a more active role? Write about your own experiences in leading discussions. Are you comfortable in the role of leader? Do you tend to ask good questions spontaneously? Do you need to prepare carefully and write questions ahead of time?

Widen Your Perspective

What type of discussion leader do you want to be? What do you need to do to improve your ability to be that kind of facilitator?

Invite Feedback

Plan and lead a discussion with a small group of students. Write the student outcomes you hope to achieve. Do you wish to emphasize students' critical thinking, creativity, or concept formation? Ask an experienced colleague or teacher to sit in on the discussion. Have someone videotape the discussion.

Redefine Your Discussion Leading Goals

In response to the feedback you received and your own assessment of the video-tape of the classroom discussion you planned and led, write a reflective critique, comparing the result to the outcomes you had hoped for.

As you watch the video, transcribe the questions you asked and categorize them according to Bloom's taxonomy. Keep a tally of the students you called on during the discussion. Were you equitable in calling on students of both genders? How did you encourage students who were reluctant to participate? If you were given an opportunity to repeat this discussion, what would you change?

Now, rewrite your statement describing the type of discussion leader you would like to be. Add the insights you gathered from this experience.

Create an Action Plan for an Engaging Discussion

Select a topic related to your unit plan (see Chapter 5). Create a set of questions and discussion starters related to your unit.

Predict the Possible Outcomes

What are the things that could go wrong when you lead a discussion? Think about it from the students' point of view. What will you do if they do not seem to understand the questions you ask? What will you do if some students sit quietly and seem hesitant to participate? What will you do if some students seem restless or bored? Write some special questions that you think will bring these three groups of students into your discussion.

Remember, some of the best feedback you can ask for is from the students themselves. Ask students to tell you what they enjoyed best about the discussion and what they did not understand. In a one-to-one situation, ask the quiet students to tell you why they did not feel like participating and what you could do to help them be more comfortable speaking in a group. Ask the bored or restless students what they needed or wanted to make the discussion more interesting or challenging.

Now, with all the valuable feedback you have received, try out your discussion with a small group of students and have it videotaped. If this video shows your strengths as a discussion leader and demonstrates growth in the areas you identified as needing attention, include it in your portfolio. Add a page to your portfolio describing this section of the videotape so that readers will know what to expect when they view it.

References

Armstrong, T. (1994). Multiple intelligences: Seven ways to approach curriculum. *Educational Leadership, 52*(3), 26–28.

Bloom, B. (1981). *All our children learning.* New York: McGraw-Hill.

Bloom, B., Engelhart, M., Furst, E., Hill, W., & Krathwohl, D. (1956). *Taxonomy of educational objectives: Cognitive domain.* New York: Longman.

deBono, E. (1967). *New think.* New York: Basic Books.

Doyle, W. (1986). Classroom organization and management. In M. Wittrock (Ed.), *Handbook of research on teaching* (3rd ed.). New York: Macmillan.

Einstein, A., & Infeld, L. (1938). *The evolution of physics.* New York: Simon and Schuster.

Gagné, E. (1985). *The cognitive psychology of school learning.* Boston: Little, Brown.

Gardner, H. (1983). *Frames of mind.* New York: Basic Books.

Gordon, W., & Poze, T. (1975). *Strange and familiar.* Cambridge, MA: Porpoise Books.

Guilford, J. (1967). *The nature of human intelligence.* New York: McGraw-Hill.

James, W. (1890). *Principles of psychology.* New York: H. Holt.

Lipman, M. (1988). Critical thinking—what can it be? *Educational Leadership, 46*(1), 38–43.

Lyman, F. (1989). Rechoreographing the middle-level minuet. *Early Adolescence Magazine, IV*(I), 22–24.

Meyers, C. (1986). *Teaching students to think critically.* San Francisco: Jossey-Bass.

Osborne, P. (1963). *Applied imagination.* New York: Scribner's.

Paul, R. (1988). *31 Principles of critical thinking.* Rohnert Park, CA: Center for Critical Thinking and Moral Critique.

Raths, L., Wasserman, S., Jonas, A., & Rothstein, A. (1986). *Teaching for thinking.* New York: Teachers College Press.

Rowe, M. (1974). Wait time and reward as instructional variables, their influence on language, logic and fate control: Part I. Wait time. *Journal of Research on Science Teaching, 11,* 81–94.

Torrance, E. (1966–1984). *Torrance tests of creative thinking.* Bensenville, IL: Scholastic Testing Service.

Teaching Strategies That Increase Authentic Learning

School experiences can be enjoyable for both teachers and students. One way to heighten the enjoyment is to use a variety of teaching strategies and activities. When learning experiences are varied, students are more likely to become actively engaged in the learning process. Their intrinsic motivation to learn is also likely to improve if the skill or knowledge they are learning is presented in a novel and unusual format. To promote the enjoyment of teaching and learning, many reflective teachers are continuously searching for new methods and strategies to motivate and engage their students in the learning process. Developing a repertoire of teaching strategies is also necessary because students' needs and learning styles are diverse. For this reason, teachers must be ready to modify lesson plans and present information in more than one way.

The purpose of this chapter is to introduce you to a repertoire of teaching strategies, and encourage you to plan engaging lessons and learning experiences for your students. As you consider each strategy, you will quickly recognize that the descriptions in this chapter are not sufficiently detailed for you to become proficient in using the new strategy. This book provides only an overview of the descriptions, illustrations, and examples you will need to employ these methods successfully. For strategies that you wish to implement in your classroom, you will need to use the reflective action of initiating an active search for more detailed descriptions of these strategies in books and journal articles or of observing experienced teachers.

As you read about or select a strategy to try in a laboratory or classroom, you will find that some of them work for you and others do not. You will need to reflect about what works for you and your students and why. You may need to combine, adapt, modify, and add your own unique strategies to the ones you read about or observe. Through this process of practice and reflection, you will discover, create, and refine your own unique teaching style.

Examples of Teaching Strategies in Action

Discovery Learning

In the 1960s and 1970s a phenomenon known as the *open classroom* bloomed, mushroomed, and then faded into obscurity. The underlying philosophy of the open classroom was that students would become more active and responsible for their own learning in an environment that allowed them to make choices and encouraged them to take initiative. To this end, the rows of desks in many classrooms were rearranged to provide more space for activity and learning centers. The curriculum of the open classroom was revised to allow students to choose from among many alternatives and schedule their own time to learn what they wanted to learn when they wanted to learn it (Silberman, 1973).

One of the teaching strategies emphasized in the open classroom was called *discovery learning*. The principle of discovery learning is that students learn best by doing rather than by hearing or reading about a concept. Teachers may still find this strategy an excellent addition to their repertoire. It can be used occasionally to provide real, rather than vicarious, experience in a classroom.

In employing discovery learning, the teacher's role is to gather and provide equipment and materials related to a concept that the students are to learn. Sufficient materials should be available so that every student or pair of students has immediate access to them. Materials that are unfamiliar, interesting, and stimulating are especially important to a successful discovery learning experience. After providing the materials, the teacher may ask a question or offer a challenge that causes students to discover the properties of the materials. Then, as the students begin to work with the materials, the teacher's role is to monitor and observe as the students discover the properties and relationships inherent in the materials, asking occasional questions or making suggestions that will guide the students in seeing the relationships and understanding the concepts. The period of manipulation and discovery is then followed by a discussion in which students verbalize what they have observed and learned from the experience (Hawkins, 1965).

A simple example at the primary level is the use of discovery learning to teach the concept of colors and their relationships to one another. Rather than telling students or demonstrating to them that blue and yellow make green, the strategy of discovery learning is to provide every student with a brush and two small puddles of blue and yellow paint on white paper and allow them to discover it for themselves. In this case, the opening question may simply be "What happens when you mix blue and yellow together?" When this relationship becomes apparent and students verbalize it, the teacher can then provide additional puddles of red and white paint and challenge students to "Create as many different colors as you can." Experiences can be designed to allow students to discover how and why some things float, what makes a light bulb light, how electricity travels in circuits, and the difference between solutions and mixtures.

Math relationships also can be discovered. Beans, buttons, coins, dice, straws, and toothpicks can be sorted according to size, shape, color, and other attributes. Objects can be weighed and measured and compared with one another. The concept of multiplication can be discovered when students make sets of objects in rows and columns. Many math curriculum projects involving discovery learning are being developed for schools because discovery is a part of the problem-solving process, currently a hot topic in education.

Inquiry Training

Closely linked to the discovery method is a strategy known as *inquiry training*. Teachers who believe that their students must learn how to ask questions and carry out other types of investigations to become active learners often plan lessons that stimulate their students' curiosity and then train them in how to ask productive questions and use critical thinking, observation skills, and variations of the scientific method to gather information, make informed estimates or predictions, and then design investigations to test their hypotheses.

As an example, a classroom teacher wanted to train her students to think like scientists do, using the skills of observation, inquiry, prediction, hypothesis testing, and experimental design to find out what they need to know. She grouped her students into pairs and distributed a clear plastic glass and five raisins to each dyad. She asked them to predict what would happen to the raisins if they were dropped into a glass of water. Most students correctly guessed that the raisins would sink to the bottom of the glass. The teacher then discussed with her students the need to keep an open mind and not jump to easy conclusions based on prior knowledge. She poured a carbonated lemon-lime beverage into the students' glasses and asked them to predict whether the raisins would sink or float. Each pair of students wrote down their prediction. The teacher generated a chart on the board showing the class predictions.

After recording the predictions, the teacher allowed the students to drop the raisins into their glasses. At first it appeared that the students who predicted that the raisins would sink were correct as the raisins fell to the bottom of the glasses, but as the students watched, several raisins began to rise to the top. In the next few minutes, the students observed a puzzling phenomenon. Raisins moved up and down in the glasses, each at its own pace.

At this stage in the lesson, the teacher encouraged the students to ask questions of her and of each other as they all tried to make sense out of what they were observing. The teacher answered their questions with "yes" and "no" answers, giving her students the responsibility of articulating the questions and gathering the information they needed to make meaning out of the situation. Soon they began to generate new investigations that would need to be undertaken to discover why some raisins moved up and down more quickly and why some settled to the bottom.

To stimulate your own curiosity and encourage you to use the reflective actions of gathering information, being creative, and being persistent in solving problems, we will not disclose the reasons for the raisins' movement. Try the experiment yourself and try to think like a scientist. If you have opportunities to learn like this yourself, you will be better able to provide your students with the encouragement and support they need without rushing to provide them with answers. You will allow them to take the time they need to inquire and experiment so that they can succeed, and fully experience the "aha!" moment, just as scientists do when their inquiries lead them to new understandings.

Role Playing

When problems or issues involving human relationships are part of the curriculum, teachers may choose to use role playing to help students explore and understand the whole range of human feelings that surround any issue. This strategy is frequently used to resolve personal problems or dilemmas, but it can also be employed to gain understanding about the feelings and values of groups outside of the classroom.

For example, to help students understand the depth of emotions experienced by immigrants coming to a new and unfamiliar country, the teacher may ask students to role play the interactions among family members who are separated or the dilemmas of the Vietnamese boat people or others who want to emigrate to the United States but are stopped by immigration quotas.

Successful and meaningful role playing has two major phases: the role playing itself and the subsequent discussion and evaluation period. In the first phase, the teacher's responsibility is to give students an overview of both phases of role playing, so that they know what to expect. The teacher then introduces and describes a problem or dilemma, identifies the roles to be taken, assigns the roles, and begins the action by setting the stage and describing the immediate problem the actors must confront.

Roles must be assigned carefully. Usually teachers select students who are involved in the problem to play the role. In an academic dilemma, the roles may be assigned to students who most need to expand their experience with and understanding of the issue. Students who are not assigned roles are expected to be careful observers.

To set up the role-playing situation, the teacher can arrange some chairs to suggest the setting of the event to be played out. During the role play itself, the actors are expected to get inside the problem and "live" it spontaneously, responding realistically to one another. The role play may not flow smoothly; actors may experience uncertainty and be at a loss for words just as they would in real life. The first time a role is played, the problem may not be solved at all. The action may simply establish the problem, which in later enactments can be probed and resolved.

To increase the effect of role playing, Leyser (1982) suggests that after playing a scene out once, the actors may exchange roles and play out the same scene so that they grow to understand the other characters' points of view. Actors may be allowed to select consultants to discuss and improve the roles they are playing.

In the second phase, the observers discuss the actions and words of the initial role players. The teacher helps the observers review what they have seen and heard, discuss the main events, and predict the consequences of actions taken by the role players. Following the initial discussion, the teacher will probably decide to have new class members replay the role to show an alternative way of handling the problem. The situation can be replayed a number of times if necessary. When a role-played situation generates a useful solution or suggests an effective way of handling a problem, the situation can be adapted and subsequent role plays can focus on communication skills that will enhance or improve the situation even further.

Role playing has many applications to both the cognitive and affective goals of the curriculum. Through role playing, students can experience history by researching the life of a public figure and taking the role in an historical interaction. Each student in the class, for example, can study the life of a U.S. president and be the president for a day. Frequently, teachers ask students to play the role of characters in books that they have read as a means of reporting their own reading and stimulating others in the class to read the book. Students can enact the feelings of slaves and slave traders, the roles of scientists as they are "doing" science, or the interaction between an author and editor as they try to perfect a piece of writing.

Students can learn new behaviors and social skills that may help them win greater peer acceptance and enhance their own self-esteem. Interpersonal conflicts that arise in the classroom can be role played as a means of helping students discover more productive and responsible ways of behaving. For example, when two students argue about taking turns with a toy in the kindergarten class, the teacher can ask the students to role play the situation in an effort to learn new ways of speaking to one another, asserting their own desires, and creating a plan for sharing the scarce resource. In a classroom, the teacher may notice that one student is isolated and treated like a scapegoat by others in the class. The dilemma can be role played with the role of the isolated student assigned to be played by some of the students who have been most critical and aggressive toward the student. Through this active, vicarious experience, students may learn to be more tolerant and accepting of one another.

Simulation

Student drivers drive simulated vehicles before they learn to drive a real car on the highway. Airplane simulators provide a realistic but safe way for student pilots to practice flying in which mistakes lead to realistic consequences without threatening lives. Simulations usually involve some type of role playing but also include other game-like features, such as a set of rules, time limits, tokens, or other objects that are gained or lost through the action of the simulation, and a way of recording the results of the players' decisions and actions. Simulations almost always focus on dilemmas in which the players must make choices, take actions, and then experience feedback in the form of consequences of their actions. The purpose of simulations is primarily to allow young people to experience tough, real-life problems and learn from the consequences in the safe, controlled environment of the classroom.

The role of the teacher during a simulation is to explain the conditions, the concepts to be covered, and expectations at the outset of the event. A practice session may be held to further familiarize participants with the rules and procedures that govern the simulation. After assigning roles or creating groups that will interact, the teacher moderates, keeps time, clarifies misconceptions, and provides feedback and consequences in response to the participants' actions. At the conclusion of the simulation, the teacher leads a discussion of what occurred and what was learned by asking students to summarize events and problems and to share their perceptions and insights with one another. At the end of the discussion, the teacher may compare the simulation to its real-life counterpart and ask students to think critically about what they would do in real life as a result of having taken part in the simulation.

An example of a simulation in economics involves the creation of small companies or stores in which students decide on a product, create the product, set up the store, price and sell the product, and keep records on the transactions. The purpose, of course, is to learn about the principles of supply and demand, as well as the practical skills of exchanging money and making change. Along with the primary goals of the simulation, there are secondary learning experiences. Students are also likely to increase their capacity for critical thinking and to learn about their own actions and decisions regarding competition, cooperation, commitment to a goal, and communication.

Students may simulate the writing of the U.S. Constitution by writing a classroom constitution. After studying various countries of the world, sixth-grade students may take part in a mock United Nations simulation in which students are delegates and face daily world problems presented to them by the teacher.

In language arts, students may establish a class newspaper to learn how news is gathered and printed in the real world. They may even establish a number of competitive newspapers to add another dimension of reality to the simulation. Students may simulate the writing, editing, and publishing processes as they write, print, and distribute their own original books.

Simulations can be used to introduce a unit or as the culminating activity of a unit. They may take a few minutes or the entire year. They may be continued from week to week but played for only a specified amount of time during each session. Some may take a full day or longer. Simulations are powerful learning experiences that can change the way students view themselves and the world.

Mastery Learning

Teaching strategies known as *mastery learning* derive from the philosophy that all students can learn if the task fits their aptitude and they have sufficient time to master the new skill or concept. The theoretical model for mastery learning was inspired by Carroll's (1963) observation that students with low aptitude for a particular subject could still learn that subject, but that it would take them more time to do so. He proposed that students have different *learning rates* rather than different ability levels.

Bloom (1974) created a practical system for instruction using mastery learning based on Carroll's (1963) theoretical model. Carroll observed that most schools are established on the assumption that learners vary in their ability to achieve. Bloom disagrees. Studies conducted under his guidance have shown that 95% of the students in our schools can achieve the educational objectives established for them, but because they learn at different rates, some students appear to be better or worse than others.

Bloom (1984) points to cases in which students are tutored to prove his point. In a controlled experiment, he demonstrated that "the average tutored student outperformed 98% of the students in the control class" (p. 5). He attributes this finding to the fact that a tutor is able to determine what each student knows in a given subject and is then able to plan an educational program that begins instruction at the student's level and proceeds at the student's own pace.

The basic structure of the mastery learning model, including adaptations known as *individually prescribed instruction* (IPI) and *continuous progress*, lends itself best to the learning of basic skills in sequentially structured subjects. Very specific behavioral objectives are written for each unit of study. Pretests are used to assess students' prior knowledge, which then determines their placement or starting level. Working individually, as students master each objective in the sequence of learning, they then proceed to the next one. Periodically, unit tests covering several objectives are given to check on the mastery and retention of a whole range of knowledge and skills.

The teacher's role in this process is quite different from teaching skills with a whole class approach. The teacher rarely instructs the entire class at one time. Instead, as students work independently, the teacher monitors their progress by walking around the classroom and responding to requests for assistance. This frees the teacher to work with small groups of students rather than devoting all of the time responding to individual needs.

The value of mastery learning is that it allows students to actively learn new material and skills on a continuous basis. Motivation to achieve also presumably increases because students are working at their own pace and have the prerequisite skills necessary for success. Also, because testing is done individually and they have opportunities to repeat what they did not learn, students should suffer less embarrassment when they make mistakes. The effective goal of mastery learning programs is to help students become independent, self-directed learners.

Contracts for Independent Learning

Because mastery learning is appropriate for use only in sequential subjects that require a great deal of independent practice, many teachers are searching for methods of promoting independence and self-directed learning in other subjects as well. An alternative to direct, whole class instruction is the use of independent or group academic learning contracts. A learning contract such as the one in Figure 9.1 is usually created by the teacher at the beginning of a unit of study. The contract specifies one list of required activities, such as reading a chapter in the textbook, finding a library resource and writing a summary of the topic, completing a fact sheet, and other necessary prerequisites for developing a knowledge base on the subject.

Figure 9.1   Independent learning contract.

Westward Expansion of the United States
Required Learning Activities

Date   **Approval**

_____   _____   Read Chapter 6 in the social studies textbook.

_____   _____   Write answers to the questions at the end of the unit.

_____   _____   Locate and read a book on the American West or Indians.

_____   _____   Write a 2–4 page summary of the book

_____   _____   Play the computer game "Oregon Trail" until you successfully reach the state of Oregon alive.

Alternative Learning Activities

_____   _____   Imagine that you are a member of a wagon train heading west. Write a series of letters back "home" describing your journey.

_____   _____   Write a play about a meeting between Indians and settlers. Find a cast for your play and present it to the class assembly.

_____   _____   Draw or paint a large picture of a scene that you imagine took place during the westward expansion.

_____   _____   Create a song or ballad about life in the west. Be prepared to play and sing it for the assembly.

_____   _____   Create a diorama or a model of a Plains Indian village.

_____   _____   Research the lives of the Plains Indians today. Be prepared to give a speech about the conditions in which they live now and how this is related to the westward expansion.

_____   _____   Create an alternative plan for a learning experience on this topic.

I, _____, agree to complete the required learning activities by the date_____. In addition, I select two to five alternative activities to pursue on my own. I will present my creative work to my classmates at our assembly on _____.

_____
      student signature

I have reviewed this contract and understand the work my child has agreed to do. I agree to support this effort.

_____
      teacher signature

_____
          parent signature

A second list of activities is offered as choices or alternatives for students to pursue. This list includes opportunities to do additional independent research or create plays, stories, songs, and artwork on the topic. When learning contracts are offered to develop independence, individuals usually select the activities they want to accomplish. A variation on this strategy would be to combine the concepts of cooperative groups and learning contracts and allow each group to sign a joint contract specifying the tasks and products they will complete.

Science investigations, social studies research projects, and creative language arts activities can be described in learning contracts. The primary advantage of this strategy is that it allows individuals at various ability levels to work on an appropriate amount and type of work during the unit of study. High-achieving students can select the maximum number of tasks and products, and lower achieving students can select fewer tasks. Theoretically, both types of students can actively learn and experience success during the same amount of time.

Group Rotations Using Learning Centers

Learning centers or stations are areas of the classroom where students can go to do independent or group work on a given subject or topic. Learning centers vary enormously in appearance, usage, and length of time for which they are set up. Teachers who use learning centers use them for a variety of purposes and with a variety of expectations.

Some centers may be informal and unstructured in their use. For example, a classroom may have a permanent science center containing a variety of science equipment and materials. Students may go to the center to do science experiments in their free time. The same classroom may have a permanent reading center furnished with a rug, comfortable chairs, and shelves or racks of books where students can go to read quietly.

Other centers are set up for a limited amount of time and have highly structured expectations. For example, to accompany the unit on settling the Western United States described in the learning contract, the teacher may have set up an area of the classroom as a research center. It would contain a computer, with the MECC computer program called "Oregon Trail" turned on and ready for students to use. It would also contain posters and maps of the Western United States and a variety of reading materials on the topic. When the unit is finished, the center can be redesigned; new learning materials replace the ones from the finished unit, and the center becomes the focus of a new unit of study.

In primary classrooms, learning centers are often an important adjunct to reading and language arts. Many teachers set up four or five learning centers or stations with different activities each week. Students in small groups travel from one station to another according to a specified schedule. For example, Ginny Bailey uses a weekly theme as the basis for her first-grade language arts program. Each week she sets up activities related to that theme in her five stations: art, math, writing, listening, and reading. To accompany her butterfly theme, students will find books on butterflies to read at the reading station, paper and directions for a writing project at the writing center, paint and brushes to create a picture at the art station, a prerecorded tape to listen to at the listening station, and a math game involving butterflies and caterpillars at the math station.

Ginny uses five centers—one for each day—and that means each group can visit each center once a week. A poster on the wall shows the schedule of groups and centers (see Figure 9.2).

In Ginny's classroom, students can go to their stations only after completing their daily work assignments. In her system, the stations extend the students' learning experiences on the weekly theme but are also used as an incentive system for students to complete their required work.

Teachers who work with students who have limited English proficiency are finding that rotations from one learning center to another give the students many rich opportunities to use the English language with their peers as well as with adults. In a kindergarten classroom at Hamilton School in Mid-City San Diego, Susan King recently completed her Cultural, Language, and Academic Development (CLAD) teaching credential. In her classroom, she wants to create a learning environment that enables her English language learners to take risks with English so that they develop oral fluency in their new language. In Case 9.1, you can read about how she changed her entire system of teaching within a few months when she became aware that her students were becoming less proficient and quieter under the conventional teacher-centered system she had been using.

Case 9.1 ⊃ Reflective Action

Establishing Learning Centers

Susan King, CLAD Kindergarten, Hamilton School, San Diego

Withitness

At the beginning of my first year as a kindergarten teacher, I organized my classroom for whole group instruction in reading and language arts. I used conventional methods in which my students all worked at the same task at the same time, with a great deal of direct instruction from me.

Define and Put the Problem into Perspective

Then I began to perceive that the room was too quiet. Students sat quietly, waiting passively for me to tell them what to do. There were very few opportunities for oral language development using this teacher-centered approach to teaching.

Figure 9.2   Learning station schedule.

Courtesy of Ginny Bailey.

Group	Monday	Tuesday	Wednesday	Thursday	Friday
Blue	Art	Math	Writing	Reading	Listening
Green	Math	Writing	Reading	Listening	Art
Red	Writing	Reading	Listening	Art	Math
Yellow	Reading	Listening	Art	Math	Writing
Orange	Listening	Art	Math	Writing	Reading

Widen the Perspective

One day after school, I was thinking about my classroom and I decided that I needed to take some risks and reorganize my entire classroom system to stimulate talking, problem solving, and cooperative learning.

Invite Feedback

Our district has designated mentor teachers who are willing to share the teaching strategies they employ with beginning teachers. I arranged to visit a mentor teacher who uses a rotation schedule for her kindergarten–first grade classroom and I learned more in that one day than I could imagine. I was able to see the physical arrangement of her classroom and watch her students travel from one learning center to another. I took pictures of the charts and schedules she used to direct traffic in her room. I also took pictures of the students working at the various centers she had established. From this visit, I was able to envision the changes that would need to be made in my classroom.

Since many of my students are English language learners, I also decided to sign up for some courses to get my Cultural, Language, Academic Development (CLAD) credential.

Redefine the Problem

The new knowledge I gained from these visits and courses caused me to become aware of the needs of the students in my class. I became aware of how important it was to include parent volunteers or peer tutors who are familiar with the primary or first language (L-1) of the English language learners in my program. In my classroom, these L-1 languages include Spanish and Laotian.

Create an Action Plan

I recruited Spanish- and Laotian-speaking parents and upper-grade students to assist me in my classroom. I also decided to use the resources of my own students who are bilingual. I began to design the materials I would need to get started. In January, I plunged into the whole new system. I set up four different learning stations in my classroom: journal writing, a reading basket, a structured activity center, and the guided reading group. Peer tutors supervised the structured activity center to help children with science, math, and social studies. In all the centers I encouraged my students to talk with each other, share ideas, help each other, and solve whatever problems were at hand. I instructed them to ask everyone in their group for help and then ask the peer tutor or group captain before coming to ask me for help. With this management system, I was free to work with the guided reading group without interruptions.

It took about 2 weeks for the children to be accustomed to the movement from one area to the next. It took even longer for them to become independent learners. At first they would stand still, waiting for me to come give them direct teaching or instruction about every little step. When I saw this response, of stillness and waiting to be spoon fed, I thought to myself, "What a disservice we are doing to children when we train them to be passive learners." I realized that the whole group teaching I had done for the first 5 months had caused this response. I had trained them to wait for my every word and not to think for themselves.

Predict Possible Outcomes

To be able to give my full attention to the students in the guided reading group, I had to find a way to organize the learning environment so that the other 25 students were busy and would not need to interrupt me. This felt like a real challenge to me because even though I had recruited parent volunteers, they did not come consistently. So, I went to my colleagues who teach upper grades and asked them to send me some helpers who would like to help in the kindergarten. The response was overwhelmingly positive. Just as my students needed peer tutors, the older children need this type of responsibility to enhance their own self-image.

A resource teacher who visited recently looked around to see the children working so independently. As he left, he told me, "I can't believe this is a kindergarten class. The children are so responsible—so in charge of their own learning."

Cooperative Learning Strategies

Cooperative groups are a welcome change of pace for many students. They enjoy the opportunity to interact with their peers for part of the school day. But teachers may be hesitant to try the strategy for fear that the students will play or talk about outside interests rather than work at the task assigned. Cooperative groups can degenerate to chaotic groups if they do not meet certain conditions.

Imagine that a teacher hears some general ideas about cooperative groups at a conference or reads the first few paragraphs of an article on the strategy. Thinking that it is an intriguing idea, the teacher may hurry back to the classroom, divide the class into several small groups, and tell them to study the Civil War together for a test that will be held next Friday. After a few moments of discussing what they have (or have not) read about the Civil War, the groups are likely to dissolve into chaos or, at best, evolve into groups who sit near one another and talk to one another as each person studies the text in isolation.

When the group has a poor understanding of the goals of the task, the results may be unproductive and frustrating. To prevent this, the teacher must clearly state the goals and expectations of each group task and provide a copy of them in writing so the group can refer to them from time to time. This includes assigning specific duties to each group member which, when combined, result in a smoothly functioning interaction.

Cooperative learning is designed to encourage students to help and support their peers in a group rather than compete against them. This purpose assumes that the perceived value of academic achievement increases when students are all working toward the same goal. Cooperative groups emphasize the notion of pride in one's "team" in much the same way that sports teams do.

Another major purpose of cooperative learning is to boost the achievement of students of all ability levels. The assumption is that when high-achieving students work with low-achieving students, they both benefit. Compared to tracking systems that separate the high achievers from the low achievers, cooperative groups are composed of students at all levels so that the low-achieving students can benefit from the modeling and interaction with their more capable peers. It is also believed that high-achieving students can learn to be more tolerant and understanding of individual differences through this type of experience than if they are separated from low achievers.

Still another point is that cooperative teams are believed to be more motivating for the majority of students because they have a greater opportunity to experience the joy of winning and success. In a competitive environment, the same few high-achieving students are likely to win over and over again. But, a classroom divided into cooperative teams, each with its own high- and low-achieving students, more evenly distributes the opportunity to succeed. To this end, the reward systems do not honor individuals, but instead depend on a group effort. As in a sports team, individual performances are encouraged because they benefit the whole team.

Johnson and Johnson (1984) provide this description of what cooperative learning is *not*:

> Cooperation is *not* having students sit side-by-side at the same table to talk with one another as they do their individual assignments.
>
> Cooperation is *not* having students do a task with instructions that whoever finishes first is to help the slower students.
>
> Cooperation is *not* assigning a report to a group of students wherein one student does all the work and the others put their names on the product, as well. (p. 8)

Slavin (1995) emphasizes the team concept in cooperative learning. For example, the teacher presents information to the entire class in the form of lectures, discussion, and/or readings. As a follow-up, students form four- or five-member heterogeneous teams to learn the new material or practice the new skills.

These learning teams are designed to encourage both individual accountability and group efforts at the same time. A baseline score is computed for each team by combining the data from individual pretests. Students then work together and assist each other in learning new material. At the conclusion of the study period, individual post-tests are given to determine how well each member of the group has learned the material. Students are not allowed to help one another on the tests, only during the practice sessions. The individual test scores are then combined to produce a team score. But the winning team is not necessarily the team with the highest combined score. The results that count are the *improvement scores,* computed by determining the difference between each individual's original baseline pretest score and the final post-test results and adding these individual improvement scores together to create a final group improvement score.

For example, students may be pretested on 20-word spelling lists. High-scoring students are grouped with lower scoring students to study and practice together, with the goal of having all students in the group earn improvement points for their team. One group's scores and points might look like this example:

Name	*Pretest Score*	*Post-Test Score*	*Difference = Improvement Points*
John	13	15	+2
Mary	17	14	–3
Jorge	12	19	+7
Carla	8	18	+10

The teacher may use the total score of 16 or calculate an average improvement score for this group, which is 16 divided by 4, for an average group improvement score of 4. This group's score can then be compared with other groups in the class and a competition among the study groups may be used to stimulate interest and motivation in working together to improve everyone's scores. If all groups do well and achieve impressive group improvement scores, then all groups can earn awards or extra privileges. Teachers can design award certificates or plan a menu of extra privileges to encourage students to work hard individually and in cooperation with each other.

Primary Curriculum Examples of Cooperative Learning

Tim Curbo, who teaches first-grade at Hawthorne School in San Francisco, describes in Figure 9.3 how he uses cooperative groups to encourage students to develop their language, problem-solving, and cooperation skills simultaneously.

Another primary example of a cooperative learning unit focuses on the theme of community. Beginning with a walking or bus tour of the commercial area, the entire group discusses the various elements that are needed for a successful community. If

Figure 9.3   A first-grade activity with cooperative groups, created by Tim Curbo, first-grade teacher, Hawthorne School, San Francisco, California.

At Hawthorne School, Monday through Thursday, students move to different classes for language arts. On Friday, they stay in their own classroom, so I use that day for cooperative group activities.

I divide the class into groups of four. Because I have many bilingual students in my class, I make sure each group has a combination of English-speaking and Spanish-speaking children.

In each group there are four different jobs or roles for children to take. I post the roles on the bulletin board. For example:

- Maria: Materials
- Jed: Reporter
- Carlos: Facilitator
- Ana: Writer

The materials person gets all the necessary materials for the task. The facilitator makes sure everyone is participating and solves any problems that arise. The writer keeps a written record of the activity. As I teach first grade, the writer may just draw illustrations, and as I circulate through the room, I record the observations of the other members of the groups. The reporter gives a report of what the group accomplished. Children get a different role each time we do cooperative group activities.

Before the first task we talk about the various responsibilities. I usually choose a simple task initially, such as a puzzle. All of the students work together to solve the puzzle. Then the writer may draw the finished puzzle, and the reporter describes the process the group used to solve the puzzle.

One of the first tasks of the group is to select a name. This is then posted on the board. The writer's report is posted next to the group's name. Other products can also be posted in this space.

From the beginning I turn questions and problems that arise back to the group. I encourage the facilitator to take leadership but to involve the others in trying to solve the problems. I tell them, "Four heads are better than one." I keep myself free to circulate, clarifying, extending the activity, and making encouraging remarks.

It's always noisy, and things are bumpy at first. Children aren't sure of their roles. There are personality clashes. We process or talk about all of these issues. Most issues are worked out with time. My students enjoy the spirit of cooperation that develops and the social interaction. Through repeated use of this strategy, it becomes evident that cooperation and problem-solving skills are prominent shared values in our classroom.

possible, some teachers extend the tour to pass by the houses of each person in the class. Given a map of the area, cooperative groups can be formed and given the initial assignment of depicting on the map the important sites they observed on the tour. Each person in the group can be given the job of locating and recording an equal number of sites on the map.

Later, the same cooperative groups can select one aspect of the community to study, such as the hospital, fire station, police station, city hall, library, churches, or the school itself. With the teacher's help, each group can invite speakers to come to the class to discuss their jobs and responsibilities to the community. Each group can also prepare a short skit (including all members of the group) that informs the rest of the class about the roles and responsibilities of the community helpers they studied.

Cooperative Learning of the Basic Skills

Cooperative learning can also be used to assist students in the mastery of basic skills such as computing the basic addition, subtraction, and multiplication facts. In a traditional classroom, teachers may prepare students for this assessment by providing them with daily worksheets for practicing and memorizing the math facts. In an effort to motivate students to improve their skills, conventional teachers may post charts for all to read that display the names of students who have reached the criteria and those who have not.

Although this type of competitive environment may please and motivate the high achievers, it is not likely to encourage the remainder of the class. To modify the process of learning math facts from a competitive to a cooperative experience, teachers could adapt the student team achievement division model to fit the needs of their classrooms.

Using a learning team approach, the teacher would begin by giving a pretest of 100 math facts to the entire class. By sorting the pretests into high, medium, and low scores, the teacher can divide the class into heterogeneous groups with equivalent ability in math facts. Each group would contain one of the top scorers, one of the lowest scorers, and two in the middle range.

How the teacher sets up the conditions and expectations for this cooperative learning experience is very important. The achievement goal and the behavioral expectations must be clearly explained at the outset. For example, the teacher may state that the groups are expected to practice math facts for a given time each day. Worksheets, flash cards, and other materials are provided, and the teams are free to choose the means they use to practice. The goal, in this instance, is to raise all scores from pretest levels as much as possible. A post-test will be given on a certain day, and each individual will receive an improvement score, which is the difference between the correct responses on the post-test and the correct responses on the pretest. The group improvement score will be computed by adding the individual improvement scores. This method of scoring encourages the group to devote extra energy to raising the scores of the lowest scorers because they have the most to gain. Top scorers, in fact, may not gain many points at all, because their pretests may already be near the total. Added incentives for this group may be devised, such as a certain number of points for a perfect paper.

The incentives to be awarded for success depend a great deal on the class itself. The teacher may choose to offer one reward for the group whose scores improve the most or reward each group, depending on their gains. For example, a single reward for the most improved group may be tangible, such as a certificate of success or temporary possession of a traveling math trophy. Less tangible incentives are also important to, say, third graders, such as the opportunity to be first in line for a week, go to the library together during a math class, or eat lunch with the teacher. To spread the incentives to all groups, the points that each group earns may be translated into an award such as 1 minute of free time per point or the opportunity to "buy" special opportunities and materials.

Once students become accustomed to helping their classmates in one subject area, they are likely to take considerable interest in assisting and supporting their members in doing well in other subjects as well. Similar groups could operate to improve spelling, vocabulary, the mechanics of writing, or other basic skills. The membership of each group would be different because students are likely to score differently on pretests for various subjects.

Cooperative Learning in Science

In many classrooms, the conventional approach to teaching science once centered on textbook reading, discussion, an occasional demonstration by the teacher, and written tests of understanding. But more recently, science curricula have been revised to include many more hands-on experiments and investigations. The current philosophy is that students need to learn how to *do* science rather than simply learn about it.

Hands-on science is an area that has a natural fit with cooperative group strategies. By participating in cooperative science investigations, students learn how scientists themselves interact to share observations, hypotheses, and methods. Although many teachers value these current science goals, they may be reluctant to try them because they are unsure of how to manage the high level of activity in the classroom when science experiments are happening. Cooperative groups can provide the support and structure needed to manage successful science investigation in the classroom.

When a topic or unit approach is taken for teaching science, each unit offers opportunities for cooperative learning. For example, different groups may study the topic of astronomy, with each studying one planet, creating models and charts of information about their planet, and reporting their findings to others.

Investigations into the properties of simple machines, magnets, electricity, and other topics in physics can be designed by establishing a challenge or a complex goal for groups to meet by a given date. Groups may be given a set of identical materials and told to create a product that has certain characteristics and can perform a specific function. For example, given a supply of toothpicks and glue, groups are challenged to construct a bridge that can hold a pound of weight without breaking. Given a raw egg and an assortment of materials, groups work together to create ways to protect their eggs when they are dropped from a high window onto the pavement below.

Science groups can be mixed and matched frequently during the year, offering students an opportunity to work cooperatively with most other members of their class. This strategy is likely to reinforce the principles of social science as well. For example, during the astronomy unit, the emphasis could be on learning how to come together as a group quickly, quietly, and efficiently when getting started on the day's project. During the bridge-building unit, the groups could practice encouraging everyone to participate, taking time to ask for opinions and suggestions from every member of the group before making an important decision. After completing each unit, the groups should participate in evaluating how well they worked together and how they demonstrated the interpersonal skill emphasized during that unit.

Literary Groups

Using conventional methods of teaching reading, three homogeneous reading groups based on ability may still be used at many grade levels. Each group reads stories, essays, poems, and plays collected in a basal reader geared to their reading ability. The teacher leads discussions of reading materials and assigns seatwork to be done while he or she works with other groups.

Many upper elementary teachers, however, prefer to use literary materials in their own format rather than as collections in basal readers or anthologies. They believe that students' motivation to read will improve if they are encouraged to choose and read whole books, novels, poetry collections, and plays. A variety of paperback books in sets of six to eight books apiece are needed to carry out this type of reading program.

At Our Lady of Mercy School in Chicago, sixth-grade teacher Roxanne Farwick-Owens has developed a system that allows choice, maximizes cooperative efforts, and holds individuals accountable. To maximize student motivation and enjoyment of reading, Roxanne believes students must be allowed to choose their reading materials. Each month she provides three or four reading selections, in the form of paperback books, to the class. Students are allowed to choose the book they want to read, and groups are formed according to interest rather than ability level. Roxanne may advise students about their selections and try to steer them toward appropriate selections, but in the end, she believes that they have the right to choose for themselves what they will read, especially because she has provided only books that have inherent value for sixth graders.

During initial group meetings, students decide for themselves how much to read at a time. They assign themselves due dates for each chapter. Periodically, each group meets with Roxanne to discuss what they are reading, but most discussions are held without her leadership. Usually, she holds the groups responsible for generating their own discussion on the book. To prepare for this discussion, all members are expected to list questions as they read. For example, each person in the group may be expected to contribute three "why" questions and two detail questions per session. Roxanne reviews the questions each day as a means of holding each individual accountable for reading the material and contributing to the group.

Another task is to plan a presentation about the books—using art, music, drama, and other media—to share with the rest of the class at the end of the month. This allows groups to introduce the books they have read to the other members of the class, who are then likely to choose them at a later date. One group made wooden puppets and a puppet stage to portray an event from Mark Twain's *Tom Sawyer*. After reading Judy Blume's *Superfudge*, a group created a radio commercial for the book complete with sound effects and background music. Familiar television interview shows are sometimes used as a format, as are music videos.

About once per quarter, two teams are formed to compete in a game show-type tournament. Questions about the books are separated into categories such as characters, plot, setting, authors, and miscellaneous. Each person is responsible for writing five questions and answers on index cards to prepare for the tournament. One student acts as emcee, while another keeps track of the points. The team with the most points wins the tournament.

Roxanne finds that this cooperative group structure increases her students' social skills, especially their ability to work with others and to find effective ways to handle disagreements. But the primary reason for the program is to help her students see that reading can be enjoyable and that instead of being a solitary pursuit, reading can have a social aspect. Roxanne believes many of her students may become lifelong readers from this one-year experience.

Peacemaking Groups

Some cooperative groups are formed for the social purpose of teaching students how to resolve conflicts, handle anger, and avoid violence in their lives. Many schools are taking an active role in training their students to incorporate conflict-management skills in their daily lives. Johnson and Johnson (1991) have created a series of learning experiences teachers can use for this purpose. Students are taught to recognize that conflict is inevitable, and that they can choose between entering into destructive or constructive conflicts. They learn how to recognize a constructive conflict through cooperative group experiences and simulations.

For example, a group of students may be told that they have just won an all-expense-paid field trip to the destination of their choice. Now comes the hard part. Where will the group choose to go? Pairs of students are formed to list their choices and create a rationale for them. Through negotiation, the group must resolve the dilemma and make a plan by consensus.

In other group sessions, students learn to identify how they personally react to conflicts and learn how to be assertive rather than aggressive or withdraw from arguments. For example, one session may be devoted to assisting students in dealing with insulting remarks and put-downs. In another they may deal with a simulated situation in which one student refuses to do her part in a cooperative group assignment. Cooperative group activities such as these are designed to encourage students to seek peaceful solutions in their school environment. Teachers who use these methods are also likely to believe they may be useful to their students as adults and may lead to future generations seeking more peaceful solutions in business, politics, or other issues in their families and communities.

Creating Well-Balanced Cooperative Groups

Assigning students to cooperative groups can be the most difficult part of the process for teachers. The philosophy of heterogeneous grouping is excellent in theory, but is sometimes difficult to achieve in a real-life classroom. A classroom is likely to have one or two superstars whose ability cannot be matched in some subject areas. Similarly, one or two students may have very unusual learning difficulties or behavior problems. For most types of learning situations, the teacher must simply make the best judgment about the combinations that are approximately equivalent in ability.

It is advisable to put non-task-oriented students into groups with highly task-oriented teammates so that peer pressure will work to keep them on task. This theory, however, does not always work out in the classroom. Angry or highly restless students may refuse to participate or otherwise prevent their team from succeeding. When this happens, the group itself should be encouraged to deal with the problem as a means of learning how to cope with and resolve such occurrences in real life.

In arranging the room during cooperative group activities, each group should have a comfortable space, and members should be able to face one another and have eye contact with every other member of the group. Separating the groups from one another is also necessary so they can each work undisturbed by the conversations and activities taking place in other groups.

Materials intended for cooperative groups may differ from those used in conventional teaching and learning situations. It is suggested that only one set of materials explaining the task and the expectations be distributed. This causes students in the group to work together from the very beginning. In some cases, each member of the group may receive different information from other members. This promotes interdependence because each member has something important to share with the others.

Interdependence can also be encouraged by the assignment of "complementary and interconnected roles" to group members. These roles will vary with the type of learning and task, but might include discussion leader, recorder of ideas, runner for information, researcher, encourager, and observer.

Tasks that result in the creation of products, rather than participation in a test or tournament, are more likely to succeed if the group is limited to the production of one product. If more than one product is allowed, students may simply work independently on their own products. Members of the group should also be asked to sign a statement saying that they participated in the development of the group's product.

To ensure individual accountability, students must know that they will all be held responsible for learning and presenting what they learned. During the final presentations, the teacher may ask any member of the group to answer a question, describe an aspect of the group's final product, or present a rationale for a group decision.

Effects of Cooperative Learning

In a school setting, students learn in classes made up of their agemates, for the most part. With conventional teaching methods, relationships among peers in a class are likely to become somewhat competitive because most students are aware of how well they are doing in relation to their classmates. Grading systems reinforce the competitive nature of school, as do standardized tests and entrance exams.

Individual competition can enhance the motivation for high-achieving students who perceive that they have a possibility of winning or being the best. However, the public nature of competitive rewards and incentives leads to embarrassment and anxiety for students who fail to succeed. When the anxiety and embarrassment are intense, students who recognize that they are unlikely to win no matter how hard they work eventually drop out of the competition in one way or another.

Even when the anxiety over competition is less intense and under control by students with average or high-average achievement, they may become preoccupied with grades to the extent that they avoid complex or challenging tasks that will risk their academic standing and grades.

Despite these negative effects of competition, it is difficult to imagine a classroom without some type of competitive spirit or reward system, and despite its obvious flaws, competition does create an energetic response from many students. Slavin's (1995) models of cooperative group structures are designed to maintain the positive value of competition by adapting it in the form of team competition so that each student is equally capable of winning.

Reflective teachers who undertake some form of cooperative learning will need to be aware of possible effects and observe for both positive and negative interactions among teammates. When using competitive teams, teachers should take steps to ensure that every team has an equal chance to win and that attention is focused more on the learning task than on who wins and loses. When anger or conflict arise within groups, teachers must be ready to mediate and assist students as they develop the interpersonal and communication skills necessary to learn from their team losses.

Slavin (1995) and Sharan (1984) also report that cooperative groups may actually improve race relations within a classroom. When students participate in multiracial teams, studies show that they choose one another for friends more often than do students in control groups. Researchers attribute this effect to the fact that working together in a group as part of a team causes students to promote more differentiated, dynamic, and realistic views (and therefore less stereotyped and static views) of other students (including peers with handicaps and students from different ethnic groups) than do competitive and individualistic learning experiences (Johnson & Johnson, 1984).

Promoting dynamic interactions among you and your students is the likely effect if you choose to learn and master the use of cooperative learning strategies for your future classroom. All of the teaching strategies presented in this chapter have the potential of creating a stimulating, motivating and highly interactive learning environment. All of these strategies enhance the relational aspects of teaching. Simulations encourage interaction; role playing encourages self-awareness and understanding of others' points of view. Discovery learning and learning centers foster independence and intrinsic motivation, and cooperative groups promote interdependence. By using many of these strategies in your classroom, you will be inviting your students to learn for the sake of learning while at the same time you are providing them with opportunities for becoming reflective and relational human beings.

Reflective Actions for Your Professional Portfolio

Your Plan for Using Cooperative Groups

Use Withitness

Visit a classroom and observe whether competition or cooperation is more highly valued. Give examples of classroom events or incentive structures to support your observation.

Put the Problem into Perspective

Do you believe in using competition, cooperation, or some of each to motivate your students to learn?

Widen Your Perspective

From your own experience, do you find cooperative groups enjoyable and stimulating or frustrating and discouraging? What type of role do you usually take in a cooperative group? Do you get impatient with others in your group and wish you could work on the assignment by yourself? How could the structure of the groups you participated in have been improved? Based on your own experience as a learner, are you likely to use cooperative groups in your classroom? Why or why not?

Invite Feedback

Visit a number of other classrooms that are using cooperative groups. This is one strategy that cannot be learned by reading alone. Observe the methods other teachers use to form the groups and to assign tasks and responsibilities. Keep a

log of the best ideas you see. Talk with the teachers to learn their best strategies for managing cooperative groups.

Redefine the Issue

After your observations, has your point of view changed? Which are you now more likely to emphasize in your class—cooperation or competition?

Create an Action Plan for Cooperative Groups

Write a brief plan for using cooperative groups in the grade level you hope to teach. Organize your plan according to subject matter or thematic units. Describe three to five types of cooperative groups you will use to accomplish different purposes.

Predict the Possible Outcomes of Various Strategies

Describe an example of a recent classroom event that you observed and tell what you would do to enhance a cooperative attitude among the students. What strategies will you employ to encourage more cooperation? How can you create more positive interdependence? Describe how you will create a climate for cooperation in your classroom.

If possible, ask for an opportunity to field test a cooperative group in one of the classrooms you are visiting. Implement it and have someone videotape the students working on the task while you assist them. Describe the field test for your portfolio. How did you form the groups? What was the task? How did you communicate the task to the students? How did you assign roles and responsibilities? How did you interact with groups as they worked on the task? Critique the results with honesty and reflectiveness, describing what you have learned in the process.

References

Bloom, B. (1974). An introduction to mastery learning theory. In J. H. Block (Ed.), *Schools, society and mastery learning* (pp. 12–21). New York: Holt, Rinehart and Winston.

Bloom, B. (1984). The search for methods of group instruction as effective as one-to-one tutoring. *Educational Leadership, 41*(8), 4–17.

Carroll, J. (1963). A model of school learning. *Teachers College Record, 64,* 723–733.

Hawkins, D. (1965). Messing about in science. *Science and Children, 2*(5), 5–9.

Johnson, D., & Johnson, R. (1984). *Circles of learning.* Alexandria, VA: Association of Supervision and Curriculum Development.

Johnson, D., & Johnson, R. (1991). *Teaching students to be peacemakers.* Edina, MN: Interaction Book Co.

Leyser, Y. (1982). Role playing in the classroom: A threat or a promise. *Contemporary Education, 53,* 70–74.

Sharan, S. (1984). *Cooperative learning in the classroom: Research in desegregated schools.* Hillsdale, NJ: Erlbaum.

Silberman, C. (Ed.) (1973). *The open classroom reader.* New York: Vintage Books.

Slavin, R. (1995). *Cooperative learning* (2nd ed.). Boston: Allyn & Bacon.

10

Integrating Technology into Your Teaching

When you think of the word *technology*, do you imagine white-coated lab technicians working quietly among rows of machines with blinking electronic lights? Do you imagine futuristic automated housekeeping or communication devices that allow almost superhuman accomplishment? For most of us, the term *technology* conjures up, at the very least, the image of a single desktop computer, perhaps linked to the Internet with a modem. Some of us work routinely at computer stations where we play computer games, word process documents, and send and receive e-mail messages. As you prepare for your career as an educator, how you define the term *technology* and how you choose to include technology in your planning will have lasting effects on the classroom environment you create. In this chapter, we seek to define technology broadly, describe some of the advantages and challenges related to its use in the classroom, and encourage you to reflect on how you will incorporate the technology of today (and tomorrow!) into your teaching efforts.

Defining Technology Broadly

As we just mentioned, the term *technology* encompasses a wide variety of meanings. If we define technology as the devices and procedures devised by humans to extend their own natural abilities (to communicate, travel, access and store information, etc.), then it is clear that each of us routinely uses a number of technological devices every day. How does that daily use of technology relate to teaching? Close your eyes and mentally glance around a classroom you've visited recently. What technology was in use? Did a public address system link each classroom in the school? Was a listening center set up in a corner of the room complete with multiple copies of a book and a tape player equipped with individual headphones? Did the teacher have access to a TV/VCR? Did students use calculators to complete or check math practice sheets?

Considered broadly, it is clear that every teacher implements in his or her daily teaching a number of technological devices. Even if there is little high-tech equipment available within a classroom, the question of how teachers can best use even low-tech materials and devices to support their work is still an important one. For example, have you ever attended a class where the teacher simply turned on a video and the students quietly watched? How did that experience differ from when a teacher played a short video clip, stopped the machine, called for discussion, and then replayed the segment to confirm or challenge student hypotheses? Or how might the situation differ if you knew as you viewed a videotape that you would soon be filming your own video on a topic? Certainly, learning to make the best educational use of every tool available to teachers is an important part of professional development and growth. One of the major points we wish to make in this chapter is that careful reflection should accompany your choice and selection of all teaching materials, not just those considered to be high-tech equipment.

Teaching with Technology: Three Challenges

No matter how they define technology, reflective educators continually seek new ways to support their teaching efforts with technological devices and procedures. The use of technology in teaching offers a number of advantages, but there are also some challenges that confront a teacher hoping to implement regular and extensive technology use into the curriculum. We first discuss three major challenges to using technology in teaching, along with creative ways teachers address these challenges. Then we highlight some of the advantages of planning for technology use in your teaching and describe some steps you may want to take in your own preparation for teaching with technology.

Issues of Access

Especially for the beginning teacher, gaining access to teaching materials, whether high or low tech, can be daunting. Access challenges can occur at any number of levels, from limited funds at the state or district level to figuring out how to help individual students best use available materials in the classroom. We have all heard of situations in which schools own too few textbooks or library books to accommodate the needs of their students. We have also heard of suburban school media centers practically overflowing with the latest children's literature and other reading materials. Although admittedly low tech in most people's minds, having access to an appropriate text or interesting library book can be critical to a curriculum of study.

The same can be true of high-tech materials. For example, some school buildings are wired for high-speed cable and other innovations, allowing teachers and students to connect easily to the Internet, often right in their classrooms. For these individuals, a net search or e-mail exchange is as close as the nearest computer keyboard. In contrast, some schools are physically and financially unable to support more than a handful of Internet connections (if they support any at all). Students or teachers who wish to access the World Wide Web or send e-mail may have to take turns at a limited number of computer sites, and then go through long waiting periods as slower modems or older equipment delay or interrupt data transmission.

It doesn't make much difference if a school is wired for Internet access, if there are insufficient funds for purchase and maintenance of appropriate hardware and software to support user needs. For example, many schools have recently thrown away outdated computers because software programs and printing materials can no longer be obtained for them, even though there are no funds to replace the obsolete systems.

Reflective educators address access issues in a number of creative ways. At many sites, they have written grants or spearheaded business/education partnerships to obtain computers, video players, etc., for the classrooms in their schools. This has enhanced school/community communication, and has often increased parental involvement in local schools as well. Some teachers have successfully experimented with Internet research teams, adapting cooperative learning strategies to take advantage of school-site technology. For example, in a school where only two computers are routinely available for web searches, teachers can divide students into small teams that work together to brainstorm research topics and note their findings. While one or two students at a time take turns with the keyboarding, one or two others take related notes and make suggestions as they observe the search results on the screen. All are involved in compiling and presenting research findings from the Internet and other sources.

Even if your school has a number of computers and Internet connections, access can also be an issue within a school site, depending on how the school has decided to allocate its computers. Computers can be located in the classroom, the media center, or a computer laboratory with its own staff. Computer labs typically have from 15 to 30 computers that students use alone or in pairs, under the direction or guidance of the computer lab teacher. The learning experiences planned for a class of students in a computer lab may include instruction about the use of computers or software programs, so that the students will be able to use these skills in other settings. This type of computer allocation makes it difficult for individual teachers to gain access to the machines for class uses.

In other cases, computer labs are used for completing students' homework or independent projects from their homeroom classes. Often, the classroom teacher and the computer specialist confer about what the students need to accomplish when they come to the lab. Occasionally, the computer specialist will initiate and manage a series of learning experiences for each grade level.

Locating computer activities in a centralized lab has certain advantages. The teacher in the lab is more likely to be familiar with the various programs and can efficiently select and instruct students in their use. Computer programs can be stored in the lab and distributed easily when students need them. On the negative side, when the entire school must be scheduled for time in the lab, each class may have only an hour or two per week to spend working with the computers.

Some schools allocate several computers to the media center so that students and teachers can access them by signing up for time on a computer. Media center computers are usually managed by media center personnel. They may designate one or more computers to be used for CD-ROM research stations. Students use these computers whenever they want to search for information on the CD-ROM encyclopedia, atlas, or other databases. Other computers in the media center may be available for a variety of uses, including word processing, tutoring programs, and literature-based software packages. When the media center has a collection of software programs available, students may be allowed to check them out and use them on a computer in the classroom. This allows them to receive assistance from media center personnel when needed.

You'll want to address scheduling and procedural issues with media center staff. Will your students only have access to the media center computers during a regularly scheduled library period? How can or should students attain access at other times of the day or week? Can a particular software program be reserved to ensure its availability for a particular project? The more information you gain from school personnel, the more smoothly your plans will function.

When you arrive at your school site, you should find out where the computers are located (in the classrooms, in a lab, in the media center, or all of these places) and how the scheduling is done. Ask about regular times, and also about how to address special needs, such as when your students are working on a special project. Scheduling problems associated with computer labs are not as serious if students have access to computers in their classrooms and in the media center.

In addition to (or in lieu of) computer labs and media center access, teachers often have from one to six computers available in the classroom. Teachers may designate one or more computers for a specific use, often reserving one computer as the teacher's computer, where records are kept and instructional materials are designed. To gain maximum use from classroom computers, many primary-grade teachers implement a rotating schedule, allowing each child to use a computer to accomplish a specified task for the week. For example, while studying addition, students may rotate through four to six stations that allow them to practice addition. One of the stations may be a computer with a program like Math Munchers Deluxe (Learning Company), focused on an addition learning activity.

Upper-grade teachers often allow students to sign up to use a computer at a particular time or for a particular purpose. Cliff Gilkey, a multiage fourth/fifth/sixth-grade teacher at Frank Paul Elementary School in Salinas, California, for example, has four computers in his classroom. He has collected a variety of software programs over the years. For some projects, he uses a rotation system that allows one cooperative group to use the computers at a time. He tries to keep the computers busy as much as possible during the day, so he rotates students to the computers for one task or another. During free time, students can choose to use the computer to play educational games.

Like all reflective teachers, Cliff keeps experimenting to find the most workable management plan for his computers. Even though he has used computers successfully for many years, he still feels like he is exploring their potential along with his students. "Computers change every year and we are all learning together," says Cliff. "That is how the kids learn, by exploring, and so do I. Computers are a wonderful tool to open doors and that's what I want for my students. I know that because they have learned to use computers in the classroom, they won't be afraid of computer technology in the workplace."

Like Cliff, you'll want to consider issues of access for your students (and for yourself). When you are considering teaching positions, you'll want to ask the interviewer(s) to describe the school's technology status and future plans. You will also want to consider how the school's goals and accomplishments mirror or extend your own technology plans.

Issues of Familiarity/Personal Knowledge

The challenge of selecting appropriate materials to support your teaching goals does not end when access issues have been successfully addressed. After all, once the materials are available, you need to face the task of becoming familiar with them so that you can assist your students in learning how to use them. And then there is the question of teaching students how to use the software. It is a time-consuming and often frustrating experience to learn how to use a word processor to create your own documents. It can be even more difficult to help a young student learn to use a word processor or other software program. Then there is the matter of deciding which program is the best one in its category and the additional burden of selecting materials that are age appropriate for your students. Given the sheer volume of materials, how can you possibly learn about all that is available and whether it will meet the needs of your students?

One of our reflective actions is to talk with your colleagues to gain more knowledge or a new perspective. Be on the lookout for individuals who express interest in and familiarity with the kinds of technology you would like to implement in your teaching. For example, if you would like to use educational videos to greater advantage, bring up the question during a faculty lunch hour or at an education course meeting. Ask your peers what they have seen or done, and take notes. Visit local school and district media centers, take their tours, and ask the directors for help and advice. If you experience an excellent presentation, stay after the meeting for a few minutes and ask the presenter what materials were used to prepare the presentation, and whether she or he has other recommendations for you to consider.

Professional publications and computer magazines are another good source of information about new computer hardware and software and other materials, as well as new uses for each. You should not, however, purchase a program simply on the recommendation of an article in a magazine. If possible, take time on your own to explore various materials and consider how they can support your instructional goals. Especially with computer software, you will find it is well worth your time to experiment with a particular program before asking your students to use it. There are several reasons for this. First, not all programs run smoothly on every system. For example, you may have a CD-ROM such as *Mario Teaches Typing 2*. When you place it in your computer, you see only a black rectangle appear on your computer screen. You may wonder if you have a defective disk. In actuality, your computer may need to be reset to run a particular program. Fortunately, most programs and modern computers are relatively user-friendly in this area, offering messages on your screen describing the problem and a way to fix it. In the *Mario Teaches Typing* example, a prompt appears on the screen noting that the program usually works best if run in 256 color mode. If you are new to computer use, this warning may sound ominous, but actually all it involves is a very minor adjustment.

During your time at the university and while you are on school sites, make a special effort to locate a technology-wise individual you can call on for help. Often, someone familiar with computers can have you up and running within moments, whereas you may spend countless hours trying to figure out something on your own. Of course, if no one is available, do not be afraid to refer to the user's manual that should accompany the software. Most software companies also have telephone help lines and Internet support addresses listed with their materials. Should you experience difficulty running or using a program, you may want to contact these sources for help. When you access the Internet address of a particular software program, you can usually access a *Frequently Asked Questions* (FAQs) section, in which many of your questions may be answered. When this happens, you'll realize you are not alone in your experience—others have hit the same snags as you!

Because the computer software market has exploded in the past few years, we have included at the end of this chapter a summary of some programs we have enjoyed (and our students, too!). We have loosely categorized the materials according to their most common use. You may want to use this list as a beginning point for your own records, adding materials as you come across them. Remember, it is important to keep good records of the materials you see and how to obtain them. Although you think you will remember a particular program when you see it demonstrated, you may be surprised to find how quickly the title and publisher fade from memory, especially as you become more involved in the busy world of teaching.

Issues of Curriculum Congruence

A third challenge for teaching with technology involves making sure that there is congruence between the teaching tool you have selected and the curriculum you are expected to promote in your particular setting. For example, you may happen upon a wonderful interactive CD-ROM about ancient Egyptian history, and yet Egyptian history is not a part of your grade level curriculum. What do you do? Perhaps you can introduce an appropriate book connected with Egyptian history into your Reader's Workshop, and then use the CD as part of the reading/learning experience. You will probably want to share your find with teachers at the grade level where ancient Egypt is part of the curriculum in your school. Of course, you will also want to note your discovery in some sort of notebook or log for that purpose, because you never know when your teaching assignment may change or a colleague will approach you for ideas.

The same is true of your general technological plans. Just because a computer or other tool is available does not mean it is the best tool for a particular learning task. Consider carefully the why of your decision to use technology as much as the how. As you review the common uses of technology described in the next section, keep in mind how each might best and most authentically be used in your classroom.

Teaching with Technology: An Inquiry Focus

One way to think about the advantages of using technology in your teaching is to visualize an inquiry continuum like the one shown in Figure 10.1. Toward the left side are technology uses that focus on drill and practice, such as a computer program that allows students to practice their multiplication tables, recall literal facts from a story, or learn to place music notes on the right line or space of the musical staff. These kinds of activities help students memorize important facts or become so practiced at a particular skill that it becomes automatic. While practice and memorization are an important part of some learning tasks, they should be kept in perspective. A curriculum centered solely at this level of learning does not promote inquiry, and students may fail to see connections between what they learn in school and the activities they engage in outside of the school setting. This can result in student behavior problems and decreased motivation to learn.

As you move toward the right on the inquiry continuum shown in Figure 10.1, activities become more open ended and require the use of higher level thinking with a distinct inquiry and research focus, such as using technology to answer self- or class-generated questions. Open-ended activities require students to raise personal questions, seek information from a number of sources to develop possible explanations, and then share those discoveries, preferably using media forms other than those in which the research was done. These kinds of activities are more like those students participate in outside of school, and generally heighten enthusiasm and learning interest. The more school learning activities resemble real-life situations, the greater the chance that skills and ideas you teach in class will transfer beyond school, truly preparing your students to be active, contributing members of society.

Remember, including technology in your lesson plans does not necessarily ensure heightened student involvement or learning. Almost any form of technology can be used in a variety of ways. Calculators can be used to solve rows of division problems (closed type of questions) or they can be used to estimate the cost of various floor cov-

Figure 10.1   Inquiry continuum.

Knowledge/ Comprehension	Application	Analysis	Synthesis, Evaluation
	Students interact with materials and may make limited choices about levels of difficulty or other ways to practice material.	Students enter and exit a learning activity from one of a number of points, can create and alter parts of the activity.	Students generate compelling questions and seek explanations from multiple sources, which they then synthesize or translate from one medium to another.

| **Degrees of Open-Endedness and Inquiry** | Students use technology as a means for practice and feedback to help them gain background knowledge, memorize facts, or achieve an "automatic" response.

Examples: Basic keyboarding, multiplication facts drill, etc. | Examples: Games requiring students to recognize or type in responses–difficulty levels may be adjusted. | Examples: Students enter some of their own thinking and writing, make choices, control output in some way. | Examples: Students respond to work of others through email and other online venues, present findings in multimedia formats. |

| **Instructional Activity:** | **Drill Programs** | **Games, Animation, Simulations** | **Interactive Materials Requiring Student Input** | **Inquiry-Based Activities, Student-Directed** |

ering options if students were to redecorate the classroom (more open-ended questions). Consider what level of inquiry you want students to achieve in their learning and then select an appropriate technological strategy that fits your goals.

Beyond thinking about the role technology can play in your lesson planning and teaching routines, you can also use Figure 10.1 to help you organize your thinking about a particular learning event and to record useful technology applications for future reference. How might this work? Let's suppose that, as part of history study, your students wonder (perhaps idly at first) what their hometown looked like 20 years before their birth. If you have the appropriate background knowledge, you could simply describe it to them, or refer them to the local library, where a yearbook of the town includes a number of pictures taken during the past 100 years. Such an intervention would fall at the far left side of the inquiry continuum. However, if you refer to Figure

10.1 and offer a bit of wise guidance, your students' wondering can be extended into an exciting curriculum project. For example, students might brainstorm interview questions and identify individuals in the town who could paint a verbal picture of their experiences there two or three decades ago. These questions could be typed into the computer (word processing), revised, proofed, and distributed to the class. Students might then fan out through the community in pairs or triads with tape recorders or video cameras, conduct their interviews, and then return to class to create a class project: *Our Town, 20 Years Ago and Today.* This (or any other) inquiry can be enhanced by carefully planned use of Internet searches, video viewing, and software exploration.

Keeping Figure 10.1 in mind, let's next review several types of technology you will want to consider regularly in planning your instruction. Again, remember that it is not your selection of a particular technology that determines the inquiry level of a learning project, rather it is how you implement the technology in your plans that sets the stage for student learning.

Audio-Video Technology

Teachers have long used films, filmstrips, and audiotapes to supplement their classroom instruction. Many of these resources can be ordered through the media center located in the school. They can be used for whole class instruction or they can be set up at a learning center so that individuals or groups of students can listen to tapes or watch a video on their own. Sometimes teachers plan for students to view a video or listen to a tape to activate or build background knowledge about a topic. At other times, teachers use these materials to evoke in students a particular sensory experience that they wish to connect to something else. For example, a teacher may show a video of a story after students have read the related story in a book, and then ask students to compare the two along a number of lines. If you think in terms of the inquiry continuum, comparing a video with a book is quite open ended and inquiry based.

With the advent of videodiscs, video cameras, and digital cameras, many new teaching strategies have emerged. Teamed with computers, these innovations allow teachers and students to create interactive video and other presentations for classroom use. An interactive format means that visual images stored on the videodisc or camera can be programmed to play on a computer or television monitor. The order of the images can be controlled by the teacher or the students by typing commands on the computer. No longer requiring film or chemical processing, digital photos can be taken, immediately loaded into a computer, and then altered with any number of techniques using programs like *Photo Suite II* (MGI Software) or *PowerPoint* (Microsoft). Video and audio clips can be dubbed from videodisc or recorded live and added to presentations. For example, as the teacher discusses Martin Luther King, Jr.'s march on Washington, the television monitor in the classroom can display him speaking on the steps of the Lincoln Memorial. When the subject is earth science, a videodisc can be programmed to display various landforms at the teacher's command.

Another interesting area for educational experimentation derives from videoconferencing technology. In this case, a digital camera is mounted on the computer terminal and linked via the Internet to another computer terminal connected to another digital camera. This allows users to see one another as they converse via the Internet. Although it offers many exciting possibilities for face-to-face communication across vast distances, videoconferencing technology still suffers from some shortcomings. Software and hardware inexpensive enough for the average classroom often feature a distracting lag time between the transmission of voice and picture. This results in a face/voice mismatch in which students hear a person's comments before the visual image moves, which can be distracting. Over time these issues are sure to be resolved however, and you will want to explore ways such technology can help you achieve instructional goals, especially those that cross cultural and physical distances.

Video technology also provides new opportunities for record keeping and practice for performance. Students' products and performances can be recorded by the teacher or an assistant for future evaluation purposes or to document an event. Students can rehearse their presentations on videotape and watch the recording to see what they need to improve. Judy used the video camera to record speeches her students gave in the unit called *Panorama of the Presidents*. In the early stages, students used the video camera to practice their speeches, so they could see themselves and hear their own voices. Preliminary viewings of their own performances caused the students to study and practice harder. She also videotaped the assembly in which they gave their final presentations. Afterwards, the class had a permanent record of their accomplishments and could share the videotape with family members who had not been present at the event. Debra taught a unit on advertising tactics and students created video commercials for imaginary products they devised. As students applied their knowledge of advertising techniques to the actual process of creating advertisements, they compared their work with actual commercials viewed on television.

Like many reflective teachers, Cliff Gilkey was searching for a method to engage the interest of his students, many from families of migrant workers, with limited English proficiency. The social studies material he had available neither matched his students' interests nor gave them positive role models. To meet these needs, Cliff created the Local Heroes Project, a social studies investigation and oral history of local Hispanic, African American, and Vietnamese leaders (such as political figures, businesspeople, researchers, and teachers).

The students decided that they would produce videotapes and publish booklets about the local heroes that students in other classes could use as well. Students were asked to identify local heroes that they would like to know more about. The heroes they selected included a Mexican American school board member, a Latina news anchorwoman, an African American police chief, the Cuban American city manager, and a Miwok Indian leader.

For this project, students worked in teams of three to four. They developed a set of interview questions by reading and analyzing biographies to see what other biographers included. After preparing the interview questions, they set up appointments to meet the individual local heroes they wanted to interview. One student asked questions as another operated the video camera. They transcribed the words of their heroes onto word processors so that they could create booklets about each hero.

This year Cliff plans to do the project again with even more technology at his command. He has a new Hyper Studio program that will allow the students to create multimedia presentations and a VCR companion they plan to use to create special effects and credits for their video production.

Calculators

Calculators are increasingly viewed as a valuable tool for investigating mathematical and scientific relationships that are complex and difficult to compute with pencil and paper. As with any teaching tool, teachers must consider which tasks are appropriate for calculators and which are not. This view is nicely articulated in the technology section of the *Mathematics Content Standards for California Schools* (Ong, 1999):

> Technology should be used to promote mathematics learning. Technology can help promote students' understanding of mathematical concepts, quantitative reasoning, and achievement when used as a tool for solving problems, testing conjectures, accessing data, and verifying solutions. When students use electronic tools, databases, programming language, and simulations, they have opportunities to extend their comprehension, reasoning, and problem-solving skills beyond what is possible with traditional print resources. For example, graphing calculators allow students to see instantly the graphs of complex functions and to explore the impact of changes. Computer-based geometry construction tools allow students to see figures in three-dimensional space and experiment with the effects of transformations. Spreadsheet programs and databases allow students to key in data and produce various graphs as well as compile statistics. Students can determine the most appropriate ways to display data and quickly and easily make and test conjectures about the impact of change on the data set. In addition, students can exchange ideas and test hypotheses with a far wider audience through the Internet. Technology may also be used to reinforce basic skills through computer-assisted instruction, tutoring systems, and drill-and-practice software.
>
> The focus must be on mathematics content. The focus must be on learning mathematics, using technology as a tool rather than as an end in itself. Technology makes more mathematics accessible and allows one to solve mathematical problems with speed and efficiency. However, technological tools cannot be used effectively without an understanding of mathematical skills, concepts, and relationships.

Technology is a powerful tool in mathematics. When used appropriately, technology may help students develop the skills, knowledge, and insight necessary to meet rigorous content standards in mathematics and make a successful transition to the world beyond school. The challenge for educators, parents, and policymakers is to ensure that technology supports, but is not a substitute for, the development of quantitative reasoning and problem-solving skills.

Just as articulated in the California standards, many teachers separate learning arithmetic skills from other problem-solving activities. When students are being asked to master the process of calculating multiplication or division or comparing fractions and decimals, calculators are not used. But for tasks designed to encourage students to explore patterns and functions, search for a variety of ways to solve problems, or create and test hypotheses, calculators facilitate and encourage the students to accept and master complex investigations. This same line of thinking can also be applied when selecting computer programs to support learning goals not only in mathematics, but in all disciplines.

Word Processing Programs

Word processing programs are among the most versatile software available for classrooms. Early experiences, especially in the primary grades, may be devoted to very simple writing assignments with a dual purpose: composing and learning keyboarding. Many programs, such as *Mario Teaches Typing 2* (Nintendo) and *Read, Write & Type* (Learning Company), are available to teach students how to type and use the special function keys on the keyboard. As students learn to identify letters and numbers, they can often begin to type them before they can hold a pencil and write them on paper. You will want to explore these programs firsthand and determine whether they meet the needs of your students. For example, one thing we like about *Mario Teaches Typing 2* is the focus on helping students select the appropriate finger for the keyboarding exercises by showing a small picture of two hands on the screen with the appropriate finger for hitting the keyboard letter highlighted in red.

Learning to operate a keyboard also provides new opportunities for students with special needs related to fine motor function. Students with visual and motor difficulties that prevent them from writing neatly or which cause them to erase and redo their work can now create neat papers. The delete key may save students from embarrassment and frustration, just as it does for adults. For this reason, we recommend allowing students to learn keyboarding skills at the same time as they are learning to write with a pen or pencil, and then allowing them to choose which form they prefer to use for assignments.

When students master keyboarding skills, they are free to compose many types of verbal products, including letters, stories, poems, essays, reports, and plays. Studies have shown that students write longer pieces on a word processor than they do by hand. Another major benefit is that the word processor greatly simplifies the editing and revision processes. Students can learn to use spelling checkers, grammar checkers, and thesaurus programs. Their motivation to write is often increased not only because of the attraction of working on a computer, but also because the final products that are printed out are neat and relatively error free. Rather than experiencing writing as drudgery, students are likely to feel pride and success related to the writing process when they are allowed to compose and edit using a word processing program.

Students with limited English proficiency can also benefit from writing and composing with a word processor. When you pair a proficient English speaker with a less proficient student, the two can work together at the computer to compose and illustrate stories and poems. In the process, they are communicating orally as well as in writing, giving the less proficient English speaker many opportunities to use the new language in a meaningful context.

By using word processing programs or more specialized desktop publishing programs, students can create newspapers, magazines, posters, invitations to events, and other materials that have the appeal of a professionally published product. Many teachers are employing these media to help students create gifts for families, such as published books of poetry or calendars illustrated by the class.

Computer-Assisted Research Projects

CD-ROM disks are fast replacing the traditional encyclopedia in most school media centers and even in the classroom. Students are able to type in a key word to call up an article on almost any subject. For many topics, they also see pictures and graphs, or even a short video of the subject they are researching. Additionally, many companies provide links between their encyclopedia product and an Internet site, allowing for constant information updates and on-line connections among researchers.

Using products like these, teachers can support the development of research skills in their students of almost any age. For example, at the Open School, an inner-city elementary school in Los Angeles, Jan Ng uses a program called *Dino Hunt* (Smithsonian) to take her first- and second-grade students to an archaeological dig where their task is to identify a dinosaur bone. The program gives clues that students use to begin their research using books and maps.

Depending on the sophistication of your school site and your experience with technology, you may enjoy experimenting with scanners to capture student work for electronic presentation. You may also want to try out one of the new electronic white boards. What you write on the white board is electronically saved to a word processing program, allowing you to save important ideas from class discussions without painstaking copying from the board.

Assessment and Tutoring Programs

Computer programs are now available for classroom use that can assess students' skills in math, reading, vocabulary, and other areas. Some prescribe lessons at the appropriate level. In teaching the lessons, computers make excellent tutors because they are endlessly patient in waiting for a student response and give the appropriate feedback without emotional side effects. An excellent example is IBM's Write to Read program, which teaches primary students how to plan, write, and edit stories and poems.

Josten Integrated Learning Systems offers an integrated package of reading and mathematics programs for the elementary school. Students are pretested on the computer in reading and math. They then begin to work at their own individual levels of mastery and progress through a series of learning activities that emphasizes comprehension and problem solving. You will want to exercise care in selecting and using this kind of program, however. It is important that the content the programs test is congruent with the content of your school and district, and that the results be considered as just one measure in a multifaceted assessment process. The activities required in many computer-based assessment programs are often somewhat fragmented, not always resembling real-life tasks. If you use a computer-based assessment/tutoring program, you will still want to plan plenty of time in your curriculum for application of the skills in other, more authentic settings.

Specialized record-keeping programs are available that allow teachers to record students' achievement. Many of these will compute average grades for report cards, maintain attendance data, and allow for custom reporting as well.

Thinking Games and Literature Links

Like manipulatives in mathematics, many computer games provide students with realistic or simulated experiences that allow them to experiment, observe relationships, test hypotheses, and use data to reach conclusions supported by evidence. Programs such as *Gertrude's Secrets* (Learning Company) offer students the opportunity to manipulate objects as they solve problems.

Two programs Debra uses often in her work at the Community Reading Center are *Crossword Maker* (Cosmi) and *Spell It Deluxe* (Davidson). Both of these allow Debra and her reading master's students to create custom learning materials for students. For example, a student learning about the *ea* vowel team can gain extra practice doing crosswords or playing games designed to feature words with the *ea* spelling (e.g., *heat, beaten, seated*).

Some game-like programs are useful in expanding students' experiences beyond the classroom walls into simulated journeys, laboratories, foreign countries, earlier periods of history, and the future. Many of these programs increase students' decision-making and problem-solving abilities by demonstrating to them the consequences of their decisions. An example is the program known as *Oregon Trail* (MECC), which allows students to simulate the experience of a wagon train journey with full decision-making power over how many supplies to bring, when to stop and restock, and how to deal with emergencies along the way. Poor choices in any of these areas lead to death on the trail. It takes most students many attempts to reach Oregon alive!

Road Adventures USA (Learning Company) builds on the well-known *Oregon Trail* program, only this time students participate in a modern-day travel adventure. They must read maps and road signs and determine a travel budget (gas, meals, lodging). Along the way, students stop at famous landmarks and explore the sights and their histories, aided by the program's 360-degree panning camera. This gives the computer user the sense of being able to look all around a particular area, almost as if standing there in person.

Another MECC program, called *Lemonade*, plunges students into the economic decision-making necessary to market a product that will make a profit. Students must decide how many lemons to buy, how many glasses to make each day, how much advertising is needed, and what price to charge based on the weather report. Good choices lead to profits, and poor choices lead to losses.

Teachers can access both the *Oregon Trail* and *Lemonade* programs through the Minnesota Educational Computer Consortium (MECC), which is available in many school districts or libraries throughout the country. MECC offers its programs to teachers for classroom use for a minimal charge. By taking their own computer disks to a MECC software library, teachers are able to copy the programs they would like to use in their own classrooms.

Debra consulted in the development of a different kind of game-like simulation in *Secret Writer's Society* (Panasonic). Students qualify to become a secret writer (like a secret agent) by progressing through six levels of writing skills (e.g., capitalization, punctuation, sequencing, paragraph structure). When students successfully complete all six levels, they receive a password that opens the way to the Secret Writer's Society. Like many others, the makers of this program maintain a web site where students using the program can interact with others, posting their writing and sharing responses.

Where in the World Is Carmen Sandiego? (Broderbund) is a multidisciplinary adventure program that allows students to explore the world in search of clues to solve a mystery. In the process, they learn about various countries and use logic and deduction to hypothesize about the solution to the mystery. After the initial success of this program, Broderbund has used the same approach to encourage students to learn history in *Where in Time Is Carmen Sandiego?* Another recent innovation in the series is *Carmen Sandiego's ThinkQuick Challenge,* which features a quiz show format where four students can compete or work in cooperative teams to respond to social studies and history questions. Programs such as these can be incorporated into unit plans or as part of a learning contract. Students can work with a partner to solve the questions and record the results in a notebook.

Another relatively new genre in the computer software market is the advent of interactive CD-ROMs linked to well-known children's books or characters from those books. For example, the Learning Company distributes a program called *Madeline* (based on the book by Madeline and Barbara Bemelmens), which features the well-known picture book character and focuses on developing reading skills for grades 1 and 2. Students even pick up a sense of France as they work through the program. Programs based on Marc Brown's *Arthur* series, Paulette Bourgeois's *Franklin* books, and several Dr. Seuss characters also focus on helping students develop beginning reading and writing skills. While none of these should replace shared and guided reading practices in the classroom, each can offer a warm connection between well-loved story characters and skill practice often essential for developing readers and writers.

Drawing, Painting, and Inventing

Many excellent software programs provide students with a blank slate for creating, inventing, and composing original works. *Kid Pix* (Broderbund) is a paint program that uses tools very similar to the ones used by professional artists and architects. Students can draw, paint, or use stamps to create designs and pictures. Patterns can be replicated and inverted, illustrating the mathematical relationships of patterns for children to see and manipulate. By becoming proficient with this child-centered program, students will be able to easily master the adult versions in later life.

Crayons (Expert) provides simple coloring book images for very young students to color in graphically, and also includes a more traditional drawing program for older or more advanced students. *Storybook Weaver Deluxe* (Learning Company) allows students to create custom scenes for stories they write, and offers the less-than-artistic child a choice of clip art to support the work. The same is true of *Stagecast Creator*

(Stagecast Software). Using this program, students can create their own visual world, painting characters and designing rules of behavior. This lends itself to the creation and modification of simulations, visualizations, stories, and games.

Another interesting synthesis of learning materials and experiences is the program called *Lego/Logo* (Lego Dacta). Students create objects with Lego building blocks and then wire their moving parts to a computer terminal. Using the computer language known as LOGO, students can type in commands that control the movement of their Lego machines and inventions from a computer terminal. This provides students with an authentic experience similar to the processes inventors now use.

Networking to Share Information

Dawn Morden, a sixth-grade teacher in Altoona, Pennsylvania, wanted to provide more relevant, authentic learning experiences to motivate her students to want to learn social studies. She noticed that her students seemed uninterested in the textbook because they saw little relationship between the text and their own lives. Dawn and a colleague, Connie Letscher, teamed up to create an interdisciplinary, technology-based project that they call *Crossroads to the World.*

They begin with literature that stimulates students' interest in traveling, then introduce computer programs such as *Oregon Trail* (MECC), *Cross Country Canada* (Didatech), and *Where in the World Is Carmen Sandiego?* (Broderbund). They also subscribe to an on-line educational telecommunications network, *WorldClassroom,* that allows students in Altoona to communicate with people all over the world. When students make contacts in other parts of the world, they share firsthand information about their communities. Turning next to word-processing programs, students write letters to their new friends.

Each student selects a travel destination and searches for information about that place on the World Wide Web. They write business letters or send e-mail messages to chambers of commerce, tourist bureaus, and embassies to gather information about their chosen destinations. To prepare their budget for their imaginary journeys, the students use spreadsheets. Before their journeys, they plan a bon voyage party, complete with party invitations to friends and family, using Print Shop (Broderbund).

During the actual *travel,* students gather information using CD-ROM, laser disks, and other traditional resources. They consult newspapers or on-line news releases to find current news about their locations, and make news reports to their classmates. They document their travels by keeping a daily log on audiotape or a word processor.

The uses of the Internet are growing every day in elementary classrooms. Students can participate in designing and managing their own web pages, providing information about their school and the issues of their part of the world to other interested researchers. If you think you might enjoy seeing a wide variety of innovative school projects on the World Wide Web, turn on your computer and surf the Internet, searching with the key words "K–12 education." You are likely to be surprised by the results—and motivated to think of an interesting project for your future students to investigate.

Managing Technology in the Classroom: Instructional Materials, Record Keeping, and Grading

In addition to student uses, teachers can use computers to create classroom materials, keep records, and compute grades. Many teachers use word processing programs to create and store curriculum plans, student worksheets, quizzes, and tests. They may also use them to write reports, proposals, and newsletters.

You will probably want to keep a log of useful web sites throughout your teaching career. Many commercial publishers (like those listed in connection with published software in this chapter) maintain Internet sites expressly for teachers. These sites often include lesson plans, tips for teaching, and special promotional offers. For example, the Learning Company hosts a site (http://www.learningcompanyschool.com) where you can find lesson plans for use with specific software, and for general academic areas. The same is true for book publishers such as Scholastic (http://www.scholastic.com). Some lesson plans are created by company employees, and others are submitted by teachers. This is common across many commercial sites.

Many noncommercial sites exist where teachers share unit plans, teaching insights, questions, and many other important ideas. Many state departments of education maintain sites for teacher input, as do numerous local school districts and even schools. Perhaps you will want to design a web page and maintain a site for yourself and for your school!

As you plan your lessons, you may want to make a special category for technology right on your planning guides, to remind you to consider which tools will best help you and your students achieve enhanced learning engagement and growth. Reflective teachers want to keep up with technological developments, and often plan their schedules in a way that allows them to attend workshops and ongoing classes, keeping their own skills fresh. Perhaps the best way to teach with technology is to spend time with the various tools available, making them a natural part of your own life. Then, in turn, you can share the marvelous advances of this computer age with your students in ways that make sense and prepare them to be the consumers and inventors of tomorrow.

Reflective Actions for Your Professional Portfolio

Your Plan for Integrating Technology in Your Curriculum

Use Withitness

Visit a classroom and observe how technology is used in the curriculum. List the types of technology you see being used and describe the type of management system the teacher uses to allow students access to the various types of technology.

Put the Issue into Perspective

What are your favorite uses of technology at this point? How do you see yourself using computers, calculators, and video cameras in your classroom?

Widen Your Perspective

Are you familiar with and comfortable using technology yourself? If you are not very familiar with some aspects of technology, will that limit your students' access to it? What can you do to become more adept at using technology? Based on your present degree of familiarity with technology, how do you see yourself incorporating it into your classroom?

Invite Feedback

Visit a number of other teachers who are using technology in interesting ways. Take notes about their favorite computer programs and how they incorporate them into the curriculum. Ask the teachers to tell you their best sources for learning more about using technology and where they get their software and other materials. Talk with the teachers to learn their best strategies for managing technology and making sure their students have access to it.

Redefine the Issue

After concluding your observations, discussions, and note taking, has your point of view changed? What is your new philosophy about using technology and making sure every student has an equal opportunity to gain access to it?

Create an Action Plan for Cooperative Groups

Write a brief plan for using technology in the grade level you hope to teach. Organize your plan according to subject matter or thematic units. Draw a classroom floor plan showing where you will place the machines and computers so that students have access to them.

Predict the Possible Outcomes

Imagine your students walking into the classroom you have sketched. Will they be motivated to learn to use technology because of the easy access to it? What will you do to motivate those children who seem reluctant to use computers? What will you do to assist those who do not seem to respond at all to this type of learning opportunity? What will you do to stimulate and challenge the students who are already very proficient at using computers? Add these contingencies to your technology plan and put this plan into your portfolio.

Software References

Drill/Practice

(Some are game-like, but with less simulation involved than the next category)

Crossword Maker. (1998). Rancho Dominguez, CA: Cosmi. (web site: http://www.cosmi.com).

Knowledge Munchers. (1997). Cambridge, MA: The Learning Company (web site: http://www.learningco.com).

Mario Teaches Typing 2. (1996). Nintendo.(web site: http://www.nintendo.com).

Math Munchers Deluxe. (1997). Cambridge, MA: The Learning Company (web site: http://www.learningco.com).

Radio Addition. (1995). San Diego, CA: Conexus.

Sound It Out Land. (1993–1998). San Diego, CA: 99VLLC. (web site: http://www.99v.com).

Spell It Deluxe. (1996). Torrance, CA: Davidson. (web site: http://www.davd.com).

Games/Animations/Simulations

Dr. Seuss Kindergarten. (1998). Novato, CA: Broderbund. (web site: http://www.broderbund.com).

Dr. Seuss Preschool. (1998). Novato, CA: Broderbund. (web site: http://www.broderbund.com).

Franklin's Reading World. (1995). Emeryville, CA: Sanctuary Woods. (web site: http://sanctuary.com).

Jumpstart Reading (K–4). (1995–1997). Glendale, CA: Knowledge Adventure.

Leap Ahead Reading (also released as Word Munchers Deluxe). (1999). Cambridge, MA: The Learning Company (web site: http://www.learningco.com).

Madeline 1st and 2nd Grade Reading. (1998). Cambridge, MA: The Learning Company (web site: http://www.learningco.com).

Reader Rabbit's Interactive Reading Journey 1–2. (1997). Cambridge, MA: The Learning Company (web site: http://www.learningco.com).

Reader Rabbit's Reading K–2. (1997). Cambridge, MA: The Learning Company (web site: http://www.learningco.com).

Reading Development Library 1–4. (1997). Cambridge, MA: The Learning Company (web site: http://www.learningco.com).

Interactive Materials Requiring Student Input

Crayons. (1997). Coral Gables, FL: Expert Software (web site: http://www.expertsoftware.com).

Middle School Language Arts, Grades 4–8. Las Cruces, NM: Pro One Software (web site: http://www.sofsource.com).

Secret Writer's Society. (1998). Panasonic Interactive Media. (web site: http://www.pimcom.com).

Inquiry-Based, Student-Directed Activities

Compton's Interactive Encyclopedia. (1996–1998). Cambridge, MA: The Learning Company (web site: http://www.learningco.com).

Encarta. (1993–1998). Redmond, WA: Microsoft (web site: http://encarta.msn.com).

Grolier Deluxe Encyclopedia. (1998). Danbury, CT: Grolier (web site: http://gi.grolier.com).

PhotoSuite II. (1989–1998) (web site: http://www.mgisoft.com).

Print Shop. (1997). Novato, CA: Broderbund (web site: http://www.broderbund.com).

Storybook Weaver Deluxe. (1998). Cambridge, MA: The Learning Company (web site: http://www.learningco.com).

World Book Family Reference Suite. (1998). IBM (web site: http://www.worldbook.com).

Reference

Ong, F. (Ed.). (1999). Mathematics content standards for California public schools. Sacramento, CA: California Department of Education. Available at http://www.cde.ca.gov /board/mcs_intro.html.

Chapter

11

Assessing Student Accomplishments

What is good work? As a teacher, you may find evaluating students' accomplishments among the most difficult judgments you have to make. You have worked hard to create authentic learning experiences. Now, how can you create an assessment system that allows students to demonstrate what they learned? How can you create an assessment system that allows students a range of possibilities to demonstrate their own particular strengths and talents? How can you create an assessment system that is fair and that your students can understand?

To be able to make fair and reasonable judgments about your students' work, you must think through the assessment process prior to teaching the lesson and communicate this process to your students. Assessment issues are present at every stage of the planning and teaching processes. That is why they are described frequently in earlier chapters of this book. Chapter 3, which outlines the processes teachers use to determine the needs of their students prior to teaching, describes many assessment devices. Cumulative files of information about students' past performance, standardized test scores describing levels of present achievement, and placement exams are all methods of assessing student accomplishments and are part of the reflective teacher's continuous process of evaluation.

Chapter 4 describes long-term goals and outcome statements. These serve as the basis for later evaluation of what students gained from their school experience. Assessment of student accomplishment is primarily concerned with measuring how much students gained and comparing the actual gain with the original goal or outcome statement.

Chapters 5 and 6 describe the creation of learning objectives that specify what teachers *expect* their students to gain during short-term learning events such as a single lesson or a short sequence of lessons. To evaluate student accomplishment in these areas, the teacher must measure what students actually gained during the lesson and compare that gain with the criteria established for each objective.

Chapters 7 through 10 describe methods teachers select for instructing students or facilitating their learning. These methods have an impact on the amount and type of accomplishment that students are able to achieve. Therefore, reflective teachers are continually assessing student progress and achievement during every learning experience to verify that the teaching strategy they have selected is working or to alter it if they find that students are not accomplishing the objective for that lesson.

This chapter on assessment and reporting on student achievement only falls at the end because of a book's linear nature. Genuine understanding of what students have accomplished in a given school year requires that reflective teachers employ a systematic process of evaluation that includes observations, testing, collecting samples of students' typical work, and creating portfolios of their best work. This process begins prior to the first day of school and continues until the last dismissal bell rings.

Assessment Terminology

The terms used in discussing student assessment can be confusing. This brief set of definitions is provided to make it easier to comprehend how each term is used in this text. There are subtle differences among measurement, assessment, and evaluation. In this textbook, *measurement* is a broad term referring to the process of obtaining a number of correct responses or a raw score for a student on any type of assessment device.

A *criterion* is a preestablished number or score that a teacher believes will demonstrate mastery of the planned objective (*criteria* is the plural form of *criterion*). The teacher makes an *assessment* by comparing the student's raw score with the criterion score and determining whether the student successfully accomplished the objective. *Evaluation*, in this text, is the reflective process of gathering objective and subjective data on a student and making a decision about how best to help that student succeed.

The current trend is to create *authentic assessment systems*. These are evaluation plans that incorporate learning of both content and thinking processes in a realistic setting. An authentic assessment is most often a task students perform that allows them to demonstrate what they have learned as well as the thinking processes they employed in completing the task. To assess student performance equitably and efficiently, many teachers establish *standards of performance* that describe what they expect from their students. They also create *benchmarks*, which are steps that mark student progress from initial introduction of a new skill to demonstrating mastery of the skill in an authentic task.

Some authentic assessment systems contain very specific, detailed descriptions of student performance that are often called *levels of learning*. Teachers evaluate each student's work by comparing it to a set of preestablished learning levels. These systems are also known as *rubric grading* systems. For example, a four-level rubric system may describe observable characteristics that can help gauge student performance. Level 4 describes the highest expectation, while level 1 describes a minimal performance level.

In this text, the term *student achievement* is used to describe the degree to which a student has demonstrated mastery of a subject or objective (usually paper-and-pencil) tests. *Student accomplishment* is meant to be a more inclusive term that indicates the degree to which a student has completed or demonstrated knowledge or skill on a variety of assessment devices, including tests, products, projects, oral presentations, performances, and creative works.

As described in Chapter 3, *criterion-referenced tests* are those created by teachers in which the test items match the specific objectives they plan to teach. Scores on criterion-referenced tests can be used to assess how well students did in relation to the criterion for success on the planned objectives. In contrast, *norm-referenced tests* are written by professional test writers and are published widely. The items may or may not match the school's curriculum. Scores on norm-referenced tests tell teachers how much a student achieved compared to other students of the same age or grade throughout the country.

Many types of tests are used in an educational program. Teachers use *diagnostic tests* prior to teaching to assess students' prior learning, especially gaps in their prior learning that must be addressed. *Placement tests* are a form of diagnostic test that teachers use to help them make decisions about the level of difficulty of material that will best match the student's present knowledge level.

A significant distinction exists between formative tests and summative tests. Although they may look exactly alike, they are used differently. *Formative tests* measure the student's progress during a set of lessons or learning experiences so the teacher can provide appropriate feedback and help the student correct errors in understanding or skill. They are *not* graded and are *not* used to make final judgments or evaluations of student achievement.

Summative tests are used at the end of a set of learning experiences to measure the progress a student has made over time. They *are* usually graded and *are* used to make final judgments or evaluations about student achievement.

Pretests are given prior to teaching a new unit or set of skills or knowledge. *Post-tests* are given directly after teaching the new set of skills. Comparing post-test and pretest scores can be an important way for teachers to learn how much their students gained from a specific lesson, sequence of lessons, or unit of study. Pre- and post-tests are often used in research to demonstrate gains students make under a certain set of conditions. Reflective teachers are likely to use pre- and post-tests just as researchers do—as a means of gathering data about the value of various teaching strategies or sets of learning materials.

Nontest measures of student achievement and accomplishment also exist. These include informal observation, student products, presentations, and portfolios. Teachers use informal observation of their students' efforts and accomplishments continuously. It may be planned or unplanned. Teachers may observe a single student or a group of students as they work together. Although it is difficult to measure any specific achievement during an informal observation, the technique does provide subjective data that teachers need to understand the objective data gathered using other assessment devices.

In this text, a *student product* is meant to include any form of written work, such as essays, stories, reports, poems, and plays that are handed in to be assessed and evaluated by the teacher. Some student products are not written but are completed works of art, music, models, machines, or other student-created items. A student product can be assessed by comparing it against a criterion or a set of criteria that fits that product type.

A *portfolio* denotes a collection of student products designed to show a progression of accomplishment from early undertakings to more recent and advanced efforts. By gathering portfolios of students' work, teachers may assess the accomplishments made over time in a given type of endeavor. There may be portfolios of drawings, showing increasing attention to detail and craftsmanship, or portfolios of student writing, showing growth in letter formation or use of grammatical conventions.

Objective measures imply that no matter who scores the assessment device, they will all get the same score. This occurs only on tests with items that have clear-cut right and wrong answers. *Subjective measures* are those that different scorers will score differently, depending on their own interpretations and values. These include essays, artwork, and any other creative products or performances.

Reliability is related to objectivity. Reliable tests consistently measure the same thing time after time. *Validity* means that a test is appropriate for the subject and contains items that will provide useful information about student achievement in that content area. Construction of both test and nontest assessment devices should take reliability and validity into account. When assessment devices are reliable and valid for their purpose, the information they provide can be used with confidence to make decisions about children's school experiences.

Public Interest in Student Achievement

Who cares about students' accomplishments in public schools? Who wants to know the difference between achievement of students in the suburbs and students in the inner cities? Why is so much energy, time, and money spent on assessment procedures in public education today? The answer is that we all care, and we all want to know at every level of society: national, state, local community, family, and individual.

At the national level, we care because we have seen signs that students educated in the United States are falling behind students from other industrialized nations. The National Assessment of Educational Progress (NAEP) measures the academic achievement of students in the basic skills in elementary, junior high, and high schools. These statistics are not reported to students or their parents. They are collected for the purpose of comparing achievement of U.S. students from year to year. Reports are made to the public and to policymakers about the achievement levels of various age groups, the changes over time, and differences in achievement in terms of gender and racial and ethnic groups. The NAEP uses the results of these tests to spot trends and forecast the future needs of U.S. schools.

State governments are also vitally interested in assessing the achievement of students within their boundaries. As described in Chapter 4, each state government has established a state department of education responsible for providing guidance and standards to local school districts in curriculum development. The state departments are also responsible for holding school districts *accountable* for achieving the curriculum standards. Many state governments use *minimum competency tests* to measure whether districts are accomplishing the state guidelines.

Classroom teachers administer minimum competency tests on a specified date. Average scores are computed for various subjects and grade levels for each school district. In some states, these average scores are ranked and reported to the public in what is known as a *school district report card*. Districts with scores above the state mean are believed to be doing a better job of educating their students than are school districts with scores below the mean. The purpose of this practice is to strengthen the feelings of accountability among school district administrators.

In some school districts, administrators choose to rank and report the results of the test by schools. In this way, they hold the principal and faculty of each school accountable for the school's educational program.

Many questions remain unanswered about the value of minimum competency tests and the practice of using the results to label schools and districts poor, good, better, and best. Some educators question whether the tests measure important student accomplishments or simply discrete, unconnected bits of knowledge. Others question whether the practice of reporting results is a valid measure of educational programming because the socioeconomic status of each school is also believed to affect test scores.

Standardized norm-referenced tests of achievement in the basic skills are a fact of life in most school districts today, and teachers must learn how to interpret and use productively the information these tests provide. But just as tests are gaining prominence in measuring and comparing achievement among school districts and states, they are also drawing severe criticism from many educators. Critics charge that testing takes too much time away from the curriculum. Schools may spend 1 to 2 weeks of a 30-week school year on district, state, and national achievement testing.

Another criticism is that norm-referenced tests may measure only limited aspects of what students have learned during the school year. Because they are written and distributed nationally by test publishers, the items on the tests are generic rather than specifically written to match what was taught in a particular school. Many items on a test may be unfamiliar to students because the material was not part of their school's curriculum.

A further criticism of standardized tests is that they cause unfair and unrealistic labeling and categorization of students. There is great concern, for example, that generic achievement tests have a built-in bias against minority students. Critics point to items, pictures, and language in early editions of such tests that were geared to the vocabulary and culture of the white middle class. Although test manufacturers now employ writers who represent various racial and ethnic minorities to develop fairer tests, the concern remains that students from minority groups may have less opportunity to learn the content of the tests, which causes them to earn unrealistically low scores.

Test results must be interpreted with caution and compared with other measures of student achievement. It is a serious breach of ethics when school districts misuse the data from standardized tests to classify students as gifted or as having learning disabilities. Neither diagnosis can be made from the limited information of a generic test of basic skills. In fact, no serious educational decision should be made using only the data from standardized, norm-referenced tests of basic skills. Overemphasizing and generalizing from test scores is likely to damage students' self-concepts and may even create self-fulfilling prophecies (Linn & Gronlund, 2000).

The emphasis given to standardized test scores varies from state to state and district to district. Some states and districts give standardized achievement tests enormous weight in labeling students gifted or low achieving, in determining children's placement in special programs, and in determining who wins awards for merit. Reflective teachers who work in schools using these practices are likely to experience discomfort. It is important, then, to challenge such practices and encourage the use of a more balanced assessment and evaluation system.

How Teachers Select and Use Assessment Methods

It is the responsibility of educators in state departments of education to create a balanced method of assessing whether students are meeting the state's standards. District administrators are responsible for creating a fair and useful collection of data about the achievement of students in the schools they serve. The principal of a single school provides guidance to classroom teachers in determining methods for evaluating the progress of the students in that school. But even with all of the direction and guidance from administrators and supervisors, individual classroom teachers retain a great deal of leeway in the area of student assessment.

Individual classroom teachers have varied philosophies of life and related curriculum orientations. Just as teachers' philosophies and curriculum orientations influence their methods of teaching, these values also greatly influence the types of assessment procedures they select and the weight they give to various measures of student accomplishment.

Teachers who believe some students are smarter than others and can learn difficult material more easily than their classmates are likely to employ summative tests early and often, recording the results in their gradebooks as evidence of how each student's achievement matches the ability or IQ tests recorded in the student's cumulative file. These teachers can be very susceptible to making and ensuring self-fulfilling prophecies about their students.

Teachers who think children's accomplishments are linked to the richness of their experiences and self-esteem are likely to employ many formative evaluation procedures in their effort to identify students' learning gaps and assist them in developing appropriate schemata. Using the information they gain from a variety of formative evaluation strategies, these teachers provide the scaffolding necessary for students to achieve mastery and succeed in their classroom. Reflective teachers are likely to hold this view of teaching and learning, and use evaluation not as a reward or caste system, but as an integral part of the learning process.

Educators committed to providing authentic learning for their students are also searching for meaningful and useful assessment systems that provide the kinds of information that allow students to move ahead and develop their skills and knowledge base.

A powerful use of assessment is to link your grading and reporting criteria with the criteria used in the learning process. When students know what the criteria for success are and see how they are linked to the learning experiences in the classroom, the learning environment seems fair to them (Guskey, 1994). Using a variety of evaluation procedures is also beneficial. No one evaluation strategy works well for all subjects, grade levels, or student learning styles. For that reason, students should be allowed a variety of ways to earn their grades.

Imagine you are a teacher planning a unit on astronomy for your classroom. You have gathered some very interesting learning materials, including filmstrips on the solar system, National Aeronautics and Space Administration (NASA) material on the space shuttles and telescopes, and many exciting books with vivid illustrations. You've planned a field trip to an observatory and invited an astronomer to visit the classroom. You have worked out a time line for several weeks' worth of individual and group investigations and projects.

But now it is time for you to think about evaluation and to clarify your values regarding complex evaluation issues. How will you know what students have learned at the end of this unit? What do you expect them to learn? What techniques will you use to find out whether they have learned what you expect? What about the possibility that they may learn something different from what you expect or even that some students who become very actively engaged in the study may learn more than you expect? How will you know what they learned? How will students know? How will you assign students science grades at the end of this unit? How will you communicate to the students' parents what each has gained from the unit?

The following sections describe a variety of assessment devices. Each one has a variety of uses and applications. Each one provides answers to different questions teachers have about evaluation. To illustrate how they compare and how they complement one another, each will be applied to the astronomy unit described previously.

Reflective teachers will consider each alternative and decide whether and how to use such measures in their own classrooms. Recognizing that this introductory text can only provide minimal information about each assessment method, the reflective teacher will want to search actively for more information about certain methods in order to fully understand their value and use before incorporating them into a program that affects children's lives.

Informal Observations

Teachers use informal observation intuitively from the first moment the students enter the classroom at the beginning of the term. They watch groups to see how students relate to one another; they watch individuals to spot patterns of behavior that are either unusually disruptive or extremely productive. To manage a classroom effectively, "withit" teachers are alert to the overt and covert actions of their students at all times.

Informal observations also have academic implications. Teachers who observe their students during a lesson are able to evaluate their understanding. Spotting a blank look, a nervous pencil tapping, or a grimace of discomfort on a student's face, the teacher can stop the lesson, check for understanding, and reteach the material to meet the needs of the students who did not understand.

As students read aloud, primary teachers observe and listen for patterns of errors in decoding words. They may also listen to the expression in the student's voice to determine whether the student is comprehending the material or simply saying words aloud. They listen for signs that indicate whether the student is interested in or bored with the material. An additional tool of informal observation is asking the student pertinent questions to check for understanding and determine the student's thought processes. This one-to-one interaction provides the type of data and information not measured by any paper-and-pencil test.

By observing the student read, asking a few questions, and comparing the results with other students of the same grade or age, the teacher is able to assess many things, including (1) the extent to which the student is able to use phonics and context clues to decode reading material, (2) the student's approximate reading level in terms of sight vocabulary, and (3) the student's comprehension level. In addition, the reflective teacher uses informal observation to gather information about the student's affective qualities, including confidence level, interest in the subject or in reading itself, amount of effort the student is willing to give to the task, and expectations the student has about success or failure in the subject.

By observing as students write or by reading what they have written, teachers can gather similar data about children's writing abilities, interests, and expectations. As students work out unfamiliar math problems, teachers are careful to observe who works quickly and who is struggling. Then they can gather the struggling students together for an extra tutoring session.

In the astronomy unit, the teacher may observe as students take part in discussions to determine the extent to which various students understand the concepts. When students are visiting the observatory, the teacher can watch them to learn about their interests in various aspects of the topic. When an astronomer visits the classroom, the teacher listens to the students' questions to assess the depth of understanding they have achieved.

Informal observations are one of the most powerful assessment devices the teacher can use to gather new information about children's learning patterns and needs. Teachers may gather data about a student from academic and psychological tests, but in the end, it is the informal observation that most teachers rely on to understand the test data and make a final evaluation about appropriate placement or a grade value for a student's work.

Performance Tasks to Show Mastery of Objectives

In contrast to informal evaluations, which provide useful subjective information, behavioral objectives are relatively formal and provide useful objective data about what students have learned. Do not assume that teachers choose one or the other of these two devices. Many reflective teachers know that it is valuable to gather both objective and subjective data. They may choose behavioral objectives as a means of gathering hard data about what students have achieved during classroom learning experiences and compare those data with the subjective information they have gathered during their informal observations.

To plan an assessment system based on students mastering certain specified outcomes or objectives, the teacher must begin before teaching the lesson. By preplanning a unit with specific outcomes or a lesson with very concrete behavioral objectives, the teacher specifies the skills that students should be able to demonstrate at the conclusion of the lesson and the criterion for success. Teachers then plan learning experiences that are linked with the outcomes. After each objective has been taught and students have had an opportunity to practice the new skill, a quiz, worksheet, or other assessment product asks students to demonstrate that they have mastered the new skill and can perform it with few errors.

When each lesson is introduced, the teacher describes the prespecified criterion for success to the students. The criterion for success may be specified as a percentage or as a minimum number of correct responses. For example, the following behavioral objective specifies 80% (or 16 of the 20 possible items) as the acceptable demonstration of mastery of this objective:

Spelling Objective: When the teacher reads the list of 20 spelling words aloud, students will write 80% of the words, using correct spelling and legible handwriting.

A criterion-referenced test such as the weekly spelling test common in many classrooms demonstrates whether the students have mastered the new skill. To record student achievement, teachers may write the percentage of correct responses that each student attained in a gradebook.

For more complex objectives, teachers design performance tasks that require students to demonstrate what they have learned. Marzano, Pickering, and McTighe (1993) describe a system that allows teachers to design performance tasks that measure growth in communication skills, information processing, and other such complex acts. For example, students may present oral reports on a NASA satellite launch and the teacher may evaluate their knowledge and communication skills by using a rubric such as the following (Marzano et al., 1993, p.85):

Rubric for Communication Skills and Oral Presentations:
   4. Clearly and effectively communicates the main idea or theme and provides support that contains rich, vivid, and powerful detail.
   3. Clearly communicates the main idea or theme and provides suitable support and detail.
   2. Communicates important information but without a clear theme or overall structure.
   1. Communicates information in isolated pieces in a random fashion.

Criterion-Referenced Quizzes and Tests

Quizzes are frequently used with behavioral objectives to determine whether students are successfully gaining each new skill or bit of knowledge in a unit of study. Quizzes are generally short, consisting of only a few questions or items, and are thought of as formative assessments, providing teachers with a way to know whether the students are learning the material day by day.

Tests, however, may consist of many items and are generally thought of as summative assessments. Tests are often given at the end of a unit and contain a variety of items that measure students' achievement of content and skills that have been taught during a period.

In both cases, the term *criterion-referenced* refers directly to the criterion established for each behavioral objective. Each item on a criterion-referenced test should match a preestablished criterion. Criterion referencing provides objective data about material that all students in the class have had an equal opportunity to learn.

Objective tests can take a variety of forms. The most common are matching, true–false, multiple choice, and short answer or completion forms.

Matching items are those that provide both the question and response. Students have only to recognize the correct response for each item and draw a line to connect the two. Items appear in a column on one side of the paper and the responses in a different order on the other side. In terms of Bloom's taxonomy, matching items are an excellent way of measuring knowledge-level objectives that require students to recognize correct responses. An example of a matching quiz related to the astronomy unit might look like this:

Jupiter	Planet with rings and many moons
Earth	Planet closest to the sun
Mercury	Planet that is ⅗ water
Saturn	Largest planet

To construct fair matching items, each right-column response must be clearly identified with only one item on the left. In our astronomy test, for example, descriptions of the planets need to contain unambiguous elements so that only one matches each planet. If several responses are vaguely correct, the reliability and therefore the objectivity of the test decline.

True–false items are also knowledge-level items, consisting of a statement that students must recognize as either true or false. These items are difficult to write, because they must be factual and objective if they are to provide useful data. If items contain unsupported opinions or generalizations, the students must guess what the teacher intended.

For our astronomy unit, we might construct a quiz with statements such as these:

True	False	The sun orbits the Earth.
True	False	Venus is smaller than Jupiter.
True	False	Mars is closer to the sun than Neptune.

These items are reliable in that the correct responses are not likely to change in our lifetime. They are also valid because every item is an element directly related to our objective of teaching students about the physical characteristics of the solar system.

As examples of less reliable and less valid items, consider these:

True	False	Venus is a more interesting planet than Uranus.
True	False	The sun will never stop shining on the Earth.

Multiple-choice items also measure knowledge-level objectives because they call for the student to recognize a fact or idea. A multiple-choice item contains a question, problem, or unfinished statement followed by several responses. The directions tell the student to mark the one correct answer. While college admission tests may contain several near-right responses and students are expected to use reasoning to determine which one is best, classroom tests should probably be constructed with only one correct response. As in other objective measures, reliability and validity of each item must be considered.

To fit the astronomy unit, two valid and reliable items are these:

1. Which planet is known as the red planet?
   A. Venus
   B. Orion
   C. Mars
   D. Jupiter

2. It would take longest to travel from Earth to
   A. Neptune
   B. Mercury
   C. Venus
   D. Saturn

Short-answer or *completion* items supply a question or an unfinished statement, and students are expected to supply a word, phrase, number, or symbol. These items are used primarily to test students' knowledge of specific facts and terminology. In our astronomy unit, two examples are these:

1. The planet Saturn has rings around it.
2. Which planet has the most moons?

The advantage of the four types of objective items that comprise most criterion-referenced tests is that they objectively measure students' knowledge of the basic content of a subject. They can be written to match directly the criteria of the teacher's objectives for the lessons. They are also relatively easy to correct, and the scores are easily recorded and can be averaged to provide the basis for report card grades.

The disadvantage of such items is that they only measure students' understanding of basic knowledge-level content and skills. They do not provide information about what students comprehend, how they would apply the knowledge they have gained, what they would create, or how they analyze and evaluate the ideas they have learned.

Mastery Learning Assessment

Some teachers prefer to use a teaching strategy known as *mastery learning* to motivate students to learn a sequence of skills. In mastery learning, individual students work through a series of learning experiences at their own pace and demonstrate mastery as they complete each objective. The teacher uses the information gained on the tests to provide helpful feedback for reteaching rather than as a record of achievement. Summative evaluations occur only at the end of a unit of study, when students are expected to demonstrate mastery of a whole sequence or unit of learning. Grades of unit tests are recorded and become the basis for determining students' grades.

In the astronomy unit, the teacher may have written a number of outcome statements, such as these:

After viewing the filmstrip on the solar system, the students will be able to match pictures of each planet with its name, with no more than one error.

Students will be able to draw and label an illustration of the solar system with the sun and nine planets in their respective orbits, with 100% accuracy.

Together these two outcomes will inform the teacher whether students have learned the names, distinctive visual elements, and locations of the planets in the solar system. To measure whether students have mastered this content, the teacher simply carries out the tasks described in the objectives after students have had sufficient opportunity to learn the material. The teacher prepares a matching quiz with a column of nine names and another column of nine pictures of the planets. For those who do not achieve the criterion of eight correct answers, the teacher can provide a reteaching experience or require students to do additional reading on their own. They can be retested until they achieve the criterion.

On another occasion, the teacher distributes blank paper and asks students to draw and label the solar system. From these two objectives and others like them, the teacher can begin to answer the question "How will I know what they have learned?" Also, the data gathered from this assessment system are more readily translated into letter grades than are the data from informal observations.

Essays Evaluated with Rubric Guidelines

Essays have the exact opposite advantages and disadvantages of criterion-referenced tests. They are subjective rather than objective. Unless they are given very specific criteria on which to base their ratings, two or more teachers rarely evaluate an essay in the same way. Essays are also very time consuming to read and mark.

However, essays provide teachers with an excellent means of knowing what students comprehend, how they would apply their new learning, and how they analyze and evaluate the ideas and concepts. Essays also provide students with opportunities to be creative by asking them to synthesize a number of previously unrelated notions into an original expression of their own. Essays can answer the question "How much more have they learned than what I taught in this unit?"

To improve the way teachers rate essays, many school systems employ a rubric guide that specifies what an essay must contain and how it must appear on the page to earn a specific mark or grade. Teachers who use a rubric to guide their assessment of essays usually limit the topic of the essay with specific parameters and may even specify what must be included in the response. For example, in the astronomy unit, the teacher may want to assess whether students can describe the concept of outer space in their own words. This will provide information about how much students truly comprehend about the subject rather than what they simply remember. For example, a teacher may present students with these guidelines for writing their essay on the solar system:

> Write a two-paragraph essay in your own words comparing the Earth's atmosphere with space. Tell why humans cannot live in outer space without life support. Use examples and provide evidence to support your ideas.

These guidelines are fairly explicit in terms of both length and content. For these reasons, this form of essay is relatively objective. To make it even more likely that two or more teachers would look for similar elements when correcting the papers, school systems may provide teachers with *rubric evaluation* samples of student work, along with specific descriptions for measuring success on a particular essay topic.

Grade	Characteristics of Essay
A	Paragraphs are well organized and contain at least six sentences. Facts are accurate and evidence is clearly given to support the student's viewpoints.
B	Paragraphs contain at least four sentences. Most facts are accurate. Examples are given to support ideas.
C	Paragraphs contain at least three sentences. Some facts are accurate, although one or more errors are present. One example is given.
D	Paper contains only one paragraph. Some facts are accurate, though no evidence or examples are given to support them.
F	Unconnected sentences contain few accurate facts. Many errors are stated. No examples given.

This format for essay evaluation is especially useful for assessing students' levels of comprehension on a topic. It also provides an opportunity for students to demonstrate their ability to analyze the topic, but limits the use of synthesis and evaluation. If students are provided with the rubric system before they begin writing, they are more likely to know what the teacher expects of them and thus be able to deliver it.

For other purposes, the *extended response essay* gives students more freedom to express ideas and opinions and to use synthesis-level thinking skills to transform knowledge into a creative new idea. In the astronomy unit the teacher may hope that students will gain a sense of responsibility for the Earth after studying its place in the universe. This affective goal for the unit may also be expressed as a series of problem-solving objectives. For example, consider this goal:

> At the end of the unit, students will write an essay entitled "The Big Blue Marble," in which they express their own hopes and fears for the future of the Earth. The essays will be edited, rewritten, illustrated, and displayed for parents to view on parent's night.

This extended-response essay calls on students to integrate all that they have learned in this unit and combine it with previous learning from geography and social studies units. Their individual experiences and outside readings are likely to affect their responses as well. Objectivity in marking this essay is very low. It is quite likely teachers will view the responses very differently from one another. Nevertheless, within a single classroom, a teacher can say or state a set of criteria or expectations that can lead students to write a successful essay. In this instance, as stated in the objective, students will have an opportunity to receive critical feedback and make corrections on their essays before the final products are displayed.

Despite the lack of objectivity of extended-response essays, there is good reason to include them in an educational program. They provide invaluable information about the creativity, values, philosophy, and maturity of students. Moreover, they encourage students to become more creative and give them practice in making difficult judgments. One of the most effective ways to provide students with the information they need to succeed is to provide them with the rubric descriptions prior to the time they write their essays. When students can see the criteria on which their work will be evaluated, they are able to meet the expectations with much greater degrees of success than when they try to guess what the teacher expects or wants from them.

Oral Reports and Examinations

Like essays, *oral reports* can be restricted or unrestricted depending on the type of assessment the teacher wants to generate. To increase objectivity and communicate expectations to students, teachers can create rubric systems describing the length and format of the oral report as well as what must be included. Examples of *restricted* oral reports include book reports in which students are expected to describe the main characters, the setting, the plot, and their favorite part of the story. In a restricted oral examination, teachers may ask questions that students must answer within specified parameters. In the astronomy unit, an oral examination may be scheduled for a certain day. Students are told to prepare for it by reading material supplied by NASA on the U.S. space program. In the examination, teachers ask questions taken from the reading material, and students are expected to respond in their own words. For example,

> Tell how the astronauts prepared for weightlessness.
>
> Describe the food astronauts eat in space.

As teachers listen to the students' responses, it is possible to make a judgment about whether their answers are right or wrong. It is also possible to assess whether the students have a poor, average, or unusually good understanding of the ideas they are speaking about. The teacher's evaluation of the students' responses can be recorded in some form, to be shared with the student later.

Unrestricted oral reports allow students more opportunities to speak about matters of great interest and importance to them. They encourage students to use their imagination to generate synthesis-level responses or to be persuasive about a matter of opinion or judgment. For example, consider these tasks:

> Describe the space journey you would like to take.
>
> Tell what you think should be NASA's next big undertaking.

Debate is a form of oral examination in that it provides students with an opportunity to prepare to speak about a subject by learning a great deal of content and evidence for opinions prior to the event. During the debate, teachers can assess the students' energy and effort used in gathering information, as well as their understanding of the topic.

In evaluating oral presentations, teachers may write comments as they listen, or they may videotape the presentations so that they can evaluate them more comprehensively later. Students may be involved in self-evaluation of their own efforts as well. They can view the videotapes and discuss with the teacher what they did well and what they need to improve.

Designing Authentic Assessment Tasks

Teachers can construct assessment tasks that measure student performance in terms of using the higher level thinking skills of analysis and evaluation, as well as critical thinking skills of observation and inference and problem-solving strategies such as the creation and testing of hypotheses. These tests can be constructed as paper-and-pencil exams, presenting a situation or dilemma and asking students to respond to it in various ways. Such a test might consist of a passage to be read that describes a problem or dilemma. Maps, charts, graphs, or other forms of data might also be available on the test. The test items then consist of questions that allow the student to observe, infer, formulate a hypothesis, design methods of testing the hypothesis, and speculate about the possible outcome.

Another common method of assessing student's authentic learning is to encourage them to do independent research on one aspect of a unit theme and to create a product that shows what they have learned. This method allows students to demonstrate their knowledge, comprehension, and all four of the higher level thinking skills on a topic. This assessment technique is appropriate for every area of the curriculum. Students can do independent research or make an independent investigation in math, science, social studies, literature, music, or art. This method lends itself especially well to interdisciplinary units.

The strategy is for the teacher to introduce a unit or theme and provide some teacher-centered instruction on it at the outset. Readings may be assigned, and quizzes and worksheets may be used to assess the extent to which the student is developing a knowledge base about the topic. Essays or oral presentations may be assigned to assess whether students comprehend the main ideas and concepts of the topic. Finally, each student selects one aspect of the main topic on the basis of individual preference or interest and begins to research that subtopic independently. Each student decides on a final product that will demonstrate what has been learned and achieved during the independent study.

The kinds of products that students might create as a result of this type of investigation are limitless. Many teachers prefer to plan their evaluations of student accomplishment to correspond with Bloom's taxonomy. Specific student products are appropriate for learning objectives at all six levels. A sample of them can be found in Figure 11.1.

Teachers may evaluate these student products using a rubric checklist or rating scale. Very specific rubric systems may be prespecified so that students know exactly what their product must demonstrate to earn a high mark or positive evaluation from the teacher. Reflective teachers who wish to encourage critical thinking and reflectiveness among their students are also very likely to involve the students in self-evaluation of their own products. When students evaluate their work critically, they learn how to

Figure 11.1   Student products related to Bloom's taxonomy.

Characteristics of Each Level	Products Associated with Each Level
Knowledge Level	**Knowledge Level**
Can recognize and recall specific terms, facts, and symbols.	Worksheet; label a given diagram; memorize poem or song; list; quiz; recognition of math symbols; spelling bee; response to flashcard.
Comprehension Level	**Comprehension Level**
Can understand the main idea of material heard, viewed, or read. Is able to interpret or summarize the ideas in own words.	Written paragraph or summary of main idea; oral retelling of story; use of math symbols and numbers in simple calculations; report.
Application Level	**Application Level**
Is able to apply an abstract idea in a concrete situation, to solve a problem or relate it to prior experiences.	Diagram; map; model; illustration; analogy; mental problem solving; action plan; teaches others; diorama; costume; diary; journal.
Analysis Level	**Analysis Level**
Can break down a concept or idea into its constituent parts. Is able to identify relationships among elements, cause and effect, similarities and differences.	Graph; survey; chart; diagram; report showing cause and effect, differences and similarities, comparisons and contrasts.
Synthesis Level	**Synthesis Level**
Is able to put together elements in new and original ways. Creates patterns or structures that were not there before.	Artwork; story; play; skit; poetry; invention; song; composition; game; collection; hypothesis; essay; speech; videotape; film; computer program.
Evaluation Level	**Evaluation Level**
Makes informed judgments about the value of ideas or materials. Uses standards and criteria to support opinions and views.	Debate; discussion; recommendation; letter to editor; court trial; panel; chart showing hierarchies, rank order, or priorities.

Created by Judy Eby from *Taxonomy of Educational Objectives: Handbook I: Cognitive Domain* by Benjamin S. Bloom et al. Copyright 1956, 1984 by Longman Publishing Group.

become more independent and responsible for revising and improving their work without an outside evaluator.

Rubrics, Checklists, and Rating Scales

When teachers wish to assess students' products or presentations, they can convey their reactions to the students in a conference or write comments on a piece of paper to give to the students. These methods suffice for informing the students, in a general way, about whether they have met the teacher's expectations with the product, and they may be adequate for evaluating an unrestricted product or presentation.

When the teacher has prespecified the criteria for a product or presentation and several important elements must be included, the teacher may choose to create a *rubric* or *checklist* to use for notation when listening, for example, to the speech. This is frequently done when the objective is for students to use effective speaking skills in a presentation. In preparing the students for the speech, the teacher might specify several important elements that the students should incorporate, such as maintaining eye contact with the audience, using appropriate volume to be heard by everyone in the room, and speaking rather than reading during the presentation. By preparing a simple checklist with these items on it, the teacher can quickly and accurately record whether each student used these skills in his or her presentations. To make the whole system even more valuable, when the teacher shares the rubrics with the students ahead of time, students are able to make much better judgments about what to study, what to include, or how to present the information they have learned.

Rubrics and checklists can record mastery of many basic skills in the primary grades. Each item on the checklist can correspond directly to a behavioral objective. Together the items on a checklist provide an overview of a sequence of objectives. Kindergarten teachers frequently employ checklists to record the letter recognition of each pupil, letter by letter. Primary teachers use checklists to record mastery of basic math operations. Intermediate and middle school teachers may use checklists to record whether students have demonstrated fundamental research skills. In our astronomy unit, for example, the teacher may combine a goal of developing research and study skills with the goal of content mastery. To record the accomplishment of these skills, the teacher may use a checklist such as the one shown in Figure 11.2.

Checklists provide useful and efficient means of recording information about the accomplishments of individual students. They are also valuable during a student–teacher conference. Both teacher and student can quickly see what has been achieved and what still lies ahead. Checklists are also valuable when teachers confer with parents about the student's progress along a set of learning objectives.

Rating scales are used in circumstances similar to those of checklists. They provide additional information, however, in the form of a rating of how well the student achieved each element or skill on the list. Rating scales are useful in providing students with feedback that rates their performance on an objective. In the astronomy unit, for example, students' products may be turned in and evaluated by the teacher, using a rating scale of important elements. In many classrooms, teachers involve the student in

Figure 11.2   Astronomy unit checklist of research and study skills.

Name _____	**Grade** _____

This is a record of research and study skills demonstrated by this student. The teacher's initials and date indicate when the skill was successfully demonstrated.

Date	Initials	Skill Area
_____	_____	A. Located a book on astronomy in the card catalog
_____	_____	B. Located a book on astronomy on the library shelves
_____	_____	C. Used the table of contents to find a topic
_____	_____	D. Used the index to find a subtopic
_____	_____	E. Orally interpreted a graph or chart
_____	_____	F. Took notes on a chapter in a book on astronomy
_____	_____	G. Summarized the chapter from notes
_____	_____	H. Wrote a bibliographic entry for the book

their own evaluation of the product and the efforts expended in creating them. In Figure 11.3, a rating scale is structured so that both the student and the teacher rate the finished product.

A rubric system is similar to a checklist, but also employs very detailed descriptions of the specific levels of mastery the teacher hopes students will attain. Student products are then compared to the levels of mastery described in the rubric system. In Figure 11.4, a rubric system is shown that allows the teacher to compare student products related to the astronomy research project against a set of very specific criteria. As has been suggested before, if students are given this rubric system prior to beginning the unit, they are empowered to make better choices about how to use their time, what to study, and how to present the material they have learned.

Learning Contracts

A learning contract is a device that can be thought of both as a teaching strategy and a means of assessment. The learning contract described in Chapter 9 listed several required activities and a number of options for the unit on settling the western United States. Teachers using this strategy meet with individual students to agree on a suitable number and type of optional activities. The activities on the contract then provide the structure for daily learning experiences. When the unit is complete, the contract is used as the basis for assessing what each student has accomplished. Just as in adult life, students are held accountable for meeting the terms of their contracts. If they succeed, they can expect a positive evaluation. If they have not met the terms of their contract, they can expect to have to explain why and describe what they will do to honor their contract.

Figure 11.3   Astronomy unit rating scale of the solar system model.

Name _____ Grade _____

To the student: Please evaluate your own product, using the following scale:

    O = OUTSTANDING; one of my best efforts
    S = SATISFACTORY; I accomplished what I set out to do
    N = NEEDS IMPROVEMENT; I need to revise and improve this element

Student's Rating	Skill Area	Teacher's Rating
_____	Did adequate research and information gathering	_____
_____	Elements of the model are accurate in shape	_____
_____	Elements of the model are accurate in scale (except for orbits of planets)	_____
_____	Labeling is accurate and legible	_____
_____	Legend is accurate and legible	_____
_____	Model is visually interesting and pleasing	_____

Learning contracts can take several forms and can even be structured so that the student makes a contract to receive a certain grade for a specified amount of work. A point system can be employed to allow students to select from among options and earn the grade they desire. For example, for the astronomy unit, a learning contract with a built-in point system for earning a grade is shown in Figure 11.5.

Learning contracts also serve as the basis for recording accomplishments. In the sample learning contract for the astronomy unit, the parent is also required to sign the contract, agreeing to support the student's efforts. This strategy is a very efficient way to communicate with parents about the goals and expectations of the class. Later, during parent–teacher conferences, the parent can see the work that was accomplished. If a student did not complete the contract, the parent can see what was left undone.

Portfolios of Student Products

Portfolios are collections of work samples designed to illustrate a person's accomplishments in a talent area. Photographers collect portfolios of their best photos; artists collect their artwork; composers collect their compositions. Assessment portfolios are used to document what a student has achieved in school. To use this technique, teachers collect samples of each student's work and put them in a file folder with that student's name on it. Some teachers collect many types of work in a single portfolio; others have writing portfolios that contain only writing samples, math portfolios filled with worksheets and tests, and others for other subject areas.

Teachers may collect only samples of a student's very best work in a portfolio to demonstrate the maximum performance of that student. However, an argument can be

Figure 11.4   Rubric grading evaluation system for astronomy research project.

To the student: Read these criteria before you begin your research so that you will know how to earn the level you want to attain.

Turn in a 5–10 page booklet on the solar system. The booklet may contain a combination of words, pictures, graphs, and any other types of illustrations that show an understanding of the physical elements of the planets, moons, and sun that make up our solar system. The booklets will be evaluated according to the following criteria:

Level 4: The student clearly and completely identifies the important planets and moons of the solar system and shows how they are related to the sun and each other in size and space. There is a combination of verbal descriptions and visual illustrations that make the distinguishing features of each planet very evident. The writing is well organized and references are given for sources of information. At least four references are provided.

Level 3: The student clearly identifies the planets and some of the most important moons of the solar system. Relationships of size and space are given, though they may be distorted in some cases. Verbal information is fairly well organized and illustrations are useful in distinguishing among the planets. At least two references are given as sources of information.

Level 2: The student correctly names the nine planets and shows that they travel around the sun. Relationships among planets are not accurate. The booklet uses more pictures than words. Only one source of information is provided.

Level 1: The student incorrectly labels planets and shows little understanding of their relationship to the sun and to each other. Verbal information is given as captions for illustrations only. No source of information is given.

---

made for collecting samples of ordinary or typical work as well. These samples demonstrate how well the individual is performing on a day-to-day basis.

Portfolios may be kept for a long or short time. Many teachers collect writing samples in the first week of school, then periodically throughout the school year. In some cases the teacher may assign a writing topic during the first week and then assign the very same topic during the last week of school. When the two samples on the same topic are compared, the growth and development of the students' writing abilities is plain for everyone to see.

A short-term portfolio may be collected for the duration of a learning unit. For example, in the astronomy unit, all of the student's work, including quizzes, essays, pictures, and photos of the model solar system can be collected in a portfolio to document that student's accomplishment during the unit. If a contract was used during the unit, the contract will be included in the portfolio along with the work samples.

Figure 11.5   Sample learning contract.

Astronomy Unit Learning Contract

I, _____ , a student in the fifth grade at Otis
School, do hereby contract to complete the following tasks during my investigation
of the solar system.

Furthermore, I agree to complete these tasks by _____ .

I understand that I am agreeing to earn _____ points, which will earn a
grade of _____ if my work is evaluated to be acceptable. I understand that the point values listed below are the maximum number that can be
earned for each task and that fewer points may be awarded.

Points Needed to Earn Specific Grades

> 90 = A	> 80 = B	> 70 = C	> 60 = D	< 60 = F

_____	10 pts	Read chapter 7 in the science text. Do exercises, pp. 145–146.
_____	10 pts	Matching quiz
_____	10 pts	True-false quiz
_____	10 pts	Multiple-choice quiz
_____	10 pts	Short-answer quiz
_____	15 pts	Drawing of the solar system, labeled correctly
_____	20 pts	Model of the solar system, labeled and scaled to size
_____	10 pts	Essay on Earth's atmosphere and outer space
_____	10 pts	Essay on "The Big Blue Marble"
_____	05 pts	per answer on NASA oral exam
_____	10 pts	Oral report on "A Space Journey I'd Like to Take"
_____	10 pts	Finished Checklist on Research Skills

Signed this day _____ at _____ School.

_____   _____
      student signature   teacher signature

_____   _____
      parent signature   witness signature

Portfolios may be used at all grade levels and for any subject or course a student takes. When portfolios are meant to be used to document student accomplishment, they must be organized so that they reveal the development of a skill or the growing understanding of a set of ideas. To demonstrate growth and change, Wolf (1989) suggests collecting "biographies of works, a range of works and reflections" (p. 37).

The biography of a work consists of several drafts of a work, showing the student's initial conception of the project, the first attempts, and the final product. By collecting these items, the teacher can document the growth and development of the student. Wolf (1989) further recommends that after completing this collection, the teacher should ask the student to reexamine all stages of the work and reflect on the process and the products from beginning to end. The student's reflection may be done in writing or captured on audiotape (and later transcribed onto paper) and should then be included in the portfolio itself. This self-evaluation is valuable in helping the student develop metacognitive abilities that then can be applied to future projects.

Wolf (1989) also suggests that teachers deliberately collect a range of works, meaning a diverse collection, consisting of journals, essays, poems, drawings, charts, graphs, letters, tests, and samples of daily work. When using the portfolios as a basis for a parent–teacher conference, this range allows the teacher to discuss and document many different aspects of the student's school accomplishments.

Primary teachers must take responsibility for collecting and filing all items in students' portfolios. At the upper grades, however, students may be asked to keep their own. The teacher may suggest items to be included, and the student may decide on others. At the end of a people and nature unit, for example, each student may have a portfolio containing the tests, lab reports, essays, creative writing, and charts created for the unit.

At the end of a unit or term, the teacher can collect the portfolios, examine them, ask for reflections on certain items or sets of items, and arrange the materials in chronological order in preparation for parent–teacher conferences. Teachers often ask students to create covers for their portfolios, which are then on display during parent open house visits or conferences.

Portfolios of student work are an excellent way to communicate with parents about a student's accomplishments. When the parent and teacher look at the writing sample together, they can both understand what the student's strengths and weaknesses are at a glance. When a parent sees the signed contract and the completed work, both parent and teacher see the same evidence to support the resulting grades.

Videotape Records

When the purpose of evaluation is to record the accomplishment of a student and allow later analysis and more comprehensive evaluation, a videotape is an excellent way to capture and store a variety of learning events. Speeches can be videotaped easily. So can dramas, skits, presentations, and displays of students' products.

Videos are also excellent ways to communicate to parents the accomplishments of a student or the entire class. They allow all interested parties to view the final products or performances of a unit of study. Teachers can store on tape a whole year's worth of accomplishments.

Video recordings also provide teachers with data they need to evaluate their own plans. By reviewing a video of a classroom learning event, reflective teachers are able to gain new understandings about what students need from their learning environment to be successful.

Cooperative Group Projects and Products

Many of the assessment methods described in this chapter can be adapted for cooperative groups. Evaluation of cooperative group efforts should include an assessment of both a task that requires a group effort to complete and an assessment of individual efforts to ensure that each member of the group takes responsibility for doing personal reading and preparation.

As an illustration of how to adapt ordinary lessons and units into cooperative lessons and units, consider the astronomy unit. To adapt this unit for use by cooperative groups, each group can function as a study team with directions to assist one another in reading and preparing for the quizzes. Group scores can be computed and recorded for each quiz at the same time that individual scores are recorded.

The contract system works very well with cooperative groups. When used in this way, there is one contract per group instead of per individual. Each group negotiates what they will accomplish together. Evaluations can include peer assessments, with members of the group providing critical feedback for one another.

Assessment of student accomplishment is a complex and multifaceted undertaking. There is no one best way to assess what students have learned or accomplished in school. Some methods work better than others at various grade levels. Some work better than others with different individuals. This chapter has provided you with a number of assessment methods that you can use to develop a repertoire of assessment devices that will become the basis for making judgments about the accomplishments of your students.

Reporting Student Accomplishments

Report cards. These two words are likely to elicit memories filled with anxiety and a variety of other conflicting emotions for most people.

In your many years of schooling, you have probably received more than 50 report cards. You probably viewed many with relief and happiness and proudly displayed them to your parents; others may have caused torment and disbelief. On occasion, you may have questioned the teacher's fairness or integrity; you may have questioned whether the teacher really got to know you or understood the effort you put into your work. Perhaps you have even approached a teacher and challenged the grade you received, showing evidence of why the assigned grade was unjustified.

Eight or 9 weeks into your first school year, you will face the task of deciding on and recording report card grades for your students. Many first-year teachers consider the responsibility one of their most difficult challenges. Experienced teachers often report that the task does not seem to get easier as the years pass. In fact, many reflective teachers find that the more they know about grades and children, the more difficult it is to sum up the work and efforts of a student in a single letter grade.

In Tracy Kidder's (1989) description of a year in a fifth-grade classroom entitled *Among Schoolchildren*, the teacher, Chris Zajac, takes a group of social studies tests home to grade:

> A stack of social studies tests lay before her on the table, slippery sheets of ditto paper, the questions in purple ink—fill in the blank questions that asked for definitions of terms such as "Tory." The test closed, as always, with an essay question; the students had to describe briefly a Famous Patriot. She stared at the stack of tests for a moment. "Do I want to?" she murmured to herself, and took the first test, Arabella's, off the pile. Chris's pen made a one-part scratching sound, inscribing red C's down most of the page, and she began to smile.
>
> "84 = B," Chris wrote across the top of Arabella's test. . . . (pp. 72–73)[1]

Although Arabella's paper proves to be a pleasure to grade, Chris later encounters the test turned in by Jimmy:

> Chris stared at Jimmy's test. He had not tried to answer more than half the questions, and had not written an essay. Jimmy was the sleepiest boy Chris had encountered in years, also one of the stubbornest when it came to evading work that required thought. . . .
>
> Chris would explain an assignment. Jimmy would say, "I don't understand." Chris would explain again. Jimmy would say, "I don't understand." Of course, he was waiting for her to do it for him. . . .
>
> Chris stared at the window. Maybe tomorrow, she thought, she'd make Jimmy take this test again. She went back to the pile. (p. 76)

Still later in the evening:

> Chris sat down again at the table. Pedro's test lay on top of the pile. She read,
>
> Tory. Like a grup of sogrs.
>
> Chris placed her hand like a visor on her forehead. She stared at the blackened window across the room and slowly shook her head. "Poor kid."
>
> . . . . He didn't often talk. He never misbehaved. He almost always tried to do his homework. It was as another teacher had said, "Poor Pedro. He works so hard to get an F." His situation had seemed intolerable to Chris the very first day when, after assigning some simple classwork, she stopped to look over Pedro's shoulder, and he looked up at her and asked, "Did I do good, Mrs. Zajac?" (pp. 79–80)

---

[1] Excerpts from *Among Schoolchildren* by Tracy Kidder. Copyright © 1989 by John Tracy Kidder. Reprinted by permission of Houghton Mifflin Company. All rights reserved.

"36 = F," Chris wrote on Pedro's social studies test. If she was not honest, she would never have the tangible evidence of progress or decline. (p. 85)

In carefully correcting and grading these tests, Chris Zajac is performing an important part of her job. She is holding students accountable for learning what they have been taught in her classroom. She is also providing them with feedback so that they can understand what they have accomplished and what they still need to work on. She is also contributing data to a growing record kept on each student so that assistance and special educational opportunities can be provided if necessary. But the task of grading is an arduous and time-consuming one, and the teacher may feel as emotional about giving grades to students as the students feel about receiving them.

Reflective teachers struggle with many conflicting ideas, thoughts, and concerns when they confront existing evaluation systems. Systems using letter grades are likely to be based on the assumption that students vary in ability and acquire learning by passively receiving knowledge from the teacher. From this assumption, it is logical to conclude that students should be evaluated by determining what they have learned and how this compares to other students of the same age. Categorizing and rank ordering of students is the next step and is done by assigning letter grades to label their respective categories of ability. Teachers with this perspective can be overheard saying "John is an A student, and Sally is a C student."

Reflective, caring teachers are often very uncomfortable with such statements. They recognize the complex mix of environmental, nutritional, genetic, and experiential factors that contribute to each student's success or lack of success in school. Moreover, according to their view of teaching and learning, it is the teachers' responsibility to determine their students' needs and then plan a series of learning experiences and the scaffolding each student needs to experience success. The competitive nature of letter grades contrasts sharply with this philosophy.

Due to the time-consuming nature of the task of correcting students' work and the complexities of the evaluation processes described previously, it is easy to see why school personnel have resorted to a form of shorthand to record and report student progress. Most teachers have too many students and too little time to hold discussions with each student's parents or to write extensive narratives of each student's learning on a regular basis. Schools use standardized shorthand methods known as *grades* and *test scores* to communicate with parents, future teachers, college admissions personnel, and future employers (Oakes & Lipton, 1990).

The practice of awarding letter grades as measures of individual achievement has been part of the U.S. educational scene for many decades. In the 1960s and 1970s, personnel in some school districts attempted to replace conventional report cards with detailed anecdotal records, describing what each student had accomplished in each subject area during the course or term. But these attempts to change the prevailing evaluation system met with opposition from parents, who insisted on a return to the letter grade system with which they had grown up. Parents were not satisfied with a description of their own child's achievements. They wanted to know how their child compared with other students. They expressed concern that these records would not be accepted at the most prestigious colleges.

In response to these debates, school boards and administrators in most school districts arrived at a compromise. While they reestablished the letter grade report cards for the intermediate and upper elementary grades, they retained the use of anecdotal report cards for the primary grades. This is the prevailing practice today. That means that if you are planning to teach at the primary grades (kindergarten through the second or third grades), you will be expected to write anecdotal report cards describing and documenting what each student in your classroom has learned. If you are planning to teach at the intermediate grades (second or third through sixth grade), you may be expected to compute letter grades every quarter for the students' report cards.

Computation of Grades

At the end of the astronomy unit described earlier, the grades for all of the reports, tests, and projects can be recorded in the teachers' gradebooks as shown in Figure 11.6.

Computation of the final grades for this curriculum unit involves a straightforward calculation of an average grade by assigning numerical equivalents to each letter grade, adding the five items, and dividing the total score by 5. The average scores can then be assigned a letter grade. After they are computed the grades are recorded in the student's cumulative folder and on the report cards that are sent home to parents. Intermediate report cards are likely to use letter grades to sum up the student's achievement in each academic subject. Some report cards may also provide checklists of subskills

Figure 11.6   Teacher's gradebook.

Name of Student	Graded Objectives						Average Score	Report Card Grade
	1	2	3	4	5			
Lisa	A	B	B	A	C			B
	4 +	3 +	3 +	4 +	2	=	16/5 = 3.1	
Peter	B	C	A	C	D			C+
	3 +	2 +	4 +	2 +	1	=	12/5 = 2.4	
Alejandro	B	A	A	B	A			A−
	3 +	4 +	4 +	3 +	4	=	18/5 = 3.6	

A = 4 points
B = 3
C = 2
D = 1
F = 0

beneath the letter grade as a means of explaining to parents how the letter grade was determined.

Writing Anecdotal Records

In most school districts, teachers are responsible for writing three or four report cards per year. These contain descriptions of each student's current level of accomplishment in each of the major areas of the curriculum, plus a summary of the student's work habits and social adjustment to school and peers. At the primary grades, report cards usually consist of either anecdotal records or checklists of skills rather than letter grades. Some school districts may use both. The advantage to this double format is that it allows teachers to describe and report their direct observations of a student's actual behaviors and accomplishments with sufficient detail so that parents understand the student's strengths and challenges. This is especially useful for such skill areas as listening, speaking, writing, study habits, social skills, and interests (Linn & Gronlund, 2000).

When a concern about a student arises, the teacher's daily observations of the student's work habits or social interactions can be important sources of data to help parents or other school personnel understand the student's particular needs and strengths. These observations may be augmented by the use of written anecdotal records of what the teacher observes. For example, if a student comes to school late, appears tired, and has difficulty sitting still in her desk, the teacher may want to document these observations by keeping a short anecdotal record for a week, recording how late the student is every morning, and describing episodes of falling asleep or inattentiveness. When this written record is shown to the parents, it is more likely to enlist their cooperation with the teacher in seeking answers to the problem than if the teacher simply reports orally that the student is "always late and too tired to work."

To be used to their best advantage, anecdotal records should be limited to observations of specific skills, social problems, or behavioral concerns. If a teacher sets out to record every behavior and event in a student's school day, the process will become too tiring and difficult to be feasible. Instead, when a student is exhibiting a particular behavior or difficulty in a skill area, the teacher can focus on daily descriptions of that one area and be successful in producing a useful document.

The major limitation or disadvantage of the anecdotal record is teachers' tendency to project their own value judgments into the description of a student's behavior or accomplishment. This is due, in part, to the tendency to observe what fits one's preconceived notions. "For example, they will tend to notice more desirable qualities in those pupils they like best and more undesirable qualities in those they like least" (Linn & Gronlund, 2000, p. 320). The recommended way to avoid this tendency is to keep descriptions of observed incidents separate from your interpretation. First, state exactly what happened in nonjudgmental words. Then, if you wish to add your interpretation of the event, do so in a separate paragraph and label it as such (Linn & Gronlund, 2000).

In general, a single observation is seldom as meaningful as a series of events in understanding a student's behavior. Therefore, anecdotal records should contain brief descriptions of related incidents over time to provide a reliable picture of a student's behavior.

Involving Students in Evaluation Procedures

For reflective teachers, the natural extension of the teaching process is the interactive evaluation process that encourages students to become active evaluators of their own efforts and products. The current writing programs organized around periodic student–teacher conferences and the grouping of students who edit one another's work are excellent examples of this type of evaluation. In classrooms that feature such writing programs, the teacher's role in evaluation is to confer with the students about their current writing projects and to ask questions that engage them in analyzing what they have written.

Teachers may use open-ended questions designed to gather information on what the student has intended to do in a piece of writing. When the teacher has a sufficient understanding of the student's goal, the teacher and student may begin to zero in on ways to improve the quality of the writing so that it more nearly matches the student's purpose. This may mean correcting the mechanics of the writing so that it can be understood by others, or it may mean guiding the student to rethink the way a passage is written and to consider new ways of stating the ideas.

The editing groups used in such writing programs encourage students to learn how to listen to and respect the work their peers are creating. Students in a group, typically, each read aloud from a current piece of writing and then answer questions about the content from the other students in the group. Through this type of interactive evaluation, students can learn how to work cooperatively, accept critical feedback, and write better at the same time.

This interactive evaluation system can be used in other parts of the curriculum as well. "What did you learn?" should form the core of the classroom evaluation. The more often this question is asked, the easier it is for students to identify and receive the help they need. It is a question children can learn to ask themselves (Oakes & Lipton, 1990, p. 132).

Providing students with self-evaluation checklists or rating scales assists them in posing more specific types of questions about their own progress and achievement. Checklists and rating scales that ask the student to evaluate specific outcomes may be developed for any learning activity, especially a unit of study that takes place over several weeks. Teacher evaluations can be entered on the same form to allow students and their parents to compare the student's self-evaluation with the teacher's assessment of the student's accomplishments. For example, in Figure 11.7, students are allowed to assess themselves after completing a research unit on leadership.

Interactive evaluation procedures are designed to breed success and enhance students' metacognitive capacities. They are as much a part of the *learning process* as they are a part of the assessment process. In fact, the long-term goals of most caring, reflective teachers are likely to emphasize the development of independence, self-responsi-

Figure 11.7   Interactive student–teacher evaluation for a leadership unit.

Name of student_____ **Grade**_____ **Date**_____

Leader selected for research _____

The student completes the left side of this evaluation and then the teacher will complete the right
side. Afterward, student and teacher discuss the accomplishments made by the student, decide on
areas that need to be improved, and plan goals for future learning experiences.

O = Outstanding   S = Satisfactory   N = Needs Improvement

Student Evaluation: **Teacher Evaluation:**

____   I completed the readings and assignments for this unit on time.   ____

____   I showed responsibility by bringing appropriate materials to class.   ____

____   I showed growth in my planning, decision-making, and organizational skills.   ____

____   I have gained skills in doing research and taking notes to gather information. ____

____   I used a variety of relevant and challenging resources to learn about my subject. ____

____   I improved my ability to speak in public.   ____

____   I gained confidence in my ability to speak in public.   ____

____   I gained independence in working on my own to achieve a goal.   ____

____   I am able to evaluate my own accomplishments and identify what
         I need to improve with accuracy and honesty.   ____

The most important thing I learned in this unit was:

Regarding my work in this unit, I am most proud of:

bility, self-discipline, and self-evaluation as important affective goals of education.
These goals are achieved through the development of metacognitive processes as children learn to understand how to succeed in any learning environment.

Reflective Actions for Your Professional Portfolio

Your Design for an Interactive Portfolio Assessment System

Withitness: Observe a Portfolio Assessment System

Visit a classroom in which the teacher uses an interactive portfolio assessment system. What system does this teacher use for recording grades? Are there elements of this system that seem useful to you? Do the students appear to understand the teacher's grading policies and expectations? How did the teacher help students understand the system? What would you do to improve their understanding?

Put the Issue into Perspective

Did you get good grades in elementary school? Do you believe that the grades you received were an accurate reflection of your effort and achievement? How will you determine grades in your classroom? If you choose not to use letter grades, what will you use instead to report student progress?

Widen Your Perspective

Given a choice, would you use letter grades or anecdotal records in your teaching? What place would portfolios have in your classroom?

Invite Feedback

Read more about portfolio assessment, especially current material by Dennie Palmer Wolf. Visit classrooms to observe the systems other teachers use to collect student work in portfolios.

Redefine the Issue of Assessment

After reading more about assessment and visiting teachers who are using a variety of assessment systems, how did your thinking change? What is your new frame on the issue?

Create an Action Plan

For the unit plan you are working on, plan an interactive student–teacher evaluation system that encourages students to use metacognitive processes to assess their own performance. Create a contract, checklist, or rating scale that students and teachers can use to look at the students' positive achievements and also to provide realistic and useful information about areas in which students need to improve.

Predict Possible Outcomes

Share your assessment plan with other prospective teachers. Get feedback from them on how clear and understandable your system is likely to be with students. Then try using the system with one student. Ask the student to tell you what is needed to make the plan clear, useful, and fair.

References

Guskey, T. (1994). Making the grade: What benefits students? *Educational Leadership*, 52(2), 14–19.

Kidder, T. (1989). *Among schoolchildren*. Boston: Houghton Mifflin.

Linn, R., & Gronlund, N. (2000). *Measurement and assessment in teaching* (8th ed.). Upper Saddle River, NJ: Merrill/Prentice Hall.

Marzano, R., Pickering, D., & McTighe, J. (1993). *Assessing student outcomes*. Alexandria, VA: Association for Supervision and Curriculum Development.

Oakes, J., & Lipton, M. (1990). *Making the best of schools*. New Haven, CT: Yale University Press.

Wolf, D. (1989). Portfolio assessment: Sampling student work. *Educational Leadership*, 46(7), 35–39.

12

Relational Teachers and the School Community

The teacher's role in the school community becomes more complex each day. Most school districts are undergoing some form of restructuring or systemic change that calls on teachers to take more responsibility for planning and evaluating school programs beyond their own classrooms. School restructuring is often compared to piloting an airplane and conducting a major overhaul while in flight.

While attempting to maintain a stable environment for students and faculty, many schools are overhauling their curriculum, schedules, student evaluation systems, and administrative relationships. Schlechty defines restructuring or systemic change as "changing the system of rules, roles, and relationships that govern the way time, people, space, knowledge, and technology are used and deployed" (Brandt, 1993, p. 8).

All of these changes make a difference in teachers' day-to-day activities as well as having long-term effects on their career paths. When restructuring is successful, teachers begin to see themselves as leaders and as inventors. "The job of the teacher, often working with other teachers, is to invent work that kids will do, and to lead them to do it," Schlechty believes. "And if teachers are leaders, then the principal is a leader of leaders" (Brandt, 1993, p. 8).

The motivation for many of these changes appears to be a shift in what people see as the basic purpose of schools. One of the first tasks of systemic change is for the faculty of the school to gather information from members of the community about what they want and need from each other and what they believe to be the purpose of the school in their community. Synthesizing the information from many disparate members of the school community into a vision, articulating it in a mission statement, and operationalizing it with a plan of action take courage, patience, and many, many meetings.

Principals, teachers, and other staff must respond by working harder and longer hours to accomplish the many complex tasks needed for a successful restructuring. They must also be able to reduce a natural tendency to become defensive on hearing criticism. Instead, teachers must be able to examine what it is the community wants them to accomplish and communicate to the community what they view as important. This process is likely to generate conflict. It is probably unavoidable and may perhaps be necessary to induce change. But reflective teachers are not afraid of conflict. Instead, they are willing to invest time and energy into building their own conflict resolution skills and using them to gain important information from all members of the school community.

Two-Way Communication with Parents

At the beginning of Chapter 4, Lori Shoults described the many thoughts, feelings, and decisions she had to make on her first day of teaching. In the week prior to that first day, Lori spent a lot of time in her classroom setting up bulletin boards and learning centers. As she worked that week, many of her new students and their parents who had come to the school for registration stopped by her classroom to see the "new teacher." Some stood outside her door looking in quietly until she approached them and introduced herself. Others came into the room and looked around, exclaiming over the brightly decorated walls. The children were all interested in trying to discern whether the new teacher was "nice" and whether they thought they would be happy in her class.

Their visits, before the first day of school had even arrived, alerted Lori to the fact that she had more than the needs of 28 students to consider. She also had to be aware of and concerned with their parents' needs.

Some parents of primary children may be especially reluctant to see the beginning of school because, for them, it marks an end to an important phase in their lives. For 5 years, they have had complete jurisdiction over the lives of their children. Now they recognize that the teacher may have almost as much influence over their children as they have. Judy has observed the parent of a first grader, for example, standing outside the school after dropping off the child, saying tearfully, "But we've had lunch together every day of his life."

For the majority of parents, many of whom work outside of the home and whose children have gone to day care centers and preschools, this leave-taking may not be so abrupt, but it is still a significant event in their own lives, as well as those of their children. Many parents feel a strong interest in, and responsibility for, determining whether this particular classroom is a healthy and welcoming environment for their children. For this reason, parents of primary schoolchildren are likely to come to school, on one pretext or another, in the first days of school, just to see for themselves that their children are in good hands.

Beginning teachers may feel somewhat overwhelmed by these visits. All of their available energy has gone into planning the curriculum, moving furniture, decorating the classroom, and meeting and becoming acquainted with other teachers in the school. When a parent suddenly shows up, unannounced, it can be unsettling, especially if the parent wants to ask questions when the students are present. When this occurs, it is necessary for the teacher to suggest politely but assertively, another time for this impromptu conference: "I'm sorry, Mrs. Jones, but all of my attention is needed in the class right now. Would you prefer to talk about this after school or tomorrow morning at 8:15?"

On many occasions throughout the school year, the teacher is expected to communicate with parents either singly or in large groups. In addition, many classroom teachers invite parents to become involved in the life of the classroom. Some students come from single-parent families, blended families in which divorced parents have remarried and have children with previous and current spouses, foster parents, and guardians. Teachers meet students who do not have the same last names as their parents. Teachers must recognize that the home lives they may have experienced may be different from those of their students. When *parents* are mentioned in this chapter, the term is meant to refer to the people who are being contacted or are meeting with the teacher on behalf of a particular child.

Fall Open House

When parents come to visit the classroom early in the year, one method of adressing their concerns is to suggest that they will be able to have many of their questions answered within a few weeks at the annual fall open house (sometimes called *Back to School Night*). This event is planned especially for that purpose in many school districts.

The fall open house is usually held on an evening in late September. To prepare for the event, teachers are asked to be ready to describe their goals for the year and give an overall picture of the school's curriculum at that grade level. The event usually begins in the school auditorium or other large meeting room, where the principal welcomes everyone to the school and describes the important events that the entire school has planned for the coming year. The teachers, counselors, other administrators, and sometimes the president of the parent–teacher organization are introduced. Special attention is given to introducing any new teachers on the faculty. At the conclusion of this general meeting, the teachers are released to go to their classrooms and make themselves ready for the open house. After a few minutes, the visitors are dismissed from the general meeting to find their children's classrooms.

When the parents assemble in the classroom, the teacher makes a short presentation to the entire group, describing what is planned for the year. A time for questions and answers of interest to the entire group is also likely to occur. Because most school districts intend the fall open house to be a time for general discussions of goals and curriculum, there is no planned opportunity for individual parents to ask teachers for specific information about their child's achievement or behavior. If parents approach the teacher and begin to discuss personal concerns, the teacher should suggest an alternate time and place for an individual conference.

Parent–Teacher Conferences

Conferences between individual parents and teachers vary greatly in purpose. Some are primarily used for addressing a problem or concern, whereas others are set up to report to the parents about a child's progress in school. Diagnostic conferences were described in Chapter 3, but are discussed briefly in this context as well because they are such valuable means of evaluation.

If either the teacher or the parent has a serious concern about a child, one or the other may arrange a conference in the first weeks of school. When teachers, for example, observe unusually aggressive, passive, depressed, or antisocial behavior in a child, they are wise to call home immediately and set up a conference right away to gain information about the nature of the child's problems. This is especially true when a child's behavior disrupts other students in the class.

Setting up a conference sends an important signal to a student who is exhibiting unusual or unacceptable behavior. It tells the student that the teacher has withitness and is going to take action to correct the problem rather than let it go. It allows the teacher to seek information about the underlying reasons for the observed behavior. In a conference of this type, it is recommended that the student attend with the parents to gain a better understanding of the adults' views of the behavior.

When the conference takes place, the teacher should describe the behavior and, if possible, supplement the oral description with written anecdotal reports of examples of the behavior. The teacher should express concern about the behavior and then ask both the student and the parents to explain why it is occurring.

"Students usually cannot explain fully why they act as they do, and teachers should not expect them to be able to do this. If the students had such insight, they probably would not be behaving symptomatically in the first place. Instead, the hope is that clues or helpful information will emerge from the discussion" (Good & Brophy, 1987, p. 293).

When the parents discuss their own views of the child's problem, the teacher may gain significant insight by learning about the home environment. For example, the parents may agree that they have observed the same behavior at home and that it seems to be related to a crisis the family is dealing with, such as a death, divorce, drugs, lost job, or move. When the teacher, the child, and the parents confront this matter together, they can begin to put together a workable plan to help support the student during this difficult period and, at the same time, help the child gain awareness about the effects of the behavior on others.

Conferences do not always result in such harmonious cooperation. Parents may not present much useful information. On occasion, they may become very defensive or resentful of the suggestion that their child's behavior is unacceptable. In their family, this behavior may be okay. For example, a fifth-grade teacher was alarmed to see a boy walk into her class on the first day of school wearing a T-shirt that read "Born to Raise Hell!" True to the message on the shirt, the child fought with other children at least once a day. When the parents were called in for a conference and the teacher described this behavior to them, the father replied, "So what? I tell my kids not to let anyone get the best of them." From the words and the father's tone of voice, the teacher learned that fighting was an acceptable behavior in that family. No happy resolution was discovered in this conference, but it did give the teacher some additional insight into the source and the depth of the boy's difficulties in social interactions with his peers.

At times, a teacher may need to involve others in the conference. Counselors may need to be present to suggest alternative ways of dealing with problems. If the teacher, parents, and counselor cannot effectively address a problem with the student, additional professional help may need to be offered to the parents. At times, parents admit that they cannot even handle their child at home.

Conferences designed for reporting on student progress rather than for diagnostic purposes usually take place in the late fall to coincide with the end of the first marking period and the first report card. In many districts, the parents are asked to come to the school for a conference with the teacher shortly after report cards are sent home. This gives the parents an opportunity to look at the report card and think about the questions and concerns they may want to raise at the conference. Some school districts require parents to come to the school to pick up the child's report card and have a conference with the teacher. In this case, the teacher explains the grades and observations to the parent as the parent views the report card for the first time. This second strategy is used primarily to make sure that parents do attend the conference.

Report card conferences are generally 15 to 30 minutes in length. They are offered during the day and sometimes at night so that parents who work during the day can be accommodated. Usually 1 or 2 school days are used for the fall conferences. In some school districts, the entire process is repeated in the spring. In the elementary school, a schedule of 30 conferences over a period of 1 or 2 days is a very tiring experience for most teachers, who may find that conference days are more exhausting than regular teaching days. This is due primarily to the tension caused by the teachers' recognition that they are responsible for the smooth flow of conversation and information. When this feeling of responsibility is multiplied by a factor of 30 or more in a few short days, it is easy to see how draining it can be.

To minimize the tension, it is extremely important that teachers plan each conference very carefully. Prior to the event, reflective teachers often write a page of notes about each student, highlighting the accomplishments and the matters of concern that the teacher wants to discuss with the parents. It is important for the teacher to be able to identify the child correctly in the conference. Teachers have mentioned embarrassing moments when parents have a puzzled look on their faces only to discover that the teacher was talking about another student and not their child.

In addition to planning what you want to say about each child, it is a good idea to make a general plan for how you will conduct your conferences. The primary purpose of report card conferences is for you to inform the parents about the child's progress in your class. But the conference is also designed to elicit information from the parents that may help you to help the child. The parents may also have concerns that they wish to discuss. To accomplish all of these things in 15 to 30 minutes is very difficult. To do so, you must act as the timekeeper and allot a reasonable amount of time to each purpose. The parent may not be concerned about going overtime, but you must be because the next set of parents is waiting outside the door for their appointment.

Linn and Gronlund (2000, pp. 396–398) suggest considering the following elements when you plan your conferences:

1. Make plans for each conference. For each child, make a list of the points you want to cover and the questions you want to ask.
2. Begin the conference in a positive manner. Making a positive statement about the child, such as "Betty really enjoys helping others" or "Derek is an expert on dinosaurs," is likely to create a cooperative and friendly atmosphere.
3. Present the student's strong points before describing areas needing improvement. Present samples of work and focus on what the child can do and what he or she still has to learn.
4. Encourage parents to participate and share information. You must be willing to listen as well as talk. They may have questions and concerns about the school and about their child's behavior that need to be brought into the open before constructive, cooperative action can take place.
5. Plan a course of action cooperatively. Guide the discussion toward a series of steps that can be taken by the teacher and the parents to assist the child. At the end of the conference, review these steps with the parents.
6. End the conference with a positive comment. Thank the parents for coming and say something positive about the student such as "Erik has a good sense of humor and I enjoy having him in my class."

The regularly scheduled report card conferences may be the only time you meet with the parents of most of your students. For others, those whose behavior or learning problems are quite serious, you will need to continue to contact the parents by telephone or in follow-up conferences to monitor whether the cooperative plan of action is being implemented and what effects it is having.

Effective two-way communication with parents is essential for assisting students with severe problems. In working with children whose behavior interferes with their learning in school, an excellent resource for both teachers and parents is Rimm's (1986) *The Underachievement Syndrome: Causes and Cures.* This book describes many of the most feared behavior problems that teachers must face: hyperactivity, passiveness, perfectionism, rebellion, bullying, and manipulative behaviors. Rimm believes these behaviors cause children to achieve much less than they are capable of in school. In her studies of underachievement, Rimm has discovered that children learned most of these behaviors in response to some elements of their home environment. Changing the behavior takes a concerted effort by the parents to isolate the causes and create new procedures to help children learn healthier, more productive behavior patterns that can lead to success.

Often it is the teacher who spots the self-defeating behavior. Parents have been living with the child for so long that they may not see that the child's behavior is unusual, and they may not be able to recognize how it affects the child's school achievement. Some examples of home situations that may lead to underachievement include the overwelcome child, early health problems, particular sibling combinations, and specific marital problems

The Overwelcome Child.

Although it has long been recognized that an unwelcome or rejected child is likely to have problems in life, it is also likely that excessive attention can cause achievement and emotional problems. When parents overprotect and overindulge, the child may develop a pattern of not taking initiative and of waiting for others to do his or her bidding.

Early Health Problems.

When children are born with allergies, birth defects, or other disabilities and parents respond by investing themselves almost totally in the child's well-being, a set of behaviors similar to those of the overwelcome child can develop.

Particular Sibling Combinations.

Birth order and sibling rivalry affect all children, but some combinations may be particularly damaging to a child's achievement. A student who is the sibling of a child with severe health problems or is considered to be extremely gifted may feel left out or inadequate in comparison to the sibling. This can lead to the development of attention-getting behavior patterns, such as clowning or mischief-making, that may prevent the child from achieving fully.

Specific Marital Problems.

A single parent may develop a very close relationship with the child as a result of seeing the child as the only purpose for living. The parent may treat the child more like a spouse or a partner than a child, thus giving the child too much power. The child may learn to expect power and may not be willing to give it up to conform to the requirements of school (Rimm, 1986, pp. 24–32).

These are only four of many possible situations that can cause children to develop behaviors that may prevent them from achieving well in school. When a teacher spots a child who is exhibiting overly dependent or overly aggressive behaviors, it is important to confer with the child's parents, to report the problem, and to learn how the behavior first developed and how the parents are responding to it. The first step toward a positive behavior change is for the teacher to describe and give examples of the behavior and its effects on the child's achievement. The parents may deny that the behavior exists or that it is serious, but if the teacher can establish a cooperative two-way dialogue with the parents, it may lead to new insights for all of them.

If parents do acknowledge the behavior, the next step is for you to describe the changes you are going to make at school to support the development of new, more positive behavior patterns and to suggest modifications that the parents may make at home. Together with the parents, set some reasonable goals for the child in terms of both behaviors and grades. Discuss methods of helping the child reach these goals, and agree on a plan that fits the child and the situation.

Rimm (1995) cautions that children will not change their behavior just because the adults in their lives want them to do so. The child must want to break the underachieving patterns and substitute them for behaviors that lead to success. Both the teacher and the parents must also confer with the child, describing the behaviors and their effects in words the child can understand and accept. When the teacher, parent, and child all have the same goal and are working together on a plan of action tailored to fit the needs of the child, it is quite possible that the child will succeed.

Independent contracts are also useful support systems for helping children change behavior. A contract can specify tasks the child is to accomplish with deadlines and expectations for success. It can also be used to specify behavioral expectations. When the teacher negotiates the contract with the child ahead of time, the child has an intrinsic incentive to complete it—after all, the child helped to create it and decide what would be required. A sense of ownership is likely to increase the likelihood of the contract being fulfilled (see Figure 12.1).

The teacher may employ additional extrinsic incentives if these seem useful in a given circumstance. It is most often recommended that students receive a reward that supports academics. For example, a student could earn points toward additional time at a learning activity or game. The major point is that the reward is something a student really would like to receive. Some things a teacher thinks would be rewarding are not rewarding to students. The types of rewards would vary by grade level.

This type of plan may be created as a result of a successful parent–teacher conference, a visit by the teacher to the student's home, or by telephone, followed by written documents specifying what the teacher expects, what the parents agree to take responsibility for, and what the student agrees to do to earn the agreed-on incentive. For example, if the teacher observes that a student is not turning in homework, the teacher may call the students' parents and ask for a conference at school or suggest that the teacher come to visit the home to discuss the matter. Alerting the parents to this concern is likely to result in a discussion of probable causes. The parents may or may not accept the teacher's perceptions of the problem and its negative consequences for their child's achievement. After a frank discussion of conditions at home that may support or interfere with the student doing homework, the parents may come to recognize that the

Figure 12.1   Daily evaluation form.

Daily Evaluation Form

Student name _____   Teacher name _____   Date _____

Assignments completed: _____ All   _____ Most   _____ Less than half

Classroom effort: _____ Excellent   _____ Satisfactory
                         _____ Fair   _____ Unsatisfactory

Behavior   _____ Excellent   _____ Satisfactory
                         _____ Fair   _____ Unsatisfactory

Comments and missing assignments:

_____

_____

_____

_____

Thank you very much for your help.

---

major cause might be the fact that the child and the family watch a great deal of television, beginning right after school and continuing up to bedtime. If the parents express a willingness to do their part to help change the child's behavior, then together they can draft an agreement or contract, specifying when the student will do homework and when he or she can watch television.

Teachers should follow up on this type of agreement by sending the parents daily reports specifying whether the homework is actually being turned in. These daily reports are likely to help everyone remember the commitment they have made. Later, when the student appears to have learned the new pattern of behavior and is more consistent about turning in homework, the reports can be sent home less frequently (see Figures 12.2 and 12.3).

One final caution about conducting parent–teacher conferences: Occasionally, participants in the conference may reveal a family problem that is unusual and extremely serious. The students or parents may describe extreme poverty, desertion, or physical or sexual abuse to a teacher as a desperate attempt to get help. The classroom teacher is advised not to try to deal with such problems alone. If this happens to you, ask the parent to allow you to discuss this matter with the school's social services personnel and immediately contact the principal, school psychologist, social worker, and other members of the crisis team to assist in the matter.

Through the Eyes of Parents

When parents send their children to school, they have many hopes and fears for their children's future. They want to be able to trust the school to create a safe, stable, nurturing environment for their students. They want their students' developing sense of self to be enhanced and their individual talents to be appreciated. But many parents

Figure 12.2   Weekly evaluation form.

Weekly Evaluation Form

Name_____   Grade _____   Date _____

Week of_____

Subject	Behavior	Effort	Grade this week (optional)	Grade to date (optional)	Teacher initials
1.					
2.					
3.					
4.					
5.					
6.					
7.					
8.					
9.					

Comments and missing assignments:

_____

_____

_____

_____

Please use the same rating for effort, behavior, and achievement:

A–Excellent   B–Above average   C–Average   D–Below average   F–Failing

From *Why Bright Kids Get Poor Grades & What You Can Do About It* by Sylvia Rimm. Copyright © 1995 by Sylvia Rimm. Reprinted by permission of Crown Publishers, a division of Random House, Inc.

Figure 12.3   Sample study plan contract.

Sample Study Plan Contract

Richard, his mom, his dad, and Mrs. Norbert agree that Richard will spend at least one hour each day, five days a week, studying and doing his homework independently at his desk in his room. He will do this before he watches TV and there will be no radio, stereo, or TV on in his room during study time. After his work is complete, his dad will review his materials. At the end of the week, if all work is complete in class and homework has been handed in on time, Richard will receive ten points, which may be saved toward a bicycle. Each point is worth one dollar toward the price of the bike. Richard may also receive extra credit points for doing special projects. Richard's mom and dad will not remind him to study, and he will take the initiative independently. If Richard has not completed his homework, he will bring all his books home on Friday and Richard will not be allowed any weekend activities until he completes all missing work.

Richard
Dad
Mom
Mrs Norbert

From *Why Bright Kids Get Poor Grades & What You Can Do About It* by Sylvia Rimm. Copyright © 1995 by Sylvia Rimm. Reprinted by permission of Crown Publishers, a division of Random House, Inc.

feel left out of the decision-making process of their children's schools. If teachers describe their goals or programs using educational jargon unfamiliar to the parents, they may be reluctant to attend conferences or meetings at the school.

When parents are involved in establishing the school's vision statement, or invited to participate on advisory groups, they may contribute many valuable ideas. In Jefferson County, Colorado, a school created a parent–teacher focus group to provide teachers with feedback on how to increase student self-esteem. At first, teachers were reluctant to have the parent observers visit their classrooms. But team members worked collaboratively to design a set of guidelines for the observations and agreed to provide teachers with copies of their observation notes after each visit. A parent–teacher retreat was held to build trust and clarify roles and expectations. The parent observers worked with faculty to develop a statement of their beliefs about how the schools could enhance students' self-esteem. Their statement includes the following:

Provide experiences that allow for individual differences.

Provide opportunities to express creativity.

View mistakes as learning opportunities.

Provide a safe/clean learning environment. (Meadows, 1993, p. 32)

While these recommendations were not new to the faculty, they were helpful in clarifying what the community wanted and expected from their school. From the team effort, both teachers and parents had a better understanding of the complexity of education.

In some communities, parents take a very active role in governance. Parents serve as members of school boards or advisory groups that work closely with the school administrators to make the important decisions about school funding and hiring and firing of personnel. On occasion, some parents have very strong views about a single issue and may try to influence school boards or administrators to provide a certain program or modify an existing program to coincide with the parents' values or philosophy. When this occurs, opinions can become very strongly stated and conflict is likely to arise among parent factions and faculty. For the beginning teacher, it is important to try to learn as much about the values of a school community prior to submitting an application for employment or accepting a teaching contract. If your own values and philosophy differ greatly from that of the majority of the school governance teams, then you are unlikely to feel at home teaching in that school district.

Teaching and Learning in a Multicultural Community

When the language, culture, and values of the parents match those of the teachers in the child's school, communication is likely to be relatively clear and agreements relatively simple to achieve. When the culture of the child's home differs significantly from the culture of the teacher, the teacher must be especially willing to listen as well as talk during parent–teacher conferences.

Before the *Brown v. Board of Education* Supreme Court decision in 1954, children who were racially different from the "white majority" were often segregated in separate (and inferior) schools. Since that time, federal mandates have required school systems to integrate both the student bodies and the faculties of their schools. But federal laws have not been able to mitigate the subtler forms of racism that still exist in some educational settings.

Although the United States is known as a nation of immigrants, a melting pot of cultures, the traditionally accepted cultural norm has mirrored the philosophy of the white Anglo-Saxon majority. Other cultures have been known as minority cultures. The prevailing belief is that children from minority cultures must be taught the language and habits of the majority. Researchers have found that "to the extent that the home culture's practices and values are not acknowledged or incorporated by the school, parents may find that they are not able to support children in their academic pursuits even when it is their fervent wish to do so" (Florio-Ruane, 1989, p. 169).

Reflective teachers are aware that their own values and expectations may vary considerably from those of the families in their school community. But rather than assume that the children and their parents should be taught to mimic the language, behavior, and norms of the teacher's own culture, reflective teachers strive to gain a better understanding of the various cultures that make up the school community and to celebrate these differences by incorporating them into the curriculum.

In parent–teacher conferences, the reflective teacher is likely to ask with great interest about the home environment and the parents' cultural values as a means of better understanding the various cultures and conveying respect to the parents. When parents sense this respect from the teacher, they are more likely to return it and to believe that the teacher shares their own concerns for their child. The teacher may need to be especially encouraging to parents of other cultures, urging them to share their own concerns and ask questions. People from many cultures were not raised to ask questions of teachers and may be very reluctant to do so. But if the teacher encourages them to ask questions or make suggestions for the child's benefit, they may feel comfortable enough to do so. This two-way communication and mutual understanding can lead to a more productive arrangement to work together in supporting the child's achievement at home and at school.

The needs of children and their parents who have emigrated to the United States are especially important, as First (1988) found when she interviewed them:

> Immigrant children and adolescents, many of whom have survived wars, political oppression, and economic deprivation, find that their problems are not over when they enter American schools. Confronted with hatred, prejudice, and violence in U.S. schools, many newcomers are left asking what they have done to deserve such treatment. One Vietnamese student spoke for many when he said, "I like school here. But I wish there would be more friendships among immigrants and American students." (p. 210)

A Spanish-speaking child revealed the following:

> I came upon a world unknown to me, a language I did not understand, and a school administration which made ugly faces at me every time I spoke Spanish. Many teachers referred to us as animals. Believe me, maintaining a half-decent image of yourself wasn't an easy thing. . . . I had enough strength of character to withstand the many school personnel who tried to destroy my motivation. But many of my classmates didn't make it. (p. 210)

The classroom teacher must demonstrate a willingness to assist culturally different children and their parents as they make the difficult transition from one land to another. One of the best ways to accomplish this is to show sensitivity and respect for the various cultures of all the children in the class. Each year, the teacher may plan a special unit of study on the contribution of the cultures represented by the class members. Parents can be invited to participate in the learning experience by visiting the classroom and sharing with children the crafts and food of their countries. They can teach the children the songs and games of their homelands. First (1988) believes that when teachers involve the parents in their children's education, they send a powerful message that the school cares about them.

However, a teacher should not feel offended if the parent does not want to be involved. This could be viewed as disinterest. However, in some cultures parents have been taught that the school is responsible for their youngster's education, and they should not be involved in the process on the school campus.

Visits to Students' Homes

When teachers care sufficiently about understanding the particular home and cultural environments that surround their students, one way to seek information is to visit the children and their families in their homes. Teachers may do this by sending home a newsletter early in the year, announcing that the teacher would enjoy meeting the parents and seeing the children in their homes, and that invitations to do so will be gladly received. This allows the parents to invite the teacher when it is a good time for them.

The visit will probably take place after school or during the evening meal. No agendas need to be established for such a visit; in fact, doing so would be counterproductive. The visit is not a structured parent–teacher conference at all. It is simply an opportunity for the teacher to understand more fully the conditions in which the child lives. As the teacher shares the family's meal, looks at their photographs, and hears some of their family stories, it greatly enhances the feelings of the child and the parents that they are respected members of the school community.

On occasion, it may become necessary for school personnel to make a more structured visit with an agenda. This may occur if a child is having extremely serious problems and is referred for special services and a psychological evaluation. In that case, the school social worker or psychologist may visit the home to determine what factor in the home environment could be causing the child's problems.

Newsletters and Notes

Many elementary teachers communicate with parents by sending home handwritten notes describing a particular behavior or accomplishment of their child. In some classrooms, a note from the teacher signifies only bad news that is sent home when the teacher wants to describe an incident or pattern of misbehavior, a poor test result, or excessive tardiness. More recently, many reflective teachers have considered how to use the note home to encourage good behavior and reward achievement. Many teachers now send home notes describing a special accomplishment, an improvement in classwork, or an act of friendliness or generosity shown by the child.

To ensure that all children benefit from this system, the teacher may send a note of good news home to a certain number of children per week until every child has had one. Others prefer not to use a schedule, but send a note whenever they observe a child doing something especially well. Without a schedule, however, it is important that teachers be careful not to favor some children over others.

In some classrooms, teachers prepare and send home classroom newsletters describing the important events planned for that week or month. The newsletter may contain items describing completed projects and new ones just getting under way. In the newsletter, the teacher can request parent volunteers for various projects and write notes of appreciation to parents who have recently helped out in some way.

In primary classrooms, the teacher generally takes full responsibility for creating the newsletter. But in intermediate and upper elementary classrooms, many teachers allow students to help write the items. They may use a computer program designed for creating newspaper-like formats. In this case, the production of the newsletter becomes more than just a method of communicating with parents. It becomes an enriching learning experience as well.

Parent Support of Educational Activities

If teachers can communicate the classroom goals for that year of school and can supply parents with regular newsletters or other reports of student progress, the likelihood is increased that the parents will support the school's educational goals at home.

Parents can support their child's education and increase the chances for his or her success in school if they understand what they can do to help and are capable of giving that help at home. Teachers vary considerably in what they ask parents to do to support their children's education. The variation seems to reflect the different expectations teachers have about what parents are capable of and willing to do. Some teachers ask parents to read aloud to their children or allow the child to read aloud to them. To support this request, many teachers are willing to lend school books and other materials to parents to use at home.

Other teachers ask parents to take their children to the library. Many also suggest that parents ask their children what they did that day in school and discuss it with them. When asked for suggested activities and games that can be used at home to support the in-class educational goals, most teachers attempt to provide parents with a list of ideas.

Most parents welcome the opportunity to support their children in school-related activities. Teachers who regularly report to parents on classroom events and ask parents to participate by doing parallel activities in the home are likely to develop very productive two-way relationships with parents that can increase the child's self-esteem and achievement and, at the same time, add to the teacher's understanding of the student's home environment.

Telephone Calls

The telephone provides an important link between school and home. Teachers often call students' homes for the same reasons as they write notes. Some use a telephone call to report a child's misbehavior and poor achievement and to enlist the support and assistance of parents in correcting the problems. Other teachers try to call home to report both positive and negative news. They may make their first call to report a problem or concern and follow up several days later with a second telephone call to report that the student is making progress in solving the problem.

Teachers are often on the receiving end of telephone calls from students' parents as well. Parents may call to clarify something about an assignment or an announcement that they cannot understand from their child's description. If parents hear confusing stories about something that happened during the school day, they may call the teacher to find out what really occurred. Responding to these promptly and in an open and informative manner promotes a positive pattern of communication between home and school.

Occasionally parents call in anger or frustration. They may disagree with the contents of the curriculum, the way a test was graded, or the way a classroom incident was handled. The teacher receiving one of these calls may easily become defensive and angry as well. Dealing effectively with these calls takes mature, well-developed communication skills. It is difficult, but very important, to listen empathetically to what the parent says. Even when the instinctive reaction of most teachers is to break into the parent's statements and present their own side of the situation, it is more productive if the teacher's initial responses encourage the parent to describe the problem in more detail and express personal feelings.

After the parent has had an opportunity to fully describe the reason for the telephone call, the teacher's side of the story can be presented in a quiet, nonthreatening, and nondefensive voice. In a situation such as this, the teacher has the responsibility for attempting to resolve the conflict and create a mutually acceptable solution.

For example, suppose a fight occurs in the classroom during the day and John is punched in the face by Dean, a much stronger boy. Because his lip is bleeding, the teacher decides to send John to the nurse. She then tries to talk to Dean to find out what prompted the fight. Dean claims he was provoked by John's name calling, and many children in the class support that claim. When John returns from the nurse, the teacher tells him that both he and Dean will have to stay in during recess for fighting. John seethes with anger for the rest of the day.

After school, the teacher is called to the telephone to find John's very angry parent on the other end. "Why did you keep my son in for recess when he got hit by that bully? And why didn't you call me immediately when he got hit? Did you know he was bleeding? I'm going to come in right now and talk to your principal about this matter, and you will be sorry you treated my son this way!"

The instinctive reaction for most teachers is to jump in and explain after the first few words are spoken. If the parent continues to question the teacher's judgment, the teacher may soon feel as angry as the parent does. But reflective teachers recognize that there will be days like this in the classroom with 30 students and one adult. They will try to keep their feelings under control and say something to soothe the parent's hurt pride and upset feelings.

"I'm glad you called, Mrs. Jones. I can understand how you feel. Tell me how John's lip is now." This type of comment will help the teacher gather information and gain time to formulate a good response. Not all such problems can be readily resolved. Perhaps the teacher and the parent will continue to have different points of view no matter how much they discuss it. If this is the case, it is necessary to acknowledge it and end the conversation with a comment such as "I recognize how you feel about this situation. I'm sorry John got hurt today, and I'll do my best to see that he is not involved in any more fights this year."

The key point of this section is expressed in the phrase "reflective teachers recognize that there will be days like this." Every school year has days like these. Values clash and feelings are hurt. The beginning teacher may be shocked the first time this happens and overreact by feeling angry, guilty, or defensive. If possible, when incidents such as these occur in your classroom, remember that every teacher experiences conflict. Conflict is unavoidable in this career, and the first step in learning how to handle it is learning to expect and accept it as part of the job.

Spring Open House and Other Special Events

In the fall, the purpose of most conferences and open house events is to allow parents and teachers to get to know each other, communicate their goals for their children (students), and make plans for accomplishing these goals. As the year goes by, the focus of most meetings between parents and teachers is for the teacher to demonstrate to the parents how these goals are being met.

Many classroom teachers invite parents frequently, perhaps as often as once a month, to attend exhibits, plays, assemblies, or other occasions for students to display what they are learning and what they have accomplished. Some of these events may be school-wide assemblies, such as Thanksgiving plays, concerts, and feasts, winter pageants, midwinter cultural fairs, and spring open houses in which collections of student work are displayed throughout the school.

Individual teachers may also invite their students' parents to school to view the performances or an exhibit of products resulting from a unit of study. These events are usually highly prized by students and parents, and are an excellent way for the teacher to interact and communicate continually with the parents.

Consider, though, how some parents might feel if they attend a spring open house and find that their own child's work is not displayed. In some competitive classrooms, teachers tend to display only the papers with "100%" written across the top. For those children who rarely get perfect papers, this can be a discouraging experience; for their parents, it is likely to be equally discouraging. If classroom displays include examples of students' work, it is important to display the best works of every student in approximately equal numbers.

To avoid creating a competitive environment, you may want to display students' work inside their portfolios on their desks so that each parent can view the work done by his or her own child alone. General classroom displays can consist of group projects and murals so that every child and parent can take equal pride in the classroom.

Community Involvement in Classroom Activities

Parents as Volunteers

Parents volunteer to do many things in schools to benefit their own children and the larger community. Many parents enjoy being members of an all-school organization known as the Parent Teacher Association (PTA) or Parent Teacher Organization (PTO). These organizations have regularly scheduled meetings and yearly fund-raising events to serve the needs of the school. In most cases, parents do the greatest part of the work on the committees, although teachers are usually represented as well.

Many elementary schools encourage parents to volunteer their time during the school day to assist teachers in educational or extracurricular programs. Parents can serve as coaches, assistant coaches, or referees for some sports events such as all-school field day events. They often serve as helpers on class field trips, accompanying the class on the bus ride and throughout the day. Usually, teachers ask each adult to be responsible for a small group of children during the trip, reducing the adult-to-child ratio from 28:1 down to 4:1 or 5:1.

In the classroom, many primary teachers invite parent volunteers to serve as assistants in the reading and language arts program. A parent can work with one small group while the teacher works with another or with the rest of the class. In this way, parents can serve many important functions. They can read aloud to a group of children or listen to an individual or a small group of children read aloud to them. Parents can write the words as a child dictates a story or can edit a piece of writing done by a child. Parents can listen to book reports and keep records of the number and type of books each child has read.

With the advent of computers in the classroom, many teachers appreciate having parents who are knowledgeable about computers volunteer to work with groups of children as they learn to operate a computer or to monitor students' progress as they work with tutorial or problem-solving computer programs.

During individualized mathematics or spelling programs, or those structured on a mastery learning model, parents can serve as assistants who correct formative tests and provide feedback to students. They can also help to organize the large amounts of paperwork, filing, and record keeping that often accompany individualized instructional programs.

Having parents volunteer to work in your classroom has many benefits, and often you will find knowledgeable and experienced parents who enjoy this type of work. Many parents have interrupted their own careers to raise children and look forward to having a regular volunteer job.

Not all teachers, however, enjoy having parent volunteers in their classrooms. Some teachers are reluctant to have parents view the ups and downs that occur in any school day. Other teachers are not comfortable with parent volunteers because the teacher must be ready with activities and materials whenever the parent arrives. For some teachers, this is a burden that outweighs the benefit of having the extra help. It is true that working with parent volunteers means greater responsibility for the teacher who must manage the other adults as well as the students in the class.

Whether you wish to use parents as volunteers in your classroom is one of those issues that you will need to reflect on, considering the benefits against the costs. One of the best ways to gather information about the efficacy of this practice in your classroom is to try it out with one subject area and a knowledgeable, experienced parent volunteer to see if it is a system you want to employ.

To increase the likelihood that the practice will work in your room, you and the parent volunteer should discuss in advance what you expect the parent to do and agree on the times the parent will visit. Usually parents do only routine tasks or monitor students as they work on a program planned by you and your colleagues. When these matters are clarified, you will probably find the volunteer effort to be very productive, allowing you to reduce the amount of time you spend on routine tasks.

Community Resources

Parents with special interests, abilities, careers, and accomplishments can also enrich your program by visiting to speak to the class about their specialties. A unit on community helpers can certainly benefit from visits by parents who are nurses, police officers, fire fighters, and others who perform community services. Parents who are manufacturers or waste haulers can provide their input during a unit on ecology. When the class is studying economics, parents who work as merchants can describe the theory of supply and demand to the class.

During the first parent–teacher conference in the fall, you may be able to discover what talents your students' parents possess and create a community resource file to draw on throughout the year. In some schools, these files are kept school-wide and parents in the file are happy to come to any classroom in the school to share their knowledge and experience with the children. The file may also contain names of adults in the community who are not parents of children attending the school but who are willing to visit as a service to the community.

Character Education Programs

The interaction between home and school becomes more complex and controversial when the school's objective changes from supporting the child's academic development to supporting the child's moral development. Nevertheless, schools in the 21st century are likely to be at the center of a growing concern about the need for greater emphasis on moral education. This concern grows out of an awareness that schools must take more responsibility for countering the influence of drugs, violence on television and other media, the fragmentation of the family, and the publicity about questionable ethical practices in business and industry (Association of Supervision and Curriculum Development [ASCD], 1988).

A panel of educators met in the summer of 1988 to discuss the schools' role in teaching values. The educators agreed that due to the enormous temptations and distractions facing children today, schools must take an active role in teaching children about the nature of right and wrong. Although the panel recognized that the increasing social, religious, and ethnic diversity of the schools makes it difficult to agree on one set of values, a few common themes appear in almost every culture. The panel recommends that schools develop community-supported programs centering on at least these four themes: *justice, altruism, diligence,* and *respect for human dignity.*

Lickona (1988) recommends that each school recruit local parents to serve on a school–parent support group to (1) arrive at a consensus of the moral values most important to that community and (2) write a moral education curriculum that will be taught at school and in the home at the same time.

Mary Ellen Saterlie (1988), a school administrator in Baltimore, illustrates how such a parent–school partnership can be formed and what it can produce. She describes the

Baltimore public schools' experience, in which school administrators created a community task force to participate in an open dialogue on community values. They purposely invited people with very different religious and political beliefs to serve on the task force. After extensive reading and debate, the task force was able to agree on a "common core" of values appropriate for a democratic and pluralistic society:

> compassion, courtesy, critical inquiry, due process, equality of opportunity, freedom of thought and action, honesty, human worth and dignity, integrity, justice, knowledge, loyalty, objectivity, order, patriotism, rational consent, reasoned argument, respect for others' rights, responsible citizenship, rule of law, self-respect, tolerance and truth. (pp. 46–47)

After identifying these community-acknowledged values, the task force wrote outcome statements for development of these moral values. The board of education then discussed and ratified their report. The PTA developed a brochure on the values education program and distributed it to all parents in the system.

The method used to implement this program allowed each of the 148 schools in the district to appoint its own values committee, which was encouraged to select certain of the task force-identified values to emphasize in its own school projects. This encouraged a creative response from most schools. Some addressed additional values such as computer ethics or academic honesty, as well as those identified by the task force. The Baltimore model linked parents, schools, and the community in a unified examination of moral and ethical issues to "strengthen the character of our students, which in turn will contribute to strengthening our free society" (Saterlie, 1988, p. 47).

As a beginning teacher, you may find that your school district is taking similar measures, and you may wish to become an active part of the task force that identifies the moral values of your community and creates school programs to educate students in these values. If you find that your school district has not yet considered such a challenge, perhaps you can be the one who initiates the idea. Reflective individuals who are committed to upholding the moral values of the community can serve as important role models for the students they teach.

Teachers Mentoring and Coaching One Another

In recent history, the school principal was responsible for observing and evaluating teachers' classroom performance. In many school systems today, however, teachers are sharing their own perspectives with each other as part of the evaluation process. Experienced classroom teachers, sometimes called *coaches* or *mentor teachers*, observe less experienced teachers as they work with children in their classrooms. Afterwards, the two teachers discuss the observed classroom events. This practice allows the mentor teacher to provide critical feedback and to share personal knowledge with colleagues. It also encourages beginning teachers to reflect on what they do, the effects of their actions, and ways to improve their teaching.

In Watsonville, California, teachers in two schools created a program called Professional Partnerships to decrease isolation and build collegial support systems. In this program, two teachers select each other on a voluntary basis to become teaching partners. They observe one another's classrooms each month for a minimum of 30 minutes each visit. The partners meet prior to each observation to define the focus of the lesson and then discuss the visit afterwards. Quarterly, the partners meet with the principal and two additional teachers in the school, who serve as facilitators. Here is how two of the teacher partners described the project:

> My partner is coming to visit so I don't let things slide. My area of interest is improving the quality of student interactions. But I've also improved management, groupings, and materials because everything surrounding the lesson affected what I wanted to have happen.
>
> The postconferences give me a chance to talk about the details of the lesson that I couldn't pay attention to while I was teaching. My partner always gives me new ideas. I feel very supported, and I'm making changes. (Stobbe, 1993, p. 41)

Teachers are also actively involved in selecting the type of staff development they need to accomplish the goals they have established for themselves. When teachers get interested in a new curriculum such as the balanced literacy approach, or mathematics programs that emphasize problem solving, they are likely to propose conferences they would like to attend and arrange to bring in consultants knowledgeable about the new methods.

Another powerful new result of the restructured school environment is the increase in the role of the teacher as a researcher. Teachers are becoming more committed than ever before to investigating areas of concern and doing active research to improve their own instructional practices. When they learn something valuable about their own efforts, they are increasingly taking the role of collaborating with other educators to focus their inquiry on issues larger than those in a single classroom.

To share the results of their investigations, many teachers are writing about their experiences and describing the investigations they have made. They submit their papers to journals and take part as presenters in local and regional conferences.

Interacting with Colleagues to Create Professional Portfolios

Beginning teachers are frequently interested in creating professional portfolios as a means of demonstrating their knowledge, awareness of issues, ability to communicate, and reflectiveness on the important issues of K–12 education. Many school systems engage experienced teachers as mentor coaches and ask beginning teachers to create professional portfolios that document their accomplishments and strengths. Judy has worked with beginning teachers as a mentor coach and finds that the most valuable aspect of creating the professional portfolio is not the product itself, but the growth that occurs during the process of selecting what to include, reflecting on each document and work sample, and talking with other colleagues and the mentor coach about the experiences that resulted in each document or page of the portfolio.

In this text, we have encouraged the creation of a professional portfolio, and have offered specific suggestions about what might be included. We also highly recommend that you view your portfolio as a work-in-progress, changing it weekly or monthly as new ideas or accomplishments occur. We also heartily recommend that you share your portfolio with other trusted colleagues and look at theirs. The ideas you will gain from one another will enable you to make your portfolio more and more interesting and useful as a means of communicating your strengths.

We hope that you have a mentor coach when you begin teaching, and that your mentor will assist you in collecting artifacts and documents for your portfolio. A mentor can be asked to photograph your classroom while you are teaching, so that you can include the photos in your portfolio. You may also ask your mentor to videotape you while you present your first unit or teach with manipulatives or lead a lively discussion. These videos are wonderful additions to your portfolio.

If there are no mentor coaches in your district during your first year of teaching, just find one for yourself. In the first few weeks of teaching, listen and watch for the teachers that have the most in common with your philosophy or curriculum orientation. Approach one and ask the teacher to serve as your informal mentor. The teacher is likely to be delighted with this invitation, because it offers both of you the opportunity to grow and learn. You will learn from the experience of your chosen coach, and the mentor will learn what's new from you. We hope that you will share this book with your coach and work on the professional portfolio pages together.

Conclusions

At the center of the changes in education, especially those leading to best practices, is the teacher. We like to acknowledge the growing power, responsibility, and respect teachers have earned. Porter and Brophy (1988) report that since the early 1970s there has been a surge of activity in research on teaching. Much of it has been predicated on a deceptively simple thesis: Effective school learning requires good teaching, and *good teachers* are those who exercise good judgment in constructing the education of their students. In our words, as we described in Chapter 1, we believe that good teachers are *relational teachers*. They may have their own hopes and expectations when they enter the profession, but they choose to use withitness and reflective thinking to put the needs of their students above their own. Not satisfied with their own self-perceptions, they consciously seek out respected colleagues to ask for feedback on their actions and plans. We hope that we have made our case in this text that there is a strong, undeniable link between *reflective, relational* and *effective* teachers.

As we discussed in Chapter 2, research shows that the most effective teachers are good classroom managers. This management skill grows directly out of reflective, relational, and democratic leadership from the first day of school. As shown in Chapter 3, the role of the teacher includes the responsibility for making accurate assessments of students' needs. Students from all cultures, ethnic groups, and economic conditions can thrive in the classroom of a caring and relational teacher who uses formal and informal sources of information to ensure that all students in the class can achieve success.

Throughout the research on effective teaching and effective schools the attribute of *teacher clarity* surfaces again and again. "Effective teachers are clear about what they intend to accomplish through their instruction, and they keep these goals in mind both in designing instruction and in communicating its purposes to the students" (Porter and Brophy, 1988, p. 81). Clarity of goal setting requires the reflective planning practices described in Chapter 4.

It is also becoming apparent that it is very effective to combine or integrate subjects into multidisciplinary units of study, as described in Chapters 5 and 6. Rather than being textbook technicians, reflective teachers prefer to create their own learning experiences either individually or with teammates. They frequently focus on interesting themes or topics in which students use and develop their reading, writing, and research skills as they gain new knowledge about a variety of subjects.

Another common element identified throughout the literature on effective teaching is that effective teachers create learning experiences in which students are not simply passive recipients of fact-based knowledge; instead, they teach their students how to use many *cognitive processes*, how to organize information in new ways, and how to solve problems for themselves. It takes a reflective, relational teacher to recognize and select the appropriate teaching strategies that will engage students in active learning, as described in Chapters 7, 8, 9, and 10.

Reflective teachers are eager to use a variety of assessment techniques, such as those described in Chapter 11, rather than rely on one objective method. This is an especially effective practice because it allows students with a variety of learning styles to demonstrate their accomplishments and succeed. Effective practitioners are also talented at providing students with useful, timely, and detailed *critical feedback* so that students know what is expected and what they must do to succeed. But we now know that simply being a good evaluator is not enough; the most effective teachers are those who cause their students to take an active role in the evaluation of their own learning by teaching them how to apply *metacognitive strategies* to become independent and self-reliant and able to monitor and regulate their own learning.

In addition to their responsibilities to their students, effective teachers are able to communicate well with the parents and other members of the school community in order to support the moral development of students, as we have described in this chapter and in Chapter 2.

The teacher's role in the educational community is changing. Teaching shows considerable promise of becoming a highly respected profession in the United States during the 21st century. This is largely due to the efforts of reflective teachers who are asking the important questions about how they can improve classroom events and children's lives. Alone or in collaboration, relational teachers are seeking new alternatives and selecting the ones they believe might improve their teaching. They are taking responsibility for evaluating their classroom practices by gathering data from their own observations and from the current research and knowledge base on teaching and learning. They are disseminating what works for them in faculty meetings, workshops, conferences, and articles in professional journals. The result is a new emphasis on inquiry, reflection, and building a knowledge base about the most successful and effective practices that create a stimulating and healthy learning community.

Reflective Actions for Your Professional Portfolio

Your Reflections on Your Role in the School Community

Use Withitness: Observe a Faculty Meeting

Arrange to attend a faculty meeting or another decision-making body at a school you are visiting. How are decisions made? Do teachers work as colleagues to propose programs or solve problems? Does the administrator respect the ideas of the faculty? Visualize yourself as a member of this faculty. What responsibilities would you be willing to assume?

Put the Issue into Perspective

Throughout this text we have used the term *relational* to refer to interpersonal interactions among teachers and students. How does this term correspond to the interactions among colleagues, administrators, and teachers? What type of relationships do you envision for yourself and your colleagues?

Widen Your Perspective

Are you a person who is comfortable or uncomfortable with decision-making power? If you work in a school district that encourages teachers to take responsibility for many important decisions, will you welcome this as an opportunity or look on it as a burden? Would you prefer to make decisions about your own classroom independently, or would you rather share the power and the responsibility with your teammates?

Invite Feedback

Ask several experienced teachers to tell you stories of their interactions with other faculty members at their schools. If there are mentor teachers at the schools you visit, talk with them about the way teachers coach one another in that setting. What are the advantages of having teachers visit one another's classrooms to offer support and suggestions? What are the possible disadvantages or fears related to these visits? In your view, how can these fears or disadvantages be minimized?

Redefine Your View of Collegial Relationships

You may have learned from your discussions with colleagues that it is difficult or impossible for teachers to please every student, every colleague, or every administrator. Whenever a controversial issue arises in a school community, your point of view will be welcomed by some, but not all, of your colleagues on the faculty. If you accept that condition, how can you present your opinions to others on your faculty who may have very different opinions from yours?

Create an Action Plan

Choose an educational issue or dilemma that you have observed in schools you have visited. Create an action plan to approach this problem that you would propose to your colleagues if you were a full-time faculty member at the school. Include a method to gather information from a variety of people who make up the school community.

Predict Possible Outcomes

Show your action plan to an experienced teacher. Get feedback on how to improve your plan or make it more realistic. What will you do if other teachers are reluctant to discuss your plan? What will you do if they think your issue is of little interest or value? What will you do if they disagree with you? Revise your plan and include it in your portfolio.

References

Association of Supervision and Curriculum Development. (1988). Moral education in the life of the school. *Educational Leadership, 45*(8), 4–8.

Brandt, R. (1993). On restructuring roles and relationships: A conversation with Phil Schlechty. *Educational Leadership, 51*(2), 8–12.

First, J. (1988). Immigrant students in U.S. public schools: Challenges with solutions. *Phi Delta Kappan, 70*(3), 205–210.

Florio-Ruane, S. (1989). Social organization of classes and schools. In M. Reynolds (Ed.), *Knowledge base for beginning teachers* (pp. 163–172). Oxford: Pergamon.

Good, T., & Brophy, J., (1987). *Looking in classrooms* (4th ed.). New York: Harper & Row.

Lickona, T. (1988). How parents and schools can work together to raise moral children. *Educational Leadership, 45*(8), 36–38.

Linn, R., and Gronlund, N. (2000). *Measurement and assessment in teaching* (8th ed.). Upper Saddle River, NJ: Merrill/Prentice Hall.

Meadows, B. (1993). Through the eyes of parents. *Educational Leadership, 51*(2), 31–34.

Porter, A., & Brophy, J. (1988). Synthesis of research on good teaching. *Educational Leadership*, *45*(4), 74–85.

Rimm, S. (1986). *The underachievement syndrome: Causes and cures*. Watertown, WI: Apple.

Rimm, S. (1995). *Why bright kids get poor grades and what you can do about it*. New York: Crown Publishers.

Saterlie, M. (1988). Developing a community consensus for teaching values. *Educational Leadership*, *45*(8), 44–47.

Stobbe, C. (1993). Professional partnerships. *Educational Leadership*, *51*(2), 40–41.

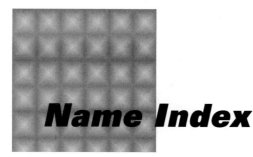

Name Index

Subject Index